Optics, Painting, and Photography

OPTICS PAINTING & PHOTOGRAPHY

M. H. Pirenne

Lecturer in Physiology, University of Oxford

Cambridge · at the University Press · 1970

Published by the Syndics of the Cambridge University Press
Bentley House, 200 Euston Road, London, N.W.1
American Branch: 32 East 57th Street, New York, N.Y.10022

Library of Congress Catalogue Card Number: 71-108109

Standard Book Number: 521 07686 2

Printed in Great Britain
at the University Printing House, Cambridge
(Brooke Crutchley, University Printer)

To my Wife

Contents

List of illustrations   *page* xi

Foreword by Michael Polanyi   xv

Preface   xxi

Acknowledgements   xxiii

1   INTRODUCTION   1
      Kepler's theory of vision   1
      Scheiner's experiment   5
      Theories of vision before Kepler   7
      Vision an active process   8
      We do not see our retinal image, nor our brain processes   8
      Pictures as representations   10
          Linear perspective and the picture surface   11

2   THE FORMATION OF OPTICAL IMAGES   13
      The concept of light rays   13
      The pinhole camera   15
      Diffraction of light   19
      Wave and quantum properties of light   20
      Theory of image formation   22

3   THE RETINAL IMAGE   25
      The optical system of the eye   25
          Blackness of the pupil   30
      Central vision   31
          Gaussian approximation   32

The retinal image as a whole   *page* 35
    Visual field   35
    Constriction of the light flux   37
    Peripheral astigmatism   38
Astigmatic eyes   40
    Effects of astigmatism   42
    The El Greco fallacy   43
Accuracy of the retinal image. Visual acuity   44

4 THE PHOTOGRAPHIC CAMERA AND THE EYE   46
Camera obscura with a lens   46
    Images in focus and out of focus   47
    Imperfections of lenses   48
Pinhole versus lens in the photographic camera   49
Purpose of the photographic camera   49

5 SPACE AND VISION. EUCLID'S OPTICS   51
Space and light   51
The apex of visual angles: the 'point in the eye'   54
Natural perspective   56
    Parallel lines   57
    Ancillary parallel passing through the eye   59
    Apparent diminution with increasing distance   59
The *Optics* of Euclid   60

6 EXPERIMENTS ILLUSTRATING GEOMETRICAL PROPERTIES OF THE   63
RETINAL IMAGE
Experiment 1   66
Experiment 2   68
Experiment 3   69
Experiment 4   69
Experiment 5   70
Conclusions   71

7 THE SIMPLE THEORY OF LINEAR PERSPECTIVE   72
Central projection   72
Retinal images   76
The effect of binocular vision   77

The effect of accommodation *page* 78
Pozzo's painted ceiling 79
   Pozzo's method of projection 79
   How the ceiling appears to the spectator 84
   Disadvantages of this kind of painting 85

8   THE PERCEPTION OF ORDINARY PICTURES 95
   Pictures seen with one eye only 95
   Ordinary pictures usually do not appear deformed 96
   Different projections of the same view 103
   Experiment 110
   The spectator's awareness of the surface pattern of ordinary pictures 113

9   OBJECTS WITH CURVED SURFACES 116
   Spheres and human figures 116
   Rows of columns 125
   Balusters and similar objects 130
   Conclusion 132

10   CENTRAL PROJECTION OF STRAIGHT LINES. SUBJECTIVE CURVATURES 136
   Advantage of a plane surface of projection 136
   Parallel lines which are parallel to the projection plane 137
   Parallel lines at an angle to the projection plane 139
   Importance of the orientation of the projection plane 140
   Orthogonals to the plane of projection 141
   Principal point 141
   Horizon 141
   Frontal projections 141
   Parallel lines at 45° to the projection plane 142
   Distance points 142
   Reconstruction of a scene depicted in perspective 143
   Subjective curvatures 145
   Luneburg's theory of binocular vision 147
   Systems of 'curvilinear perspective' 148
   Curvatures in Doric temples 149

x CONTENTS

11 HOW PICTURES LOOK WHEN VIEWED FROM THE WRONG   *page* 151
    POSITION
    Influence of preconceived ideas   151
      Theoretical ambiguity of perspective   151
      Perspective illusions in architecture   152
    Theoretical deformation of pictures viewed from the wrong position 154
      Stable elements in pictures   160
      Relatively stable elements under special conditions   160
    Ordinary pictures viewed with both eyes   161
      Deformation in anaglyphs   163

12 IMITATION IN PAINTING   165
    Limitations of pictorial representation   166
    Some psychological problems of the artist   168
    A painting can fix an aspect of reality   174
    Note on the historical evolution of the theory and use of perspective 175
    Conclusion   183

    Bibliography   184

    Index   193

Illustrations

CHAPTER 1

1.1   Formation of the retinal image in the vertebrate eye, according   *page* 2
        to Descartes
1.2   The retinal image *ab* of an object *AB*, in focus on the retina   3
1.3   Light convergence in the vertebrate eye   3
1.4   Formation of the retinal image in a compound eye   4
1.5   Principle of Scheiner's experiment   6
1.6   Scheiner's Experiment   7

CHAPTER 2

2.1   Camera obscura with two pinholes, according to Leonardo da Vinci   16
2.2, 2.3   The pinhole camera   17
2.4   Pinhole photographs obtained using holes of various sizes   18
2.5   Diffraction of light by a small aperture   19

CHAPTER 3

3.1   Horizontal section through the human eye   26
3.2   View of the posterior half of a sectioned human eye   27
3.3   View of the anterior half of a sectioned human eye   28
3.4   The crystalline lens of the eye   29
3.5   The nodal points in the human eye   33
3.6   The limit of peripheral vision   36
3.7   Oblique astigmatism of the eye   38
3.8   Formation of the image over the whole retina   39
3.9   Effect of corneal astigmatism   41
3.10 Images of an object point formed by an astigmatic eye   42

CHAPTER 4

4.1   Formation of an image by a biconvex glass lens   46
4.2   Refraction of a light ray by a biconvex glass lens   47

CHAPTER 5

5.1   Astronomical refraction   53
5.2   Oval figure of the horizontal sun or moon   54
5.3   The appearance of sunbeams in the atmosphere   58

CHAPTER 6

6.1–6.5   Retinal images of arrays of small electrical lamps, observed   *page* 64
      through the wall of the eyeball in an intact albino rabbit's eye.
6.1a   Experimental arrangement relating to Fig. 6.1   65
6.2a   Experimental arrangement relating to Fig. 6.2   65
6.3a   Experimental arrangement relating to Figs. 6.3, 6.4 and 6.5   65

CHAPTER 7

7.1   The principle of linear perspective   73
7.2   Piero della Francesca's 'Flagellation'   74
7.3   Plan and elevation of the scene represented in Piero della   75
      Francesca's 'Flagellation'
7.4   The interior of the church of St Ignazio in Rome   80
7.5   Pozzo's painting on the ceiling of the nave in St Ignazio   81
7.6   Elevation of the interior of the church of St Ignazio   82
7.7   Plan and elevations of the imaginary architecture painted by Pozzo   82
      on the ceiling of the nave of St Ignazio
7.8   Part of the perspective drawing made by Pozzo for the nave   83
      ceiling in St Ignazio
7.9   Method of construction of the perspective on the curved ceiling of   83
      St Ignazio
7.10   Photograph of part of the Pozzo ceiling, taken from the marble disc   86
7.11   Photograph of the same part of the Pozzo ceiling as in Fig. 7.10   87
      taken from a position away from the marble disc.
7.12, 7.13   Photographs of the other end of the Pozzo ceiling taken from   88, 89
      a position away from the marble disc
7.14   Photograph of the whole Pozzo ceiling taken from a point in the   90
      transept, well away from the marble disc
7.15   Photograph of the Pozzo ceiling taken at a position 20 m above   91
      the floor of the church
7.16   Engraving by Pozzo of the perspective of the cupola he painted   92
      in St Ignazio

CHAPTER 8

8.1   Deformation in a photograph of a photograph   97
8.2   Another photograph of a photograph   98
8.3   Sketch by Einstein   100
8.4a, b   Two pinhole photographs of the same statuette taken from   101
      different distances
8.5a   View of Venice by Canaletto 1697–1768   102
8.5b   Enlargement of part of Canaletto's painting Fig. 8.5a   103
8.6a, b   Two pinhole photographs of the Arch of Janus in Rome   104, 105
8.6c   Plan of the arrangement for taking the photographs of Fig. 8.6a   106
      and b
8.7a, b   Two pinhole photographs of the so-called Temple of Neptune at   107
      Paestum
8.8a, b   Two pinhole photographs of the Temple of Neptune at   108, 109
      Paestum, taken on a vertical and an inclined plate
8.9a, b   Two pinhole photographs of the same set of cubes and cylinders   111
8.9c   Arrangement for making the photographs of Figs. 8.9a and b   112
8.9d   Plan of the arrangement for viewing Figs. 8.9a and b   112

CHAPTER 9

9.1   Diagram of the central projection of a sphere upon a plane   *page* 117
9.2   Pinhole photograph of spherical architectural ornaments   118
9.3   Pinhole photograph of a set of five spheres on top of five cylinders   119
9.4   Composite pinhole photograph of fifteen spheres on top of cylinders   119
9.5   Diagram of the arrangement for making Figs. 9.3 and 9.4   120
9.6   Raphael's School of Athens   121
9.7   Detail of Raphael's School of Athens   122
9.8   Pinhole photograph of columns of the so-called Basilica at Paestum   124
9.9   Another pinhole photograph of the Basilica at Paestum   124
9.10   Engraving of the cloister of the Charterhouse at Rome   125
9.11a Elevation and plan of the set of eighteen cubes, two perspectives   126
       of which are given in Figs. 9.11b and 9.11c
9.11b Central projection of the set of eighteen cubes   127
9.11c Another central projection of the set of eighteen cubes of Fig. 9.11a   127
9.12a Elevation and plan of a set of eighteen cylinders, two   128
       perspectives of which are given in Fig. 9.12b and 9.12c
9.12b Central projection of the set of eighteen cylinders of Fig. 9.12a   129
9.12c Another central projection of the set of eighteen cylinders of   129
       Fig. 9.12a
9.13a Elevation and plan of another set of eighteen cylinders, the   130
       perspective of which is given in Fig. 9.13b
9.13b Central projection of the set of cylinders of Fig. 9.13a   131
9.14   Pinhole photograph of a balustrade on the roof of the Church of   132
       St Ignazio in Rome
9.15   Banqueting scene. Painting from Pompei   133
9.16   Pinhole photograph of small cups and other solids of revolution   134
9.17   Saenredam: Interior of S. Bavo, Haarlem   134

CHAPTER 10

10.1   Distance points   142
10.2   Principal point and distance points   144
10.3   Demonstration of subjective curvatures   146
10.4   Straight parallel alleys may look curved   147

CHAPTER 11

11.1a, b The perspective arcade by Borromini in the Palazzo Spada,   153
          Rome
11.1c Plan of the Borromini arcade in the Palazzo Spada   154
11.1d Diagram of the perspective effect produced by the arcade in the   154
       Palazzo Spada
11.2a, b The Piazza of the Capitol in Rome   155
11.2c General plan of the Capitol   156
11.2d, e Diagrams of the perspective effects of the Piazza of the   157
          Capitol
11.3   Theoretical effect of displacements of the eye on the appearance   158, 159
       of a perspective

CHAPTER 12

12.1   Detail from Hogarth's engraving 'A Modern Midnight   *page* 169
        Conversation'

12.2   Drawings of the planet Saturn made by astronomers previous to   170
        Huygens

12.3   The phases of Saturn according to Huygens   171

12.4   Sketches of two phases of Saturn by Huygens   172

12.5   Egyptian limestone bas-reliefs of the XIth Dynasty, *c.* 2100 B.C. 176, 177

12.6   Central projection of a plane figure on another plane parallel to   178
        the plane of the figure

12.7 a, b   Egyptian drawing of a woman painting her lips   179

Foreword

The first part of this book explains in terms of optics and physiology the way we perceive external objects and reproduce them in paintings. It recalls, in doing so, the historical roots of this enquiry, all the way back to Euclid. I am no expert in these branches of science and history but can appreciate the author's penetration and lucidity. His guidance is invaluable.

The rest of the book explains how we see a painting as a picture. Dr Pirenne pursues here a problem presented by a combination of two facts that have been generally ignored, one having been set aside as a mere curiosity and the other neglected because its familiarity bred indifference to it. The first of these facts was the strange behaviour of the picture covering the curved ceiling of the Church of St Ignatius in Rome, done by the Jesuit Andrea Pozzo about the turn of the seventeenth century. This painting shows, among other figures, a set of columns which appear to continue the pilasters supporting the ceiling, but can be seen thus only from the middle of the aisle. From other parts of the floor the columns appear curved and seem to lie at angles to the supporting structure of the church.

The strange behaviour of the painting becomes even more surprising, when we realize that this is precisely what the theory of linear perspective should make us expect. It has always been recognized that a perspectivic design could be seen as such only from its centre of projection. Pozzo himself had rightly explained on these very grounds the distorted appearance of his painting when viewed at an angle. It is indeed the *absence* of such distortion, when viewing ordinary paintings from a point away from the centre of perspective, that presents a problem. This question has been often raised in a tentative manner, but has not been seriously pursued.

Dr Pirenne offers the following theory to meet this problem. In his view Pozzo's ceiling shows that only when the perspectivic illusion of the painting is so perfect that it makes the painting appear three-dimensional, does skew viewing produce a distortion of appearance. Other paintings are deemed insensitive to the angle of viewing, mainly because their perspectivic design is not fully convincing, owing to the fact that the viewer remains aware of facing a flat canvas. This awareness reduces the illusionary powers of the perspective, and enables us thereby to retain at skew angles of viewing, the particular appearance we see from the correct centre of projection. Our eyes seem to select this appearance for all positions of viewing, because it resembles the way the painted object is seen in nature.

When telling that in looking at a painting we are aware of its flat canvas, Dr Pirenne calls this a 'subsidiary awareness' of the canvas and he refers to my writings as the origin of this term. In the past seven years, since Dr Pirenne first publicly connected his ideas with my work, I have sketched out further developments of our joint interests.

To speak of *subsidiary awareness* is to discriminate against both focal *awareness* and *unawareness*. Take Pozzo's painting. We are so deceived by the perfection of its perspectivic design, that we are totally *unaware* of the hemicylindrical vault on which the image is painted. Unawareness obviously excludes subsidiary awareness, but focal awareness also excludes it and this is not so obvious. As a case in point, suppose that we look at close quarters at the brush-strokes and the canvas of a painting. This would make us lose sight of the painting. For a painting can be seen only from a distance by a subsidiary awareness of its brush-strokes and canvas. Subsidiary awareness lies thus midway between unawareness and focal awareness.

Subsidiary and focal awareness exclude each other because subsidiary awareness has a *function* which focal awareness lacks. This function consists in pointing away from itself, in the way our subsidiary awareness of brush-strokes and canvas make us see these particulars, jointly as a painting.

A simple illustration of the function of subsidiary awareness is found in a pointing finger. We are obviously not unaware of the finger; but we do not look at the finger focally, as we would in order to examine it, but look along it with a view to attending focally to something else at which the finger is pointing.

Thus we form a triangle: ourselves in one corner, the pointing finger in a second and the object the finger points at in a third corner. This scheme is akin to the way gestalt psychology regards parts of a whole forming the whole. The observer does not look at these parts in themselves, focally, but sees them as bearing on the whole to which he is focally attending. In this sense a painting can be regarded as a whole, the parts of which are the paint and the canvas which are seen jointly as the painting.

In his *Art and Visual Perception*[1] Rudolph Arnheim considers a painting to be based in this way on the laws of gestalt psychology. But my past attempts to base a theory of knowledge on the principles of gestalt has taught me that gestalt as a process of equilibration cannot account for creative thought. It must be made to include the powers by

---

[1] Arnheim, R. (1967). *Art and visual perception: a psychology of the creative eye.* London: Faber Paper Covered Editions.

which we can deliberately integrate even sharply conflicting clues to a novel kind of experience.

Let me go back then to the viewing of an ordinary picture over a range of different angles. The behaviour of Pozzo's ceiling teaches us the fantastic distortions our 'retinal image' of a painting may receive when we view a picture from an angle. Deformations are particularly striking here because the surface is curved and the scene it represents is a continuation of the actual architecture of the building. But we have additional evidence from pictures called anaglyphs; these represent two different perspectives in different colours, so that, when viewed through a corresponding pair of coloured glasses, the image appears fully stereoscopic. Such three-dimensional images show strong deformations when viewed from different angles. There is evidence also from photographs of a painting taken at an angle. The photograph would produce the same retinal image as that formed when we look at the painting from the same point as the photograph is taken and it shows the extravagant distortions of these retinal images. This is illustrated by Dr Pirenne in Figs 8.1 and 8.2.

Thus we may take it that, as we walk past a picture, we are facing a row of wildly distorted aspects of it and yet we unhesitatingly see these aspects as having the same undistorted appearance. Moreover, we see that Dr Pirenne's explanation of this remarkable integration of incompatibles implies the joint operation of two such integrations, for it assumes that we see the whole array of distorted impressions in one single undistorted way because, along with the brush-strokes of the painting, we are subsidiarily aware also of its canvas. The mutual contradiction of the several distorted aspects may be said to be integrated to one and the same undistorted sight, each distorted aspect being integrated also to the awareness of the canvas which contradicts its perspectivic appearance.

To go deeper into this integration of contradictories, remember once more the peculiar appearance of Pozzo's ceiling as compared with normal paintings. Pozzo succeeded in producing the compelling illusion of a three-dimensional scene; whereas, however effective the perspective of a normal painting may be, the picture will not be mistaken for the sight of its real objects. Its appearance has depth and this is an essential feature of it, but this depth is not deceptive: it is felt to have flatness in it. It has the quality of a mixture of depth and flatness.

Gestalt psychologists have fully realized that wholes have a sensory quality not to be found in the separated parts. They noticed for example that when we integrate the features of a person to the appearance of his physiognomy, we create a novel sensory quality. But in such cases we link together complementary elements of experience and this can be interpreted as an equilibration in the sense of gestalt formation, while to view a painting by integrating its conflicting elements goes well beyond this.

It corresponds to the kind of process in which experimentally produced sensory contradictions are resolved in terms of a sensory innovation. A subject, being made to practice doodling while wearing a right–left inverting prism, soon feels his hand to be at the place where his eyes wrongly show it to be. When asked to write down blindfolded some letters and figures he writes them right–left instead of left–right.[1] Moreover, a far-reaching integration of conflicting clues in the terms of sensory innovations has been found to underly the way one finds one's way wearing inverting spectacles. The work of Kottenhoff (1956)[2] has shown that the visual image remains inverted and the subject learns to find his way by reintegrating the inverted image to all his proprioceptive, auditory and gravitational clues. Sensory innovations of this kind fuse conflicting clues in the same way as the viewing of a painting fuses the conflicting clues of brush-strokes and canvas.

Integrative powers of this kind may work effortlessly, as they do in combining the sight of brush-strokes with that of the canvas, but they may require days of persistent efforts, as in learning to see rightly with inverting spectacles. In neither case is explicit guidance of much use. To be told that the Pozzo ceiling is painted on a hemicylindrical vault will not affect its deceptive impression nor its distortions when seen at a forbidden angle; it is not *the information* that paintings are based on a flat background, but *the sight* of their flatness which sets off the integrations showing us paintings as correct perspectivic pictures.

When integration is achieved by an effort, this is the effort of the imagination. It is the painter's imagination that senses the possibilities of making a painting on certain lines and it is his imagination that leads him further from stage to stage, in his effort to complete his work and get it right. And it is once more by the power of the imagination that the viewer achieves the appreciation of a painting of an unfamiliar type and learns not to ask questions that are meaningless in regard to these paintings.

At the turn of the last century, writers wishing to emphasize that a painting possesses value irrespective of its imitative powers, have declared that a painting has an independent reality. We can appreciate this point by imagining the transformation of a painting into a trompe-l'oeil. We realize instantly the abysmal triviality to which a still life by Cézanne would be reduced were it somehow made to convey the illusion of real fruits and vegetables placed in a recess in the exhibition's wall. It is as well that the integration of brush-strokes and canvas lends to all paintings a distinctive artificial quality which isolates them from all natural sights. This secures the artistic reality of a picture and thus guards its distinctive powers from dissolving in the surroundings of factual reality.

[1] Irving Rock and Charles S. Harris, 'Vision and Touch', *Scientific American*, 1967, pp. 96–104.
[2] Kottenhoff, H. 'Was ist richtiges Sehen mit Umkehrbrillen?' *Psychologia Universalis*, Vol. 5, Meisenheim am Glan 1961.

It has been observed that the colours and shapes available to the painter cannot equal the variety of details we meet in nature (though it is still possible to paint patterns and pictures which appear to be three-dimensional objects). There is also a powerful movement which would deny any significance to the simulation of objects by the painter. Dr Pirenne's theory adds a new kind of limitation on the endeavour to imitate nature. It teaches that a painting achieving trompe-l'oeil illusion remains undistorted only over a quite insufficient range of viewing. The painter must aim therefore from the start to produce an essentially untrue painting. He must strictly limit himself to producing a work of the imagination which will serve in its turn the viewer's imagination. The objects that it represents must remain parts of an imaginary reality.

MICHAEL POLANYI

Preface

This book discusses from the standpoint of optics, physiology and psychology, certain aspects of pictorial representation. It deals with the making of pictures; that is, with the representation of objects or a scene upon a *surface*, the surface of the picture. In recent times, some have seemed to take it for granted that this was an easy technical matter, of no great interest; while others, at the opposite extreme, have appeared to argue that there could be no real objective basis for such a representation. Now, however, Professor E. H. Gombrich's book on *Art and Illusion* has succeeded in breaking through the barrier of incomprehension surrounding the subject.

While Gombrich's book is based largely on the psychology of perception, the present book, on the other hand, takes as its starting point the meaning of the geometry of pictorial representation in terms of physical and physiological optics. Leonardo da Vinci's writings remain of central importance to this subject. In a sense, the present work constitutes a commentary on Leonardo. Instead of merely relying on texts, however, it deals on an experimental basis with problems which confronted Leonardo. Some of the experiments were specifically made for the present purpose. The book also deals with relevant aspects of the history of optics, from Euclid to Einstein. Again, just before the revolution produced by photography, the geometry of pictorial representation had been examined by La Gournerie: his searching analysis, which has become largely forgotten, helped the author to frame his main argument, which can be summarized as follows.

The depiction on a surface of the shape and arrangement in space of the objects, figures, etc., constituting a given scene, involves two different, though related, steps. The first relates to the (invariable) geometrical properties of human vision. This already was Euclid's concern: it is *natural perspective*. The second (very variable) step consists of the partial, or in rare cases the full, use of *linear perspective*: for the picture is made on a surface, and linear perspective, which derives from natural perspective, deals with the projection of a scene or objects on a surface. (Even the 'perspectiveless' depictions made by the Egyptians rest on one theorem of linear perspective.) Now the central thesis of this book is that in the usual case of ordinary pictures, the spectator is aware of some of the characteristics of the picture surface *at the same time* as he perceives the scene represented by the picture. This gives stability to his percept of the depicted scene when he views it from the wrong position. It also raises difficulties which have led to controversies on the use of linear perspective. The perception of trompe-l'oeil pictures, in which the picture surface, *qua* surface, is 'invisible', is a much simpler matter: there the spectator simply sees a scene in three dimensions. In the case of ordinary paintings, the spectator's awareness of the painted surface is a fundamental factor in the artistic impression produced by the painting.

To-day the teaching of perspective has almost disappeared from Art Schools, at any rate in the United Kingdom where students may obtain the Diploma of Art and Design without ever having heard of perspective (Ministry of Education, 1960). It has been stated that the teaching of perspective 'may endanger the students' spirit of enquiry'. This suggests that the very significance of perspective must have become lost to many artists. Yet it may be regained. For as Monsieur Jourdain did with prose, all representational artists make use of linear perspective even if they are not aware of the fact.

Very little previous knowledge of optics, and only a knowledge of elementary geometry, are needed to read this book. Much of its contents has been the subject of controversies, yet these are not insisted on. The book rather attempts, like a textbook, to re-state the whole argument, always on the basis of experiment, and tries to ascertain what is right, rather than who is right—which would be too great an enterprise.

It is hoped therefore that it will be of some use to those whose business it is to make representational pictures, from artists to photographers, and also to those who are interested in visual communication and in the meaning and evolution of pictorial art. It should perhaps be explicitly stated that the author's aim is not to tell painters, draughtsmen and photographers what they should do, but rather to investigate from the general standpoint of optics what actually has been done in the course of the centuries.

Such a study could be extended indefinitely. The main subject selected is the so-called 'depiction of space'. The references relate mainly to this subject. They do not, and could not, give a complete bibliography of pictorial representation. Omission of some work from the references does not imply that it has been thought of no value or relevance. 'Better a tacit than an obvious agreement.'

While the preparation of this book was started in earnest about ten years ago, the author has always been interested in the subject. His father, Maurice Pirenne (1872–1968), was an artist who steadily painted for some eighty years, and who was for a long time Curator of the Musée Communal at Verviers, Belgium. The author himself is an amateur painter, or rather draughtsman. He preferred the study of science to that of painting, but since his school days has been interested in the relationship of optics to painting and to pictures in general, and he eventually studied optics and vision precisely on account of this.

Acknowledgements

First of all I am deeply grateful to my father for all he taught me since I was a schoolboy. Again I am greatly indebted to Professor Michael Polanyi, who wrote the Foreword; to my late friend Dr G. ten Doesschate, of Utrecht, for discussions and encouragement extending over many years; to Mr B. A. R. Carter, of the Slade School of Fine Art in University College, London, who read an early draft of the MS. and made important suggestions, besides all the information he gave me in conversation; to Dr M. Zanetti, architect, for discussions, information, and unfailing help, especially with regard to those illustrations coming from Italy; and to Dr F. H. C. Marriott, my collaborator in visual research, who read the final MS. and suggested valuable changes and additions. I alone, however, am responsible for the opinions and errors contained in the book.

I am also greatly indebted, among many others, to the late Mr W. A. Sanderson, and Mr J. C. Thornton and to the Calouste Gulbenkian Foundation who helped with grants and enabled me to make my first visits to Italy; to Mr J. B. Ward Perkins, Director of the British School at Rome where I stayed a number of times and gathered invaluable information; to the Reverend G. Giachi, S.J., Rector of the Church of St Ignazio in Rome, who gave permission to take photographs inside this church and on its roof; to Mr A. S. Evett who took photographs, drew diagrams, and helped me in any number of ways; to Mr A. Austin, of the Photographic Department of this Laboratory, who taught me what I know of practical photography, and endlessly gave help with regard to the illustrations; and to the staff of the Cambridge University Press, without whose unfailing help this book and its complicated illustrations would not have been suitably printed.

I am grateful to the following for permission to reproduce illustrations in this book: Oxford University Press (Fig. 2.1); Longmans, Green and Co. (Fig. 3.1); Istituto Centrale del Restauro, Rome (Fig. 7.2); Mr B. A. R. Carter and *J. Warburg and Courtauld Institutes* (Fig. 7.3); Chiesa di S. Ignazio, Rome (Figs. 7.4 and 7.5); the British Broadcasting Corporation (Fig. 8.1); Associated Press, Ltd, and Wide World Photos (Fig. 8.2); the Trustees of the National Gallery, London (Figs. 8.5 and 9.17); the Mansell

Collection, London (Figs. 9.6 and 9.7); Museo Nazionale, Naples (Fig. 9.15); La Société Hollandaise des Sciences (Fig. 12.4); the Trustees of the British Museum, London (Fig. 12.5); Museo Egizio, Turin (Fig. 12.7a); Spring Books, and J. R. Harris (Fig. 12.7b).

Acknowledgements are due to the Cambridge University Library for providing photographs for Figs. 1.1, 1.4, 4.1, 11.3, 12.2, 12.3, 12.4; to the Library of Trinity College, Cambridge, for Fig. 2.5; to the Library of Christ Church, Oxford, for Figs. 7.6, 7.7, 7.8, 7.9, 7.16; and to the Bodleian Library, Oxford, for Figs. 9.10, 11.1c, 11.2c.

I also wish to thank Dr M. D. McIlroy and Mr J. E. Stoy who made Figs. 9.11b and c, 9.12b and c, and 9.13b by computer, and Signorina S. Calza-Bini who took special photographs of the paintings in St Ignazio.

Finally I wish to express my warmest thanks to the Physiology Department of the University of Oxford, and especially to Professor E. G. T. Liddel and to Dr R. V. Coxon, for their support and encouragement over the years.

University Laboratory of Physiology, Oxford   M.H.P.

1 *Introduction*

Kepler's theory of vision

'Vision, I say, occurs when the image of the whole hemisphere of the external world in front of the eye—in fact a little more than a hemisphere—is projected onto the pink superficial layer of the concave retina.'

So in 1604 wrote Kepler, the astronomer, in his *Ad Vitellionem Paralipomena*, a book which marks the beginning of the era of modern optics.[1] Kepler was the first who clearly understood that the light coming from external objects forms an inverted image of these objects on the retina, the light-sensitive layer which lines the inside of the eyeball and which is connected to the brain by the optic nerve.

As illustrated by Fig. 1.1 from Descartes's *Dioptrique*, published in 1637 together with his *Discours de la Méthode*, and by the modern diagram of Fig. 1.2 from Helmholtz, the optical system of the human eye functions as a camera obscura.

The retinal image is formed by a mechanism of light convergence. Consider a single point source of light S situated in front of the eye of a man in a dark room (Fig. 1.3). This source emits light in all directions around it. First it will be noted that by far the greater part of this light fails to enter the eye, but strikes the walls of the room, the face of the man, his eyelids, the white of his eye, etc.; this part of the light is absorbed, reflected or scattered by the objects on which it falls, and can play no direct part as far as seeing S is concerned. But a small part of the divergent light flux originating from the point S does pass through the transparent cornea of the eye, through the aperture constituted by the pupil, and through the lens. It is thus able to reach the retina which lines the posterior chamber of the eye. And as it passes through the cornea and the lens, the light flux is refracted in such a manner that, if the eye is properly focused on S, the light from S converges onto a 'point' s on the retina, s being the retinal image of S.

Figure 1.2 which relates to the vision of an object AB in focus on the retina, shows that the light flux sent into the eye by any object point such as A starts outside the eye as a cone the apex of which is at A, and ends inside the eye as a second cone the apex

[1] Kepler, J. (1604). *Ad Vitellionem Paralipomena*, Cap. V, 2, 'Modus visionis'.

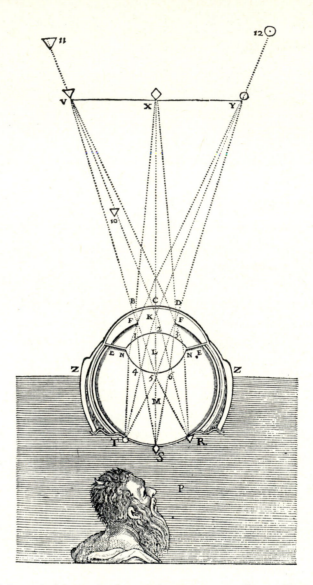

1.1   Formation of the retinal image in the vertebrate eye, according to Descartes

The rays from the object points *VXY* form an inverted image *RST* on the retina. This figure relates to an experiment which was first performed by Scheiner (1619). The membranes at the back of an ox's eye, for instance, were cut out so as to uncover the vitreous humour, and a piece of thin white paper was placed on the aperture so obtained. The eye was fitted into a suitable hole made in the shutter of a window, so that the paper screen faced the inside of a darkened room. Then a small inverted picture of the illuminated objects outside the window could be observed on the screen *TSR*. The experiments of Chapter 6 on the albino rabbit's eye were based on the same principle, but there the translucent white wall of the eyeball itself was used as a screen to study the retinal image. (From Descartes (1637), *La Dioptrique*.)

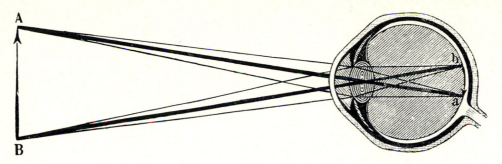

1.2   The retinal image *ab* of an object *AB*, in focus on the retina

This diagram illustrates a simplified construction, which in any case is valid only for retinal images close to the optical axis of the eye. All the *main rays*, such as the straight lines *Aa* and *Bb*, are taken to cross at one optical centre, inside the crystalline lens, to define the position of the retinal images of the different points of the object. (From Helmholtz (1884), *Vorträge und Reden*, Vol. I.)

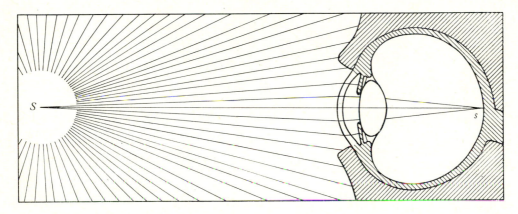

1.3   Light convergence in the vertebrate eye

Some of the divergent rays emitted by a point source *S*, having entered the eye, are made convergent by the optical system of the eye and are re-united at a point *s* on the retina. (From Pirenne (1967*a*), *Vision and the Eye*.)

of which is the image point *a* on the retina. To another object point such as *B* corresponds another similar pair of cones, the light flux from *B* becoming concentrated on the retina at the point *b*. While the light from any object point is divergent, the separate conical fluxes reaching the eye from all the different object points converge towards the eye and cross one another within the pupil of the eye. Consequently the retinal image, relative to the external objects, is inverted. What is of primary importance for vision, however, is the fact that the optical system of the human eye thus achieves a 'point to point' correspondence between the object and its image cast on the nervous layer receptive to light.

A similar correspondence is also achieved by eyes in which the principle of the optical

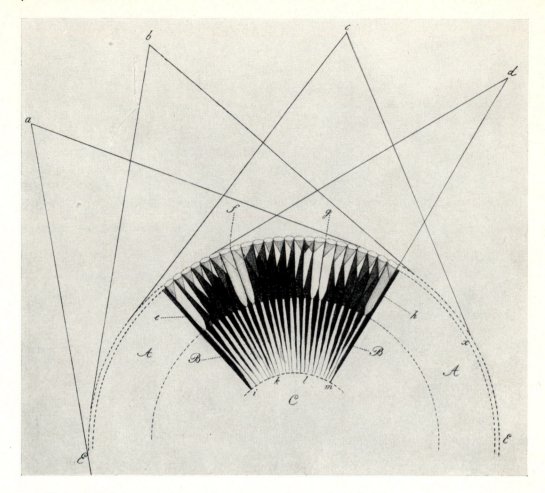

1.4 Formation of the retinal image in a compound eye: Müller's theory.

The external surface of the eye is *EE*. The eye consists of individual elements, the ommatidia, which form the layer *AA* and each of which corresponds to one facet of the eye. Each ommatidium may be regarded as a transparent tube surrounded externally by black pigment. The tip of each tube contains the light-sensitive ending of a nerve fibre, the layer of the nerve fibres being *BB*. When light emitted by such point sources as *a*, *b*, *c* or *d* falls on the surface of the eye, it is able to penetrate to the tip of only those few tubes whose axes are nearly directed towards the corresponding source. In the other tubes the light strikes the black wall of the tube and fails to reach the tip. Thus an erect, convex, retinal image is formed at the level of the nerve fibres in contact with the tips of the ommatidia. (From J. Müller (1826), *Zur vergleichenden Physiologie des Gesichtssinnes.*)

system is entirely different, namely the compound eyes of insects (Fig. 1.4). Here the mechanism essentially consists of the separation, effected by individual components each of which corresponds to one of the facets of the eye, of light fluxes coming from various directions. Light fluxes originating from different points of the objects and converging towards the eye are thus able to reach different sensitive elements of a convex retina. The retinal image is erect, not inverted as in the human eye.[1]

The notion of 'point to point' correspondence between external objects and their retinal image is subject to very important qualifications. The phrase 'image point' has been used above largely as a manner of speech; it should of course not suggest that an image point is a mathematical point, which would imply that the retinal image could be absolutely accurate. In eyes such as the human eye the retinal image even of the smallest light source is always a light patch of finite dimensions. On account of the effect of light diffraction, this would be so even if, which is not the case, the optical system of the eye were entirely free of defects or aberrations.

Scheiner's experiment

A simple experiment was described by Scheiner in 1619, which shows that our eye does function according to the general principles enunciated by Kepler. At the basis of this experiment lies the fact that vision through one small aperture remains fairly sharp for a very wide range of distances, independently of whether for the naked eye the objects are in focus or not. Thus the normal eye is quite out of focus for an object held a few centimetres from it; yet the object can be clearly seen through a pinhole. This is so because the cone of light admitted through the pinhole is much narrower than that which would be admitted through the full extent of the eye pupil. The corresponding cone formed inside the eye is also proportionately narrower. Even though the apex of this cone is situated well behind the retina, its intersection with the retina will therefore be a much smaller area than would be the case for the naked eye.[2]

Consider a point c which forms an image f in focus on the retina (Fig. 1.5, diagrams 4 and 6). Now suppose that an opaque screen pierced with two small apertures a and b is placed in front of the eye—the distance between a and b being a little less than the diameter of the pupil of the eye, and the screen being held so that the light from c passing through both apertures falls into the pupil. These apertures then isolate two narrow light pencils within the conical light flux which normally would enter the eye through the pupil. Since this whole conical light flux, after being transformed by refraction into a second cone inside the eye, would converge onto the point f, the light of the two pencils will also converge onto this single point f. According to the theory, the interposition of the screen with apertures should therefore interfere but little with formation of the retinal image, apart from cutting down the amount of light reaching the

---

[1] For a more detailed account, see for example Pirenne (1967a), *Vision and the Eye*.

[2] The use of a very small aperture would, however, defeat its purpose on account of the effects of light diffraction. The Scheiner experiment succeeds well with holes $\frac{3}{4}$ mm in diameter. The holes should preferably be made in a thin sheet of metal.

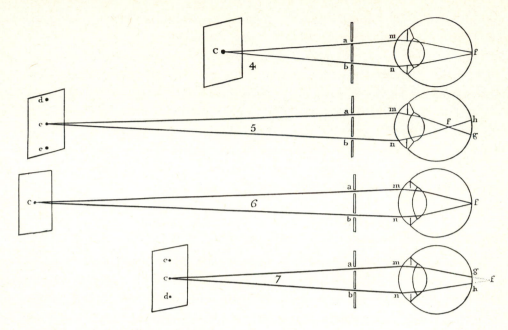

1.5 Principle of Scheiner's experiment

Explanation in text. (From Smith (1738), *A Compleat System of Opticks*.)

retina. In fact an external object seen sharply with the naked eye still appears single, but dimmer, and rather less sharp, when it is looked at through two pinholes in such a manner.

If, on the other hand, the eye is not in focus for the point c, as in Fig. 1.5 diagrams 5 and 7, the narrow pencils admitted into the eye through a and b will form two separate images of c where they strike the retina at h and at g. Therefore the point c, which to the naked eye appears blurred, and single, will be seen much more sharply, but will appear double, when viewed through the two pinholes.

Figure 1.6 from Scheiner's book, shows the appearance of a distant turret, out of focus for the naked eye, viewed through two pinholes under such conditions. The two large overlapping circles in this Figure correspond to the two 'images' of the pupil of the eye, cast on the retina by the light passing through each of the holes, and which limit the field of view in the experiment. In the region of overlap of these circles the turret is seen double.

If three holes are used in the same manner instead of two, objects out of focus are seen treble; and a corresponding result is obtained if more than three holes are used. Objects in focus, however, still appear single. Again, the interposition in front of the eye of a slit, instead of a system of holes, does not prevent those objects for which the

1.6 Scheiner's experiment
The appearance of a distant turret seen through two pinholes situated on a horizontal line. The eye used in this experiment possibly was myopic, since it must have been out of focus for the distance considered. (Copy of illustration from Scheiner (1619), *Oculus*.)

naked eye is in focus from being seen clearly. This corresponds to the case of the eye of such animals as the cat, whose pupil contracts to a slit in bright light, whereas in man the pupil remains circular.[1]

Theories of vision before Kepler

Kepler called his book a 'Commentary on Vitellio'. Now the book on vision by Vitellio, who lived in the thirteenth century, amounts to little more than a commentary on Alhazen, the Arab astronomer, who lived about the year 1000. Thus progress was very slow, even though Greek philosophers and scientists already had been deeply interested in the theory of vision. The first treatise on optics still extant is that of Euclid (*c.* 300 B.C.). Most of the conclusions of this work, which deals mainly with the geometrical aspects of human vision, remain valid to this day. Yet nineteen centuries were to elapse until, with Kepler, the optical functioning of the eye became understood.

Many of the Greek theories of vision were *centrifugal* theories. Theories of this kind, which radically differed from all our modern conceptions, held their own until at least the thirteenth century. They were based on the hypothesis that visual rays were *emitted* by the eye. These visual rays were supposed to reach out from the eye to the external objects, rather like long thin tentacles. In a medium of even density the visual rays were assumed to be straight lines, however. This explains why Euclid, for instance, reached correct conclusions even though he based his reasoning on a centrifugal theory.

The main rival theories of vision among the Greeks were *centripetal* theories, according to which 'images' of the objects somehow left the surface of objects and were eventually received into the eye. Alhazen's theory was a centripetal one, more intelligible than its predecessors, but based on *ad hoc* assumptions. Alhazen accepted, at least to some extent, the physician Galen's (A.D. 129–?199) belief that the receptive surface in the eye was the surface of the crystalline lens—not the retina. He believed that each separate object

[1] This is an old problem, mentioned for instance in A.D. *c.* 200 by Sextus Empiricus (1961), Bk I, § 47.

point sent its image to the receptive surface. In order to explain this 'point to point' correspondence between object and image, he had to assume that only some of the rays striking the surface of the lens (and of the cornea which he wrongly believed to be concentric with it) were effective in stimulating the receptive layer. The effective rays he supposed to be those rays which fell perpendicularly on the curved sensitive surface. This was a quite arbitrary assumption. Yet it is curious to reflect that the optical arrangement of the compound eyes of insects does precisely achieve a result of this kind.[1]

Vision an active process

Almost any attempt to see accurately and reliably requires a considerable effort of attention. Vision is an active, not a passive process. In order to see, it is necessary to look. Such phrases as 'casting a glance' ('jeter un regard'; 'einen Blick werfen') are still in current use. The old theory of the emission of visual rays gave a direct suggestion of the active part played by the observer in visual perception. In the modern theory this might appear to be left out of account. For the formation of the retinal image by light coming from the outside world is a purely physical process which takes place in the living eye as it does in a dead one, or as in an inanimate object such as the photographic camera. This might lead to the erroneous conclusion that we merely are passive 'receivers of images'. Apart from psychological considerations, the ceaseless movements of the eyes indicate that this is not so.

Besides the large displacements of the eyes which of course occur when we shift our gaze from an object to another, the eyes also undergo small continual movements in their orbits. It has been recently realized that normal vision is entirely dependent upon these movements of the eyes. If we succeed in maintaining the eye sufficiently steady in one position, or if artificial means are used to keep the image steady on the retina in spite of the natural motion of the eye, then after a lapse of a few seconds vision fades and becomes very blurred and imperfect.[2]

We do not see our retinal image, nor our brain processes

Prior to Kepler, others, including Leonardo da Vinci, had been led to the idea that an optical image of external objects was formed inside the eye on the principle of the camera obscurra. But they could not reconcile themselves to the idea that the image was inverted. For they believed that this would be incompatible with upright vision of the

---

[1] On the history of optics and vision see for example Hirschberg (1899), Ronchi (1956), ten Doesschate (1962) and the historical notes in Helmholtz (1962), *Treatise on Physiological Optics*.

[2] For a critical discussion of this phenomenon, see Barlow (1963).

outside world. The answer to this difficulty is that we do *not* see our retinal image. So the fact that this image is always inverted in the natural use of our eye is irrelevant—as is the fact that the compound eyes of insects give an erect retinal image.

As Le Grand has said epigrammatically, the eye is the only optical instrument which forms an image which has never been intended to be seen. This is the great difference between the eye and the photographic camera. Failure to realize this lies at the root of many misunderstandings.

The 'retinal image', or more precisely the succession of retinal images formed in the two eyes in the course of their continual motion, constitutes only the first stage of the visual process. The light reaching the retina is absorbed by sensitive substances contained in the retinal receptor cells (the 'rods' and the 'cones'), thus producing in these receptors various degrees of nervous excitation. This excitation, after having undergone considerable transformations in the complex nervous structure of the retina, is propagated to the fibres of the optic nerves and eventually reaches the visual cortex in the brain. Relatively very little is known concerning the further propagation of these excitations in the brain, and the manner in which the brain, so to say, 'makes use' of them. As to the problem of the precise relationship between the physiological events occurring in the brain and the psychological processes of vision, it is part of the philosophical riddle of the relationship between body and mind, and largely remains a mystery.

It can be stated, none the less, that we do not see the 'pattern' of excitation which occurs in our brains as the distant result of the excitation of the retinal receptors by the light which forms the retinal image, any more than we see the pattern of excitation produced in the retina, or the light flux which enters the eye and causes this retinal excitation.[1]

---

[1] Modern anatomical and physiological research has shown that there is a (complicated) correspondence between the pattern of excitation of the retina and the pattern transmitted by the optic nerve to the visual cortex of the brain; see for example Pirenne (1967a). Descartes in his *Dioptrique* had already postulated that the retinal excitation pattern was conveyed to the brain, so that a picture ('une peinture') was formed there, bearing a certain resemblance to that formed on the retina and therefore to the external objects. But Descartes himself insisted that it was *not* by virtue of the resemblance of this 'picture' with the objects that we see them '*as if there were again other eyes within our brain with which we could see it*' (see Pirenne, 1950). It will be seen that the retina, and therefore the retinal image, extends over considerably more than a hemisphere inside the eyeball. Again it must be borne in mind that, on account of the continual movements of the eyes, the pattern of nervous action in the retina changes many times per second, even when we look at an unchanging external scene. The resulting pattern in the brain changes in a corresponding manner. The more one considers the characteristics of the nervous visual process, the less it seems possible to conceive how vision could occur as a result of somehow 'seeing' the spatial pattern, formed by these processes, in the way we see a picture. Of someone who stated that the Impressionists 'painted their retinal image', a psychologist, the late Professor George Humphrey, said: 'He believes that he sees his retinal image: he would have a shock if he could.' We are hardly aware of the nervous processes occurring in our body. What an artist sees and paints on his canvas is not his retinal image, nor the stimulation pattern formed in his brain.

We see the objective world which lies outside our eyes. Sometimes we also see 'things' which definitely do not belong to the external world, for example the floating spots caused by small bodies inside the optical media of the eye, which intercept the light on its way to the retina. Again, if we suffer from migraine, we may see bright scintillating designs caused by a disturbance occurring in the visual cortex of the brain. Now we see such 'things' in front of us, outside our eyes. We do not see the floating spots inside our eyes, even though the small bodies which cause them are inside our eyes. Neither do migraine sufferers see scintillating designs inside their brain, even though the disturbance which lies at their origin exists there only. What we see always appears to be external to our eyes.

Pictures as representations

Our visual perception of the external, physical, world is selective, incomplete and often erroneous. Again, the percepts of one observer differ from those of another, even when they both look at the same things under the same conditions. Nevertheless, in any given observer under given conditions, all the subsequent stages of the nervous processes relating to the vision of a set of objects are dependent on the first stage, the pattern of excitation produced in the light receptors by the retinal image. And this nervous pattern does itself depend on the characteristics of the complex light flux which, originating from the objects, strikes the eye.

Now imagine for the sake of argument that a representational painting or a photograph could be made so as to send into the eyes exactly the same distribution of light as would be sent by the objects depicted by the painting. In such an ideal state of affairs, it would follow that, in any given observer, under given conditions, the pattern of retinal excitations produced by the painting would be essentially the same as the pattern produced by the actual objects. Other things being equal, later stages of excitation in the nervous system and in the brain would also be the same. Accordingly the painting would be mistaken for the real objects it represents. This would be true for all observers. The percepts would differ from observer to observer. But for each and every observer, objects and painting (when viewed under the same conditions) would give the same percepts. Thus, *in theory*, a trompe-l'oeil might be painted which would totally deceive the eye, and the mind, of any observer. (Pozzo's painted ceiling, discussed in Chapter 7, comes fairly close to a realization of this ideal experiment.)

This brief argument may be enough to show that a representational painting is *not* the artist's psychological, subjective, percept. The painting is an *object*, which does produce visual percepts in the observers, that is, the spectators or the artist himself, which resemble those which would be given by the (actual or imaginary) scene represented.

A painting or a photograph which would be a perfect imitation of the scene depicted would give to each observer the same subjective percepts as the scene would give him, because it would *act upon his eyes* in the same way as the actual scene.[1]

In almost all cases, as will be seen, paintings, and photographs also, fall very far short of such an ideal of perfect imitation. Yet, almost by definition, the picture made by a representational painter always must, at least in some respects, *act upon the eyes* of the spectator in the same manner as the actual scene he wishes to depict would act upon them. From an optical standpoint, a representational painting is an object which sends to the spectator's eyes a complicated light flux resembling to a certain extent the light flux which would be sent by the scene it purports to represent.

For this reason, some of the relationships between optics and representational painting can be discussed in spite of an incomplete knowledge of the physiology and psychology of the visual process. An instance is given by linear perspective, which was developed and discussed before even the formation of the retinal image was understood.

Linear perspective and the picture surface. This book is to a large extent devoted to problems relating to linear perspective, which is the geometrical basis of representational painting and of photography. Perspective provides a linear structure for the depiction on a surface of the apparent shape, size, and relative position of the objects constituting a scene in three dimensions: that is, for the representation of form, or for what is sometimes called the 'representation of space'. The geometry of perspective rests on the fact that, while we can hear round corners, we cannot see round corners, because light propagates itself in straight lines.

[1] Such a pictorial representation of a real scene would send to our eyes a complicated light flux of exactly the same kind as that which is sent by a plane mirror in which we see the reflection of this scene: but with the all-important difference that the representation would do so when the scene was not there. Such a representation would, like the mirror, give a total illusion. It would, like the reflection in the mirror, be perceived differently by different observers, since they perceive the scene itself in different ways. But this ideal representation would be a perfectly objective one, containing no trace of the personality of the man who would have made it. Consequently, it could not somehow *be* the personal, subjective percept of any one man viewing the scene.

A plane mirror, or to be quite exact a system consisting of two plane mirrors suitably arranged, sends to every eye the actual light flux which comes from the real scene. Consequently, what we see in the mirror is reality itself. The illusion produced by the mirror is thus of a very special kind. The mirror does not *represent* reality, it *presents* to us reality.

Accordingly the phrase 'an artist wishing to hold a mirror to Nature' can only mean an artist whose ideal is an objective, exact, complete representation of reality. Now an artist's representation of reality does in fact necessarily depend on his knowledge of reality. But an artist is a man, and all human knowledge is personal knowledge. Even in science, as Polanyi (1958) has emphasized, there is no completely impersonal knowledge. The personal psychology of the artist will, perforce, intervene even if the only aim he is striving after is a completely objective representation of the reality before his eyes—and such an aim can only be an unattainable ideal. (This problem is examined further in Chapter 12.)

The problem of the use of linear perspective in pictorial representation would be a relatively straightforward one but for the following fact—which seems to have been almost completely overlooked. When ordinary pictures are viewed in the usual manner, with both eyes, the spectator is aware of the characteristics of the picture surface, including its shape and position. This is very important for his perception of the picture. It is only in exceptional cases or when special arrangements are being used that this 'subsidiary awareness' of the picture surface, *qua* surface, fails to arise: then the picture is a trompe-l'oeil, perceived as a scene in three dimensions. In most cases this special awareness of the picture surface is present, a fact which has important consequences with regard both to the practical usefulness of pictures as representations and to their artistic effect.

First, awareness of the surface works in some ways *against* illusion, by bringing to the spectator's notice the so-called marginal distortions of exact perspective, which 'distortions' should on a simple theoretical basis remain undetected when the spectator is at the right position. Secondly, this awareness of the surface does, in other ways, work *for* illusion, by giving stability to the perception of the scene represented in spite of the spectator's displacements relative to the picture. Such displacements should, again on a simple theoretical basis, cause deformations in the appearance of the scene represented: yet in practice these deformations are hardly noticeable. Finally, the fact that, while he concentrates his attention on the scene represented, the spectator at the same time is subsidiarily aware of the picture surface, as a surface, means that, unwittingly at least, he must be influenced by the composition and other characteristics of the painted pattern itself. That is, he must be influenced by specifically artistic elements which representational painting has in common with non-representational painting.

2 *The formation of optical images*

The concept of light rays

The concept of light rays probably arose originally from a consideration of such phenomena as the shadows cast by illuminated objects, and the beams of sunlight the straight paths of which are made visible by the presence of dust or smoke in the air when they enter a darkened room. Such observations led to the idea that any beam or pencil of light consists of a very large number of rays propagated independently of one another, the path of each ray being a straight line in any medium of even density.

'The least Light or part of Light, which may be stopp'd alone without the rest of the Light, or propagated alone, or do or suffer anything alone, which the rest of the Light doth not or suffers not, I call a Ray of Light.' This was Newton's definition.[1] (It is only at the end of his *Opticks*, in Query 29, that Newton put forward his corpuscular theory of light: 'Are not the Rays of Light very small bodies emitted from shining substances?')

The preceding definition was formulated so as to take account of the finite speed of propagation of light, whereas older definitions did not: 'Mathematicians usually consider the Rays of Light to be Lines reaching from the luminous Body to the Body illuminated, and the refraction of those Rays to be the bending or breaking of those lines in their passing out of one Medium into another. And thus may Rays and Refractions be considered, if Light be propagated in an instant...' (Newton, 1730). This was essentially the concept used by Kepler. It remains of the greatest practical value in many optical problems, but can give only approximate solutions to them. It was eventually found that the light-ray theory was unable to explain diffraction, which always accompanies the propagation of light. Experiment shows that it is not possible, for instance by using very small apertures, to isolate the single light rays of the ray-theory.

A primary source of light, that is a self-luminous body such as the sun, emits light which falls on innumerable other bodies, themselves not self-luminous, but which scatter or reflect in many directions part of the light they receive from the primary source. Not only ordinary solid objects but, say, the clouds, the drops of rain and the dust contained

[1] *Opticks* (1730), Bk I, Pt I, Def. I.

in the atmosphere, and the very air of the atmosphere itself, act as secondary light sources. The light coming from the secondary sources falls on other bodies, which again scatter or reflect part of it. Even black objects as a rule scatter appreciable amounts of light. They look black, not because they send no light at all to the eye, but because they send relatively much less light than neighbouring light-coloured objects.

According to the light-ray theory, therefore, each luminous point, whether it belongs to a primary or to a secondary source, sends innumerable light rays into surrounding space. Consequently, in the air in which we live and move, light rays coming from all directions must intersect at every point. 'The air is full of an infinity of straight and radiating lines intersected and interwoven with one another without one occupying the place of another.'[1] So wrote Leonardo da Vinci (1452–1519). On this basis he explained that the optical images of illuminated objects are, *potentially*, present everywhere in the space around them. In his writings Leonardo returned repeatedly to this fundamental concept which he demonstrated with the help of the camera obscura.[2] Using a pinhole camera, which casts on its screen the images of objects situated in front of its small aperture, he observed that such images are produced for any position of the aperture. This does prove that the light reaching any small region of space conveys the images of surrounding bodies. On the basis of his concept of light rays, Leonardo went further and concluded, but wrongly, that even a most minute aperture should be able to transmit optical images.[3]

'All bodies together, and each by itself', wrote Leonardo, 'give off to the surrounding air an infinite number of images which are all in all and each in each part, each conveying the nature, colour and form of the body which produces it.'[4] This recalls the poet Lucretius's (95–52/51 B.C.) account of the centripetal theory of vision which dates back to the philosophers Democritus (d. 361 B.C.) and Epicurus (342–270 B.C.): 'I maintain therefore, that replicas or insubstantial shapes of things are thrown off from the surface of objects. These we must denote as an outer skin or film, because each particular floating image wears the aspect and form of the object from whose body it has emanated.'[5] But this ancient theory was, indeed, incomprehensible, whereas Leonardo did understand how images can be conveyed by light.[6]

---

[1] Richter & Richter (1939), No. 64A.
[2] Richter & Richter (1939), Nos. 58, 59, 61, 63, 64, 64A, 65, 66, 67, 70.
[3] It does not appear that Leonardo was aware of the limitations of his light-ray theory—even though he made the suggestion that light propagates itself by a wave motion (Richter & Richter (1939), No. 69).
[4] Richter & Richter (1939), No. 61.
[5] *De Rerum Natura*, Bk VI. Trans. Latham (1958).
[6] Leonardo rejected the centrifugal theory of the emission of visual rays by the eye, saying that even if the eye consisted of a million worlds, this would not prevent its being consumed in the projection of its visual power (Richter & Richter (1939), No. 68).

Alhazen (Ibn Al-Haitham, A.D. *c.* 965–1039) used the pinhole camera obscura in astronomical studies and understood its theory (Winter, 1954; Schramm, 1963; Lindberg, 1967). It is probable that Leonardo da Vinci was acquainted with the optical works of the great Arab physicist. But in any case his own writings are here of special interest because of their connection with the theory of representational painting.

The pinhole camera

In a passage entitled 'Prove how all objects, placed in one position, are all everywhere and all in each part'[1] Leonardo wrote: 'I say that if the front of a building, or any open piazza or field, which is illuminated by the sun has a dwelling opposite to it, and if, in the front which does not face the sun, you make a small round hole, all the illuminated objects will project their images through that hole, and be visible inside the dwelling on the opposite wall which should be made white; and there, in fact, they will be upside down, and if you make similar openings in several places in the same wall you will have the same results from each. Hence the images of the illuminated objects are everywhere on this wall and all in each minutest part of it. The reason, as we clearly know, is that this hole must admit some light to the said dwelling, and the light admitted by it is derived from one or many luminous bodies. If these bodies are of various colours and shapes the rays forming the images are of various colours and shapes[2] and so will the representations be on the wall.'[3]

One of Leonardo's diagrams is reproduced in Fig. 2.1. It shows how two separate inverted images of the set of the three bodies *a*, *c* and *e* are formed in the same camera obscura, one by a hole situated at *n*, the other by a hole situated at *p*.

The diagrams of Figs. 2.2 and 2.3 illustrate the principles of this type of camera obscura. Into the dark chamber *O* no light can enter except through a small aperture, the 'pinhole', havings its centre at *H*. The surface of the camera wall opposite the aperture constitutes the screen which receives the image of illuminated objects situated outside. Consider three luminous object points *A*, *B* and *C*, each of which sends light rays in all directions. Each point of space in front of the camera lies at the intersection of three light rays, coming from *A*, *B* and *C* respectively. This applies to the point *H*, the centre of

---

[1] Richter & Richter (1939), No. 70.

[2] 'Stampe' in the text; this word, translated as 'Shapes', refers to the array of rectilinear light rays, which carries the imprint of the objects like a stamp or mould.

[3] The beginning of Leonardo's *Treatise on Painting* contains a brief paragraph entitled 'Basis of the science of painting' which says that the image of a plane surface is entirely contained in another plane surface placed opposite to it, and in any point of this surface (McMahon (1956), No. 2; Richter & Richter (1939), Vol. 1, *Paragone*, No. 3, p. 32). This is clearly the same idea as in the passage just quoted, although, as given in the *Treatise*, without further explanation, it appears as a rather puzzling statement.

the pinhole. The rays *AH*, *BH* and *CH* continue their path in straight lines inside the dark chamber, impinging on the screen at *a*, *b* and *c*.

Disregarding diffraction, consider the light rays diverging from any given object point in straight lines. The edges of the aperture in the camera will define among the rays originating from this point a cone which enters into the chamber, and which is intercepted by the opposite wall or screen (Fig. 2.3). Accordingly the image of any object point is the

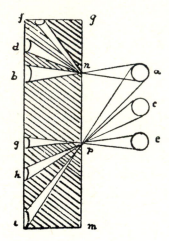

2.1 Camera obscura with two pinholes, according to Leonardo da Vinci

The two holes *n* and *p* form each an image of the three objects *a*, *c* and *e* on the opposite walls of the darkened room. (The rays which should join *c* and *e* to *n* are omitted in the drawing.) (From Richter, J. P. and Richter, I. A. (eds.) (1939), *Leonardo da Vinci: Literary Works*, No. 66.)

central projection of the camera aperture on the screen, the centre of projection being the luminous object point. In the arrangement of Fig. 2.3, where the plane of the aperture is parallel to that of the screen, the image of any object point is a light patch the shape of which is geometrically similar to that of the aperture—it will be a circle if the aperture is circular. The image of an illuminated object consists of innumerable light patches of this kind, which overlap one another, and each of which corresponds to one point of the object. Now the centre of each patch is defined by the central projection of the corresponding object point according to Fig. 2.2. That is, the general shape of the image is the central projection of the objects on the screen, the centre of projection here being the centre of the 'pinhole'. As the image of every point of the object is expanded into a patch of light, the result for a fairly large aperture is that a blurred (and sometimes a misleading) inverted image of the whole object is formed on the screen (Fig. 2.4).

Now on the basis of the light-ray theory it is obvious that if the aperture is replaced by a smaller one, all the cones of light rays of Fig. 2.3 will become narrower, so that the corresponding patches on the screen will be smaller, and the image of the object will be sharper, as shown in Fig. 2.4 for holes 3·0, 1·0 and 0·38 mm in diameter. It will also be dimmer, since the amount of light entering the camera to form the image decreases as the area of the aperture decreases.

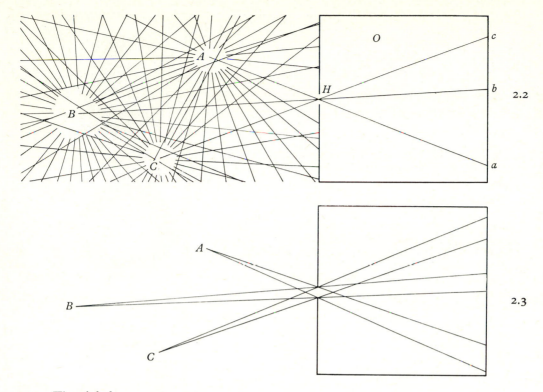

2.2, 2.3 The pinhole camera

Whereas each luminous point sends divergent rays into its surroundings (Fig. 2.2), the pinhole camera does select certain cones of rays (Fig. 2.3) from among all the rays which fill the whole of space, so that the *main rays* of these cones do now *converge* towards the centre of the pinhole. These main rays are shown in Fig. 2.2 as the lines *AH*, *BH* and *CH*.

The fact that image-forming systems so select certain cones of rays in each of which the rays diverge from its object point, while the cones themselves all converge towards the image-forming system, is the crux of the matter with regard to the formation of 'real' optical images.

The situation is essentially the same for the eye—except that inside the eye, as well as inside the lens camera, the rays of each cone are made to converge, whereas inside the pinhole camera they remain divergent. Outside the eye, the narrow divergent cones of rays coming from the different object points all converge towards the pupil. The main rays of all these individual cones thus form a *visual pyramid* or a *pyramid of sight* which geometrically diverges from the eye, even though physically the light goes towards the eye. From a geometrical standpoint, therefore, the mathematical lines representing light rays diverge from all the object points, but the main rays, each of which relates to an individual object point, do also diverge *from the eye*—a fact evidently related to the ancient theory of the emission of visual rays.

On the basis of the light-ray theory, the diagram of Fig. 2.3 thus suggests that it should be possible to make each of the pencils of light entering the camera as thin as one might wish, simply by reducing the size of the pinhole. A most minute aperture used as a pinhole should cast on the screen, as the image of each luminous object point, a corre-

Diameter of 'pinhole'
used for each photograph

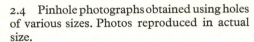

3 mm.

1 mm.

0·38 mm.

0·09 mm.

2.4   Pinhole photographs obtained using holes of various sizes. Photos reproduced in actual size.

The diameter of the circular hole used is indicated with each photograph. The test objects were placed at a distance of 46 cm in front of the pinhole, and the photographic plate was 14 cm behind it. Holes 3·0, 1·0 and 0·38 mm in diameter gave images of increasing sharpness when the hole used was smaller, as expected on the basis of the light-ray theory. But on account of the effect of diffraction, the smallest hole, 0·09 mm in diameter, gave an image less sharp than that given by the hole 0·38 mm in diameter. The smallest C-test object is resolved only in the photograph obtained with a hole 0·38 mm in diameter. This smallest C is at the centre of the largest C, but is hardly visible in the present reproduction. The second smallest C, however, is seen to be more blurred for 0·09 than for 0·38 mm.

It will be noted that the largest hole (3 mm) produces an image which is not merely blurred, but in part misleading. One of the black C's, on the right, is imaged as a central black patch surrounded by a grey halo. Such effects of 'spurious resolution' must be expected when the image of each object point is expanded as a circle. They depend of course on the size of this circle relative to that of the image of the object. Jurin (1738) studied the theory in detail with regard to retinal images out of focus in the eye. (Photos by A. S. Evett.)

spondingly minute patch of light. The sharpness of the inverted image of the objects should therefore increase indefinitely as the pinhole is progressively reduced in size. This, it seems, is what Leonardo would have expected to happen.

In fact, however, for pinholes smaller than a certain critical size, the sharpness of the image no longer increases according to this prediction. The image for a hole 0·09 mm in diameter is less sharp than that for 0·38 mm in Fig. 2.4. The sharpness decreases on account of light diffraction, as the size of the patch corresponding to each point source now *increases* when the size of the hole decreases.[1]

Diffraction, which is inseparable from the propagation of light, always occurs in such experiments. But, to be easily demonstrated, diffraction phenomena require the use of an intense source of light, which must be either very small or be used in conjunction with a very small aperture.

Diffraction of light

The term 'diffraction' was introduced by Grimaldi (1618–63) who was the first to observe and study this phenomenon. As is universally known, diffraction effects are now accounted for on the basis of the wave-theory of light, whose origin goes back to Christian Huygens (1629–95).

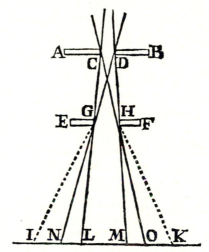

2.5 Diffraction of light by a small aperture
The light patch *IK* is considerably larger than the largest image *NO* expected on the basis of the theory of light rays. See text. (From Grimaldi (1665), *Physico-Mathesis de Lumine, Coloribus et Iride.*)

In one of Grimaldi's experiments (Fig. 2.5), light from the sun was made to enter a darkened room through a very small aperture *CD* in the window shutter *AB* (the aperture *CD* then acting as a small light source) and made to pass through a second small aperture *GH* in an opaque screen *EF* (this aperture *EF* acting as the pinhole of a camera obscura). The light having passed through both apertures was made to fall on the white screen *IK*. If light propagation were strictly rectilinear, the patch of light should be confined within the area extending from *N* to *O*, the extent of which is limited by the intersection of the straight lines *DG* and *CH* with the screen *IK*. No light should fall on the screen beyond

[1] In experiments such as Leonardo's, however, it will be shown presently that the effect of such small apertures can hardly be tested, for the simple reason that the image they cast on the screen becomes too dim to be seen clearly.

the *penumbra* as defined by *NL* and *MO*, which surrounds the fully illuminated central area *LM*. Now Grimaldi found that the light patch extended markedly beyond *NO*, from *N* to *I* and from *O* to *K*. This he determined by comparing the observed diameter *IK* of the patch with the diameter *NO* of the theoretical penumbra calculated on the basis of the dimensions of the experimental arrangement. (Figure 2.5 is a diagram in which the size of the apertures is much too large in comparison with the distances between apertures and screen.) It must be concluded, therefore, that in such an experiment light is, to a certain extent, 'bent into the shadow'. Grimaldi also observed that, while the middle of the light patch on the screen was white, its edges were coloured.

Returning to the diagram of Fig. 2.3, experiment shows that when the aperture of a pinhole camera is made progressively smaller, the 'image' of a very small and bright light source first becomes smaller, for geometrical reasons, and then becomes larger. For smaller and smaller apertures below the critical size, the light patch on the screen becomes larger and larger; it also becomes rapidly dimmer. Eventually for an extremely small aperture, the light transmitted by the aperture extends over the whole screen, so that the camera then fails altogether to produce an image of the luminous point.

Accordingly, as illustrated in Fig. 2.4, there is an aperture of optimum size, depending on the distance of the aperture to the screen, and of that of the lighted objects to the aperture, which must be used in order to obtain the sharpest image in a pinhole camera (Hardy & Perrin, 1932; Wood, 1934; Clerc, 1946).

The light patch formed by a small light source and a small aperture is a complicated pattern. As a rule the centre of the patch is surrounded by concentric darker and brighter fringes, which become fainter as one moves away from the centre. When the light of the source is white, the fringes show colours. The very centre of the patch may be bright, but under some conditions, strangely enough, it is dark.

Similar diffraction fringes can be seen at the edges of the shadow of solid objects cast on a screen by a sufficiently small and bright source. The reason why these characteristic diffraction fringes are not apparent, say, in the shadows ordinarily cast by the sun, is that the fringes due to all the individual points of the extended source are smoothed out by overlapping and become confused within the penumbra.

Wave and quantum properties of light

Newton wished to explain such diffraction phenomena, which he referred to as the 'inflections' of light, by the hypothesis that individual, independent, light rays became bent as they passed close to the edge of opaque bodies. The whole development of optics since the beginning of the nineteenth century, however, has made it impossible to retain this concept of independent light rays. In the experiment first performed by Thomas

Young (1807), the arrangement consists of one small light source, two small holes pierced close to each other in the same diaphragm, and a screen. The light patch formed on the screen then contains a particular pattern of sharp bright and dark fringes, which is absent when only one hole is used at a time. Thus the characteristics of the light pattern received on the screen change entirely when one of the holes is covered or uncovered. The sharp fringes given by the two holes together are impossible to account for on the supposition that the light intensities of the two patches given by each hole separately are simply added together, as should be the case if the holes transmitted light rays independent of one another. The explanation is that the light passing through one of the holes *interferes* with the light passing through the other, because light is propagated, not by independent rays, but by a wave-motion.

It is unnecessary to point out the importance of diffraction and interference phenomena in modern physical optics. It was their thorough investigation which led to the complete acceptance of the wave-theory of light in the nineteenth century. A further, fundamental, development was the theory that light waves are electromagnetic waves, light being a form of radiant energy, like radio waves, infra-red radiation and X-rays.

In the present century the quantum theory arose when this electromagnetic wave-theory was found incapable of explaining some further experimental facts (see Rosenfeld, 1936). This does not mean, however, that the classical wave-theory has been overthrown. It has only been modified by the introduction of quantum considerations. It is necessary to ascribe to light sometimes wave properties, and sometimes quantum properties. Roughly speaking, light when in transit may be regarded as consisting of waves, but when it is emitted or absorbed by matter, it must be regarded as consisting of the *photons* of the quantum theory, which are indivisible packets of light energy. That is, light possesses 'corpuscular' properties, but of a very peculiar kind. A 'photon in transit' can only interfere with itself. The *same* photon passes through the two holes in Thomas Young's experiment.

That light thus seems to possess two sets of apparently incompatible properties has been, and still is, a major subject of discussion among theoretical physicists. But the fact itself, that light sometimes behaves as waves, and sometimes as indivisible packets of energy, is not in question.

Newton had cautiously discussed the physical nature of light, suggesting that it consisted of material particles, the light rays of mathematicians representing the trajectories of these particles. This corpuscular theory of light was taken up more dogmatically by Newton's successors—later to be entirely superseded, for a while, by a purely undulatory theory.

It must be emphasized that the concept of the photons of the modern quantum theory is different from that of the 'very small bodies' of Newton's theory, because quantum properties become apparent only when light is emitted or absorbed by matter. Light in transit does not behave like, say, a stream of machine gun bullets, or like drops of rain falling from the sky, whose trajectories could be accurately plotted. Light in transit behaves like waves.[1]

As can be seen by casting pebbles into a pond, waves can cross one another and afterwards continue to spread undisturbed—even though they do interfere with one another while they cross. As light in transit behaves like waves, this helps to explain that different fluxes of light can cross in space, in the pinhole of a camera, and in the pupil of the eye, whereas if light consisted of 'very small bodies' in motion, or of thin lines as suggested by the ray-theory, the light fluxes might be expected to hinder one another on their respective paths.

Theory of image formation

The wave-theory explains why too small a pinhole casts very blurred images on the camera screen. It also solves the general problem of the irreducible inaccuracy of all optical images, even when formed by the best optical systems. Thus it explains quantitatively the theoretical limits of the resolving power of such instruments as the telescope and the microscope. The success of the modern optical industry is based on the wave-theory.

The basic idea of the theory of the resolving power of image-forming instruments is that the maximum accuracy attainable by the instrument, on the assumption that it is entirely free from defects, is determined by the spatial extent of the light flux which enters into it through its aperture—because of the finite length of the wavelength of light.

This refers to the geometrical dimensions of the optical system, for instance to the angle of the cones of Fig. 2.3, not to the total quantity of light entering it. This quantity of light is implicitly assumed to be always large enough to produce the best image which the system can give. If there is too little light the quality of the image deteriorates for reasons ultimately connected with the quantum properties of light.

In the case of the telescope, which forms the image of distant objects, it is theoretically the area of the object lens which limits the resolving power, that is, the amount of detail contained in the image. The best optical system is incapable of increasing the accuracy of the image beyond this limit. The use of a more powerful eye lens will only increase the apparent size of this image; it will not increase the amount of detail contained in it. Ideally, the resolving power of a telescope depends only on the size of its object lens.

Accordingly the light from illuminated objects passing through a sufficiently large area in the neighbourhood of any given point in space does indeed contain potentially an

---

[1] The beginning of Dirac's book (1958) gives a clear non-mathematical exposition of the principles of quantum mechanics.

'image' of these bodies. But this potential 'image' is more accurate when the area considered is larger—and if the area is too small the light passing through it is unable to form any image.

Consider a photographic camera the lens of which has been removed, thus changing it into a camera of the pinhole type, the 'pinhole' in this case being the large aperture previously occupied by the lens. Needless to say, the light flux entering this large aperture will only produce a very blurred, useless, image—whereas the same light flux will of course form a sharp image if the aperture is fitted with the right lens. Now the point is that an image at least as good as this would be obtained, *without a lens*, if the length of the camera were sufficiently increased.

Suppose that the lens of the camera is replaced by a simple pinhole, of optimum size for the actual length of the camera. The accuracy of the image given by this pinhole will be lower than that of the image given by a good lens. But the essential reason for this is that the aperture is smaller in the case of the pinhole than in the case of the lens. It is not that the pinhole camera is without a lens. Indeed for a pinhole of the optimum size it is not possible to improve the accuracy of the image by placing a lens in front of the pinhole.

Thus the use of a lens in a camera obscura is not essential in order to obtain maximum accuracy, provided the size of the aperture and the aperture-screen distance are suitably related to one another. Lord Rayleigh (1910) who has given the theory of this, calculated that the image thrown by a hole 5 mm in diameter (that is, of the same order of size as the pupil of the eye) on a screen situated at a distance exceeding 20 m, should be at least as well defined as that seen direct by the eye—provided it is bright enough. Experiments show that a surprisingly sharp image of the sun (18 cm in diameter for a distance of 20 m) can be obtained under such conditions, showing the sun spots and other details (Wood, 1934). As the minimum distance required to obtain the best image accuracy increases as the square of the diameter of the aperture, however, a quite impracticable distance would be required to rival the resolving power of a telescope. Thus for an aperture of 10 cm the distance should be at least 8 km.

When the minimum distance corresponding to a given aperture is used in a 'pinhole' camera the physical luminance of the image on the screen is inversely proportional to this minimum distance. Consequently when the long distances corresponding to fairly large apertures are used the images of illuminated objects become too dim for their details to be seen clearly. For a distance of 20 m and an aperture 5 mm in diameter, the luminance of the image of an extended object on a white camera screen is roughly 100 million times dimmer than the object itself. This means that an object in sunshine will throw on the screen an image which is about a hundred times dimmer than the object itself would be if it were lit by the moon instead of the sun. Moonlight is roughly one million times dimmer than sunshine.

For a distance of 20 cm and the corresponding optimum-size aperture, 0·5 mm in diameter, the luminance of the image only reaches a value about equal to that of the object lit by the full moon. Now Leonardo da Vinci formed the image of sunlit objects, not of the sun itself. As screens for his camera obscura, he used the actual wall opposite to the aperture, as explained above, and also a very thin sheet of paper, looked at from behind, which he placed nearer the aperture.[1] Even with the latter arrangement (which is similar to that of the ground glass screen in a photographic camera) the image was most probably too dim for its details to be clearly visible when an aperture of optimum size was used. It seems likely, therefore, that Leonardo never was able to ascertain the deterioration of the image caused by the use of apertures smaller than the optimum size, simply because such apertures would have given him images he could hardly see. Thus his actual observations must have given him no serious cause to doubt the truth of his light-ray theory, according to which optical images are potentially present even in the most minute regions of space. For his light, and therefore his sight, began to fail just as the theory was beginning to fail.

As to the fact that our ability to distinguish details decreases at low illuminations, becoming very poor at levels lower than those corresponding to moonlight, this must ultimately be accounted for, not by the wave properties of light, but by its quantum properties. Light is absorbed by the retinal receptors in single photons, or quanta of light energy. Now the eye is one of the most efficient detectors of light in existence. It is still able to function when the quanta thus acting upon the retina are few and far between. Under these conditions we may still be able to see, say, the main features of a very faint image thrown on a screen, while being unable to distinguish any of its finer details. This is so essentially because the effective light stimulus, that is the random pattern of quanta causing nervous stimulation in the retina, is itself too imprecise to register those details.[2]

---

[1] Richter & Richter (1939), No. 71.

[2] The rod cells of the retina are those receptors which are responsible for night vision, the human retina containing about 100 million rods. An extended luminous field can still be distinguished from complete darkness when, on an average, each rod cell 'catches' only one quantum per hour. One quantum is the smallest amount of light energy which can be absorbed by matter. It is as it were an 'atom of light'; but, unlike atoms of matter, it cannot be split. The energy of a quantum of light from the middle of the visible spectrum is of the order of 4×10^{-12} erg, an exceedingly small value.

One quantum absorbed by the retina is not sufficient for seeing, however. A number of the order of 10 quanta is required, under the best conditions. On account of some of the light being lost in the eye, this corresponds to a light energy equivalent to about 100 quanta striking the eye. A small brief flash of light delivering such an amount of energy can just be seen. On this basis it is easy to calculate that the mechanical energy of a pea falling from a height of one inch, would, if transformed into light energy and used without loss, be sufficient to give a faint impression of light to every man who ever lived. The bearing of the quantum theory of light on the physiology of vision is discussed in Pirenne (1967a) and, in a more detailed manner, in Pirenne and Marriott (1962). See also p. 45.

3 *The retinal image*

The optical system of the eye

The shape of the human eye approximates to that of a sphere, about 2·5 cm in diameter (Fig. 3.1). The eyeball is not made of rigid materials, but retains its shape by virtue of fluid pressure within it. Most of its outer coat consists of a dense fibrous membrane, called the *sclera*. In front of the eye the sclera is replaced by a transparent horny window, the *cornea*, which is more convex than the sclera. In the living eye the anterior part of the sclera is seen between the eyelids as the white of the eye. The coloured (blue, green, brown, grey) front of the *iris* is seen through the cornea. The back surface of the iris is lined with black pigment, however, so that the iris constitutes a diaphragm opaque to light. The *pupil* is the opening in the middle of the iris, through which the light passes to reach the retina. The pupil in the living eye appears as a black circle in the middle of the iris. The iris is able to expand or contract, thus altering the size of the pupillary aperture, the diameter of which can vary between about 2 and 8 mm. The pupil normally is small in bright light and dilated in dim light.

Most of the inside surface of the sclera is lined with the *choroid*, a layer containing many blood vessels. The choroid in turn is lined with black pigment, which backs the retina. The *retina* is a thin nervous layer, having a very complicated structure, which covers the greater part of the inside of the eyeball (Figs. 3.1, 3.2 and 3.3). It contains the very numerous receptors cells, the rods and the cones, which are stimulated by the light pattern which constitutes the retinal image. These light-sensitive cells are connected, through the intermediary of other nerve cells contained in the retina, to the many optic nerve fibres which converge together towards the *optic disc*, the place where the optic nerve emerges from the eyeball to go to the brain (Fig. 3.2). Arteries and veins enter the eye through the middle of the optic disc and spread over the retina to form a network of blood vessels between the vitreous humour and the retina—which thus receives nourishment and oxygen both from this network in front and from the vessels in the choroid at the back of it. In a sense the retina may be regarded as a very complex, light-sensitive expansion of the optic nerve, and thus of the brain itself.

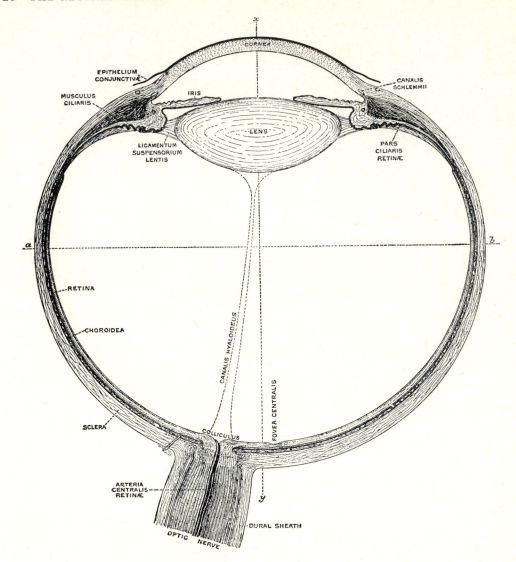

3.1 Horizontal section through the human eye

This is an adult right eye seen from above. The fovea is to the right of the axis *xy*, the optic disc to the left. According to Schäfer, the eyeball measures nearly an inch (24·5 mm) across from *a* to *b*, but slightly less along the axis *xy* (24 mm) and still less from above down (23·5 mm). There are of course individual variations from eye to eye. The wall of the eyeball is about 1 mm thick. (From Schäfer (1894), *Quain's Anatomy*, Vol. III, Pt III.)

The *fovea centralis* is a small depression situated near the axis *xy* of the eye (Fig. 3.1). It is also shown in the centre of Fig. 3.2. The fovea is much less conspicuous in the retina than such features as the optic disc and the blood vessels seen spreading from this disc in

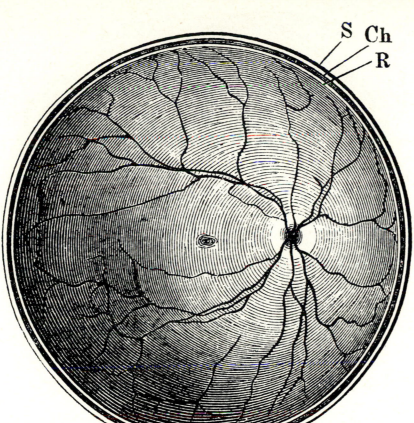

S Ch
R

3.2   View of the posterior half of a sectioned human eye
This is a vertical meridional section through a right eye. The fovea is seen in the middle of the engraving, the optic disc to the right. In the section of the wall of the eyeball, *S* is the sclera, *Ch* the choroid and *R* the retina. (From Helmholtz (1884), *Vorträge und Reden*, Vol. 1.)

Fig. 3.2. In spite of this and of its small size the fovea is the most important region of the retina with regard both to accuracy of vision and to colour vision. When we look at an object to see it clearly, we automatically turn our eye so that its image falls in the fovea. This is the *fixation reflex*. Any point on which we fix our gaze forms its retinal image in the middle of the fovea. Except for the centre of the fovea the retina contains both rods and cones. The centre of the fovea is the only part of the retina which contains only cone receptor cells. These cones are so connected to optic nerve fibres that they may work as if they each had a 'single line' to the brain. This certainly cannot be so for all the cones and rods of the human retina because their numbers are much greater than the

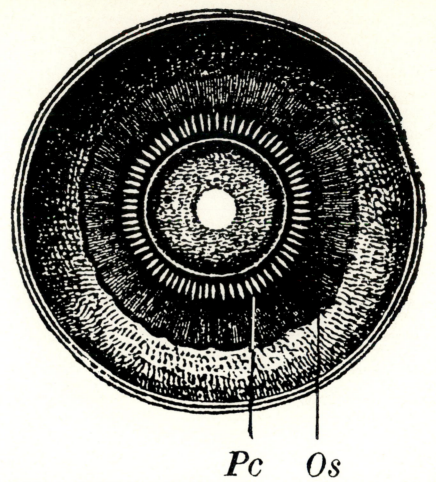

Pc   Os

3.3 View of the anterior half of a sectioned human eye

Taken together with Fig. 3.2, this gives a view of the whole of the inside of the eye. In the middle of the figure, the iris and the bright aperture of the pupil in the centre of it are seen through the lens. The lens is held in position by the suspensory ligaments which are attached to the ciliary processes *PC*, the edges of which are white. The retina, which is drawn in a lighter shade in the lower part of the figure, covers a large part of the front half of the eyeball, its edge being at *Os*. The retina thus extends over an area considerably greater than that of the half-sphere shown in Fig. 3.2 (cf. Fig. 3.1). The inside of the eye is a dark chamber into which light enters only through the opening of the pupil. It is lined with black pigment. The light-sensitive retina, in front of this pigment, receives the luminous image formed by the cornea and the lens, which reach it through the transparent vitreous humour. (From Helmholtz (1896), *Handbuch der Physiologischen Optik.*)

total number of fibres in the optic nerve: there are about 1,000,000 optic nerve fibres, 6,000,000 cones and 100,000,000 rods. But all the finest work of the eye is done by a few thousand cones in the fovea.

The layer of dense black pigment situated between the choroid and the retina prevents the light reaching the retina by diffusion through the wall of the eyeball. This layer of black pigment is continuous with that which lines the back surface of the iris. Accordingly the retina lines the greater part of a round enclosure opaque to light, pierced by the aperture of the pupil. Consequently, under normal conditions, the retina is stimulated only by the light having entered through the pupillary aperture—that is, by the retinal image (Figs. 3.2 and 3.3). (This is not so in the eyes of albino men and animals, in which the black pigment is missing; in albino eyes light does diffuse through the front part of the wall of the eyeball, that is, through the white of the eye, and casts on the retina a luminous veil which interferes with vision.)

The crystalline lens of the eye is situated just behind the pupil; its anterior surface is in contact with the iris. The lens is held in position by a number of filaments, the *suspensory ligaments* which anchor it to the wall of the eyeball through the *ciliary* processes. These form a complicated circular arrangement situated behind and around the iris (Figs. 3.1 and 3.3). The lens has a complex structure. It is not a rigid, but an elastic body; left to

3.4   The crystalline lens of the eye
The lens, removed from the eye, assumes a convex shape by virtue of its own elasticity. (From Helmholtz (1884), *Vorträge und Reden*, Vol. 1.)

itself it assumes a convex shape (Fig. 3.4). When the eye is focused on distant objects, the lens is flattened by the radial pull of the suspensory ligaments and ciliary processes. The eye is then said to be in a state of relaxed *accommodation*. When the eye does accommodate to focus for near objects, the pull of the suspensory ligaments is reduced and the lens becomes more convex, especially on its front surface, by virtue of its own elasticity. This relaxation of the tension of the suspensory ligaments is the result of the contraction of certain muscles attached to the ciliary processes. (In *presbyopia* or old sight, the lens progressively loses its elasticity and the eye therefore loses the power of accommodating for short distances.) The fact that the lens does become more convex in shape when the eye is focused on near objects is beyond doubt. The increase in curvature of the lens can be observed in the living eye by watching, through the cornea and the iris, the reflections of a source of light on the front and back surface of the lens. These reflections are very faint compared with that which is produced by the front of the cornea, but in favourable cases they can be seen and even photographed: their sizes and positions vary when the eye looks at near or at distant objects.[1]

The chamber between the cornea and crystalline lens is filled with a fluid called the *aqueous humour*. The larger chamber between the lens and the retina is filled with a watery jelly, the *vitreous humour*. These humours and the lens are transparent. The crystalline lens, however, has a yellow tinge, and this yellow colour becomes deeper with increasing age.[2] The lens is optically denser than either the aqueous or the vitreous humour. To reach the retina, light must pass through the cornea, the aqueous humour, the lens and the vitreous humour, which are called the *optical media* and which, with the pupil, constitute the *dioptric apparatus* of the eye.

Blackness of the pupil. The outer surface of the cornea, which is covered by a thin film of tear fluid, reflects outwards about 2 per cent of the light striking the eye. Thus the cornea acts as a small convex mirror, giving a diminutive image of external objects. This *corneal reflex*, which plays no part in the visual process, is particularly conspicuous in front of the dark circle of the pupil. Now, if the pupillary aperture usually looks dark, it is not because none of the light having entered the eye is able to come out of it again through the pupil. The light which forms the retinal image is not absorbed entirely by the retina and the layer of black pigment lying behind it. A small fraction of the light forming the retinal image is scattered back, and some of it does emerge from the pupil. But it so happens that under usual conditions, none of the light coming out of the observed eye can enter the pupil of the observer's eye. Because of the optical principle of the reversibility of the paths of light rays, this light entirely returns to the external sources which have originally sent it into the eye. Referring to Fig. 1.2, it will be seen that a point *a* of the image in focus on the retina must scatter light in many directions and that some of this light must emerge from the pupil. But this light retraces the path of the

[1] Cataract is an eye complaint in which the crystalline lens progressively loses its transparency, thus causing partial blindness. The surgical operation for cataract consists in bodily removing the defective lens from the eye. Distinct vision is restored by the use of spectacles: but of course the power of accommodation is lost.

[2] In the same person, the increase in the yellowing of the lens may take place at different rates in the two eyes. Thus the late Professor C. G. Douglas told me that with one eye he saw aubretia flowers as purple, that is, as most people see them, but that with the other eye he saw them as red. No doubt this was because the greater yellowing of the lens in this eye prevented the blue part of the purple light reflected by the flowers from reaching his retina.

rays which have come from the original source A, and therefore returns to A. This is why the pupil looks completely black—so that if one tries to gaze 'into' someone else's eye, all that one sees is a reflection of oneself. 'My face in thine eye, thine in mine appears.'

Albino animals, such as albino rabbits, have 'pink' eyes, that is, their pupil is filled with a characteristic reddish glow, because their eyeball is not lined with black pigment. The pupil here is no longer the only place of entrance and exit for the light: light also enters the eye through the white of the eye and illuminates the retina diffusely. By bringing one's eye close to that of an albino animal, details of its retina can sometimes be seen, the dioptric apparatus of the animal eye playing the same role as a strong magnifying glass placed in contact with an illuminated object.

In principle, the *ophthalmoscope* consists of a partly reflecting, partly transmitting, mirror which makes it possible to throw light onto the retina of a normal eye, through its pupil, in such a way that the light scattered back by the retina does enter the observer's eye. The pupil of the observed eye then is also seen filled with an unusual pink glow. Either with or without the help of a suitable lens, the retina then can be observed through the pupil of the eye. The magnified view of the retina thus obtained is of course of considerable value in medicine.[1]

Central vision

The aqueous and the vitreous humours both consist mostly of water, and their optical properties are very similar to those of pure water. Thus, whereas the pinhole camera and the photographic camera are filled with air, the eye is essentially a camera obscura filled with water. The cornea and the lens are responsible for the refraction of the light entering the eye. The greater part of this refraction occurs at the cornea, which may be regarded simply as a convex surface separating the air outside from the aqueous humour inside the

[1] In a darkened room, in the presence of a light source (but not in the total absence of light) the pupil of the human eye is sometimes seen to glow without the help of an ophthalmoscopic device. This is so when the eye examined is not in focus for the light source, as some of the light scattered by the retina then can emerge from the pupil in directions other than those leading back to the light source. The eyes of animals such as the cat are also observed to glow in this way, more often than human eyes. (The green glow of the cat's pupil is due to the fact that in this animal the retina is lined, not with black pigment, but with a *tapetum* which is greenish in colour.) Helmholtz was helped by earlier investigations of this glow of animal eyes when in 1851 he invented the ophthalmoscope. After the event, but only after the event, one might perhaps wonder why this remarkable though simple invention was not made earlier, at least once the formation of the retinal image had been explained by Kepler. Before Kepler, it seems likely that the blackness of the pupil was a puzzle and a considerable hindrance to the understanding of the functioning of the eye.

A full discussion of the blackness of the pupil and of the ophthalmoscope will be found in Helmholtz (1962), *Treatise on Physiological Optics*; a simple account is given in Pirenne (1967a).

eye. If the crystalline lens were absent, the rays from a distant luminous point, after passing through the cornea, would converge in the eye toward a point situated about 1 cm behind the retina. The lens bends further the rays which reach it through the pupil, thus increasing their convergence sufficiently to bring them in focus on the retina. (The lens of the eye, if used in air, would have a much greater converging power than it has in the eye where it is surrounded by water.) As has been explained, changes in the shape of the lens with consequent alteration of its converging power are responsible for accommodation. Focusing is thus achieved in an entirely different way in the eye than in the ordinary photographic camera, in which it is the length of the camera which is adjusted to focus an object on the sensitive plate.

Gaussian approximation. According to the theory developed by Gauss in the nineteenth century, the main geometrical properties of the image formed by a complicated optical system such as the human eye can be defined merely by the positions of a few *cardinal points* situated on its axis. The positions of these points have been determined for the human eye largely on the basis of painstaking studies of its individual components, the result obtained corresponding to the properties of an 'average' young normal eye (Helmholtz, 1866; Le Grand, 1952). It must be emphasized that the Gaussian theory is valid only for images formed close to the optical axis of the eye, and is no longer so for the images cast on peripheral parts of the retina. As the *fovea centralis* is situated near the optical axis (Fig. 3.1), the Gaussian approximation is applicable to the image formed on this important part of the retina.

Now as far as the geometrical construction of the accurately focused retinal image of an object is concerned, only two cardinal points, the *anterior* and the *posterior nodal points*, need to be considered according to the Gaussian theory. These points are situated inside the crystalline lens, near its posterior surface (Fig. 3.5). To find the position of the image point of a given object point, a straight line is drawn from the object point to the anterior nodal point, and then a second straight line, parallel to the first, is drawn from the posterior nodal point to the retina. The intersection of this line with the retina is the image of the object point. The two nodal points are only one-third of a millimetre apart from one another, so that in many cases it is sufficiently accurate to consider them as one single point, and to draw through this point a straight line from the object point to the retina. This is the construction used in Fig. 1.2. The two nodal points, regarded as one, therefore play in the human eye the same role as the optical centre in a thin lens, which is discussed in the next chapter.

This simple approximate construction only applies to images of objects close to the optical axis of the eye, in focus on the retina. Bearing this in mind, it may be concluded that the image of external objects formed on the central retina by the dioptric system of the eye has almost the same size, shape and position as the image which would be formed by a pinhole camera filled with air if the small pinhole of this camera were situated in between the nodal points of the eye, the camera screen being the retina. But the retinal image is of course sharper and brighter than the image which would be given by such a

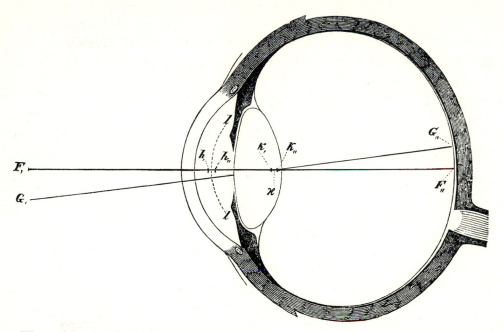

3.5   The nodal points in the human eye

The anterior nodal point is at $K_{\prime}$, the posterior nodal point at $K_{\prime\prime}$. Both are situated inside the lens near its posterior surface. The average distance of the posterior nodal point $K_{\prime\prime}$ to the fovea in the unaccommodated eye may be taken as 16·68 mm (Le Grand, 1952). The image of a distant point in focus on the retina is obtained by drawing a straight line to $K_{\prime}$, and a parallel to this line through $K_{\prime\prime}$ until it reaches the retina.

The point κ midway between $K_{\prime}$ and $K_{\prime\prime}$ is the optical centre of the eye used in the approximation of Fig. 1.2 in which the main rays Aa and Bb cross at κ. All this applies only to retinal images formed near the optical axis $F_{\prime}$, $F_{\prime\prime}$ of the eye, including the fovea whose centre is at $G_{\prime\prime}$. (From Helmholtz (1896), *Handbuch der Physiologischen Optik*.)

pinhole camera, because the aperture of the dioptric apparatus of the eye, namely the pupil, is much larger than the pinhole.

Thus Leonardo da Vinci's intuition was right when it led him to the idea that the eye worked like a pinhole camera obscura and that 'the images of objects received by the eye intersect within the crystalline humour of the eye'.[1] He postulated the existence of a 'point in the eye' which was the apex of his 'pyramid of sight': 'Perspective is nothing else than seeing a place or objects behind a pane of glass, quite transparent, on the surface

[1] Richter & Richter (1939), No. 71.

of which the objects that lie behind the glass are to be drawn. These can be traced in pyramids to the point in the eye, and these pyramids are intersected by the glass plane.'[1] Again: 'By a pyramid of lines I mean those which start from the surface and edges of bodies, and converging from a distance, meet in a single point. A point is said to be that which [having no dimensions] cannot be divided, and this point placed in the eye receives all the points of the cone.'[2]

For images focused on the central retina, the point in the eye may be taken to be the optical centre κ of Fig. 3.5, that is, the crossing point of the straight lines Aa and Bb in Fig. 1.2. Leonardo's *pyramid of sight* here consists of *main rays* such as Aa and Bb. When dealing with the problem of visual angles and of perspective, the exact determination of the apex of the pyramid of sight is, however, rather a delicate matter because the images of objects at different distances from the eye cannot as a rule be focused simultaneously on the retina, and especially because the eye continually rotates in its orbit (see Chapter 5).

In spite of these complications, a fundamental point will be clear by now. While the light originating from each and every object point is *divergent* (Fig. 1.3) there are certain lines, the 'main rays' of Fig. 1.2 which do *converge* towards a point in the eye from all the different object points and which determine the retinal image of the external scene or objects as a whole. These convergent straight lines, outside the eye, form the pyramid of sight, the intersection of which by the picture surface is the image of the objects in linear perspective on this surface (Chapter 7). The 'main rays' constituting the pyramid of sight are the same lines as Euclid's 'visual rays'. They define the visual angles subtended by the objects, which angles are the main subject of natural perspective (Chapter 5). We now know, while Leonardo did not know, that the main rays, like all light rays, are mathematical abstractions—but they remain as useful a concept as ever.

The cardinal points of Gaussian theory also are mathematical abstractions. Knowing the straight path followed in air by a given ray before it strikes the cornea, the theory makes it possible to determine the straight path which the ray will follow, in the vitreous humour, from the posterior surface of the lens to the retina. But the actual paths followed by the rays inside the crystalline lens, for instance, cannot be calculated on the basis of the cardinal points of the eye. The lens of the eye is not a homogeneous body, like a simple glass lens, but consists of many layers of different densities, the inner layers being the denser; consequently light rays actually follow curved paths inside the crystalline lens of the eye. (Moreover all this of course is geometrical optics, based on the concept of light rays, which leaves out of consideration the wave and the quantum properties of light.)

[1] Richter & Richter (1939), No. 83.
[2] Richter & Richter (1939), No. 50. Here again we meet Leonardo's concept of light rays as mathematical lines which could all cross at a mathematical point, based no doubt on his false belief that a pinhole camera with a most minute aperture would project an accurate image; see Chapter 2.

The Gaussian theory offers the great practical advantage that it makes it unnecessary to enter into the details of problems such as that of the path of light inside the lens of the eye. It finds its main value with regard to the design of spectacles, which are intended mainly to improve central, foveal, vision.[1]

The retinal image as a whole

Visual field. The visual field of each eye is the region of outside space in which objects can be seen by this eye when it is in one fixed position, and does not rotate in its orbit. The visual field of each eye can be regarded as 'attached' to this eye. Thus, if the head is kept immobile but the eye rotates in its orbit, the visual field moves with the eye, and with the point of fixation, which corresponds to the middle of the fovea. Consequently the total *field of view* covered by the moving eye is considerably greater than the visual field itself. We are hardly aware of the properties of the different parts of our visual fields since we always tend to turn our eyes so as to use foveal vision when something attracts our

---

[1] *The spherical errors of refraction* of the eye may be briefly discussed here. These are defects of eyes whose optical system is symmetrical around its axis—astigmatism will be discussed later in this chapter. An eye is said to be *emmetropic*, that is, normal as far as refraction is concerned, if it brings into focus a distant object when its accommodation is relaxed. An eye which under these conditions is in focus only for near objects is called *myopic*. One that is out of focus for all distances when its accommodation is relaxed is called *hypermetropic*.

Hypermetropia, or long-sight, may be corrected automatically by always using some degree of accommodation, even for distant objects. Accordingly young subjects sometimes are unaware of this defect in their eyes. Suitable positive lenses, that is, lenses thicker in their centre than at their edges, are used to correct hypermetropia. With their help the unaccommodated eye is in focus for distant objects, like the emmetropic eye.

Myopia, or short-sight, is corrected by suitable negative lenses—thinner in their centre than at their edges. Such lenses, in effect, render the eye emmetropic. Accommodation is of no help to myopes for distant vision: it would only make matters worse. But vision through a pinhole can be of great help to them, for the reason explained in the section on Scheiner's experiment in Chapter 1. Partly closing the eyelids has a similar effect, as this leaves only a small part of the pupil in use; the word 'myope' comes from the Greek *muōps* (*muō* shut + *ōps* eye).

The emmetropic eye (as well as the hypermetropic and the myopic eye so corrected by lenses that they are in effect rendered emmetropic) must accommodate to see clearly objects nearer than about 6 m, the amount of accommodation required increasing rapidly with decreasing distance. Now with increasing age the power of accommodation is progressively lost, because the lens of the eye loses its elasticity. This is *presbyopia*, or old sight, which must not be confused with hypermetropia. The emmetropic eye therefore must wear a positive lens for near vision, when it has become presbyopic. The presbyopic hypermetropic eye needs a positive lens for distance and a stronger positive lens for near vision. The presbyopic myopic eye still needs a negative lens for distance, and, in principle, a weaker negative lens for near vision.

The myope is able to see distinctly objects held closer to his eye than is possible for the emmetrope. Thus the unaided myopic eye is able to see finer details than the normal eye. A strongly myopic eye is able to see such details as well as a normal eye helped by a magnifying lens. It has been suggested that some very fine work in medieval manuscripts was made by myopic artists, at a time when spectacles and magnifying glasses were not in use.

attention. Yet peripheral vision is of great practical importance as it gives a broad view of things, and enables us to detect moving objects 'out of the corner' of the eye: it would be hardly possible to move about safely without peripheral vision.

The visual field of the human eye covers a very large solid angle. Kepler, who stated that 'a little more than the hemisphere of the external world' is projected onto the concave

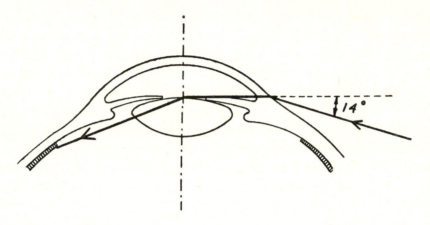

3.6   The limit of peripheral vision

This schematic diagram shows how light rays at an angle of more than 90° from the axis of the eye can still reach the retina, near its forward edge, on account of their being bent inwards by the cornea and the lens. We can see, although very indistinctly, objects which are situated somewhat *behind* the eye. (Redrawn after Hartridge (1919), *J. Physiol.*, **53**, xvii–xviii.)

surface of the retina, remarked that we would be able to see our own ears, each with the eye on the same side of the head, if they were a little longer. Again a man can see at the same time the sun and the shadow cast by his head. Objects situated on the side of the temple of the head at angles somewhat greater than 90° from the axis of the eye can still be seen, albeit very indistinctly. Figure 3.6 shows diagrammatically how light coming from such a direction can reach the retina as a result of its inwards refraction at the surface of the cornea. The retina covers a great deal more than the posterior half of the inside of the eyeball, extending forward to the beginning of the ciliary processes (Figs. 3.1 and 3.3). The retinal image of objects seen by extreme peripheral vision is thus formed behind a part of the white of the eye which can be seen when the eye is turned inwards or outwards.[1]

[1] Kepler in 1604 (*Ad Vitellionem Paralipomena*, Cap. v, 2, p. 175) gave an incorrect explanation of extreme peripheral vision, suggesting that it was made possible by rays passing through the pupil and in between the suspensory ligaments, but *not* through the lens, to reach the most forward part of the retina. He was driven to this view by the erroneous belief that the lens was

The shape of the visual field is not a regular geometrical figure. Again, vision becomes more and more indistinct towards the edges of the visual field. If therefore the field is measured with test objects placed in various angular positions with regard to the point of fixation, the field defined on this basis is found to be smaller when smaller test objects are used.[1]

Constriction of the light flux. Consider the cone-shaped flux of light which diverges from an object point situated away from the optical axis of the eye, and the (approximately) convergent light flux into which it is transformed after passing through the cornea, the aqueous humour, the pupil and the lens. Relative to the original light flux in the air outside the eye, the whole of the flux in the vitreous humour has undergone a general bending towards the axis of the eye. This is shown diagrammatically in Fig. 1.1 from Descartes for the points V and Y, which form their images respectively at R and T on the retina. (The diagram of Fig. 3.6 shows an extreme case of this bending.) It is only in the case of the point X, which is on the axis of the eye, that the conical fluxes the apices of which are at X and S have a common axis XS. Thus there is a general 'squeezing' of the light fluxes from all external object points into a narrower compass as they enter the eye: this helps to increase the angular extent of peripheral vision (see also Figs. 3.7 and 3.8). It is essentially due to the fact that the eye is filled with aqueous media, denser than the air outside the eye.

For central vision the Gaussian approximation does take this general constriction of the light flux into account. Helmholtz's diagram of Fig. 1.2 is approximately correct with regard to the construction of the image ab of the object AB in focus on the retina. But this construction, or the more accurate construction based on the two nodal points, becomes less and less applicable as one considers a retinal region extending farther and farther towards the periphery. That is, the retinal image as a whole cannot be determined

placed deep inside the eyeball, and widely separated from the pupillary aperture in the iris. Figure 1.1 from Descartes is also anatomically incorrect, but to a lesser extent. The oldest detailed diagram of the eye, from an Arabic manuscript dated 1197, puts the crystalline lens in the centre of the eyeball. The anatomist Vesalius still does the same in his *De corporis humani fabrica* published in 1543. Scheiner's diagram published in 1619 is more accurate than Descartes's but the iris is not depicted in contact with the lens. These three drawings are reproduced, with a number of others, in S. L. Polyak's book, *The Retina*, 1941.

[1] It may be pointed out that, contrary to what has sometimes been stated, the visual field, or rather its projection on a surface, does not correspond to what the artist paints on his canvas. We are normally unaware of the peculiarities of our visual field. It would be truer to say that the artist depicts part of his field of *view*, which takes into account eye movements and changes of fixation. Accordingly there is no physiological reason why the marginal parts of his canvas should be painted in less sharp detail than the middle of it—even though, of course, there may be artistic reasons to leave the outlying parts of a painting relatively indistinct. See the section on the Purpose of the Photographic Camera in Chapter 4.

on the basis of one single optical centre, or of one single pair of nodal points: this will be clear by reference to the case of extreme peripheral vision (Fig. 3.6). The image projected on the concave surface of the retina 'by rather more than a hemisphere of the external world' is not an exact central projection of this region of the external world.

Furthermore, on account of the very strong curvature of the retina, the image of a given object (even a spherical object) must be expected to change its shape, and its size, as eye movements displace it, say, from the periphery to the centre of the retina.

Peripheral astigmatism. Further complications arise in peripheral vision, especially at high angles from the axis of the eye. Figure 3.7 shows how the cone of rays coming from the object point P, which is in a position away from the eye axis, is refracted by the

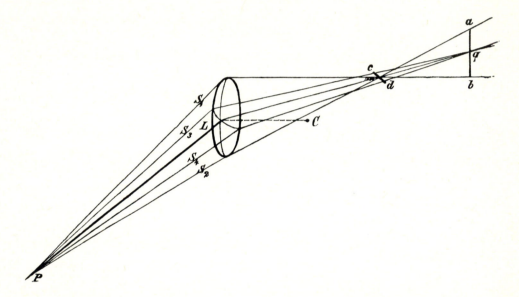

3.7   Oblique astigmatism of the eye

The point source P sends a cone of rays at an angle to the axis of the cornea, which is assumed to be symmetrical around its axis. After refraction by the cornea the rays are never re-united at one focus point, but merely concentrated into two focal lines cd and ab at two different positions. It will be noted that the cone of rays as a whole is bent towards the axis of the cornea after refraction. (From Fick (1879), 'Dioptrik'. In Hermann's *Handbuch der Physiologie*, Vol. III, Pt I.)

cornea of the eye. These rays are nowhere re-united accurately at one image point. Even though the optical system is here assumed to be symmetrical around its axis, it is *astigmatic* for rays at an oblique incidence. The rays from P are partly re-united after refraction at one *focal line cd*, and again partly re-united further away, at a second focal line ab, which

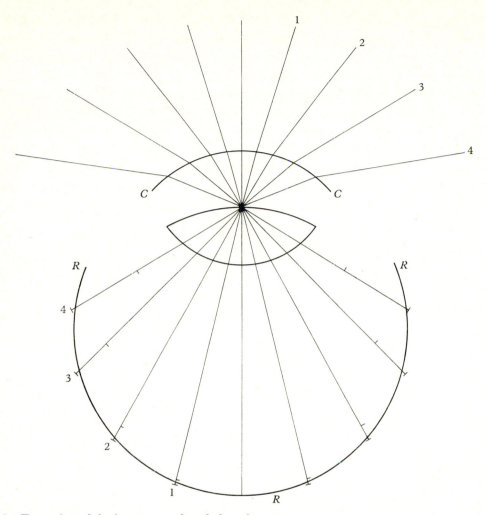

3.8 Formation of the image over the whole retina

This diagram shows the path of the main rays, numbered 1, 2, 3 and 4, coming from four distant object points situated at various angles to the axis of the eye. After refraction by the cornea *CC* and the lens each light flux forms two focal lines, the positions of which are indicated in the drawing. The first focal line is at right angles to the plane of the paper, the second in the plane of the paper. The second focal lines are close to the curved surface of the retina *RRR*. A plane retina tangent to the eyeball at its posterior pole would receive in its periphery a very blurred image in comparison with the actual retina. It will be noted that, as already shown in Fig. 1.1, the whole flux of light entering the eye is constricted by refraction on account of the bending illustrated in Fig. 3.7. (Redrawn with modifications after Fick (1879), 'Dioptrik'. In Hermann's *Handbuch der Physiologie*, Vol. III, Pt I.)

lies in a plane perpendicular to that of *cd*. (The cone of rays oblique to the axis is thus refracted here, by a symmetrical cornea, in the same manner as the rays originating from a point on the axis of the eye would be refracted by an asymmetrical cornea—as will be described below under the heading 'Astigmatic eyes'.) The presence of the lens of the eye (not taken into account in Fig. 3.7) does not, as a rule, remove this astigmatism.

Figure 3.8 shows the result of theoretical calculations giving the directions inside the vitreous humour of the four main rays 1, 2, 3 and 4 of four pencils of rays after these pencils have been refracted by the cornea and the lens. The figure also gives the position of the respective focal lines. It is seen that the second focal lines are formed close to the actual position of the retina. The fact that the retina is strongly curved thus enables it to receive a relatively sharp image of peripherally situated objects—whereas a plane retina perpendicular to the axis of the eyes would only receive an image utterly out of focus for such objects. This peripheral astigmatism increases when the object is at an increasing angle from the axis of the eye; it is of negligible importance near the axis, for instance, for the fovea.

Thus, the formation of the retinal image must be expected to be less accurate in peripheral than in foveal vision, the more so when the angle of the rays with the axis of the eye is greater. In fact there are individual differences from one eye to another. Furthermore, in one and the same eye, the degree of accommodation which gives the best focusing of the image near the axis may differ from that which gives the best image away from the axis (Ferree, Rand and Hardy, 1931; Le Grand, 1956). Accordingly the determination of the shape and accuracy of the retinal image as a whole presents a very difficult problem. It has received much less attention than the easier problem of the formation of the image near the axis of the eye, because it is the improvement of this image which is the main purpose of the design of spectacles.

Astigmatic eyes

It has been assumed so far that the optical system of the eye had symmetrical properties with regard to its axis. Now, by the nature of things, it can hardly be expected to be exactly so. For instance, in many eyes the curvature of the cornea is found to vary with the corneal meridian considered. If this variation is smooth and regular, the curvature is maximum for a certain meridian, and minimum for the meridian in a plane normal to that of the first meridian. This causes *regular astigmatism*.

Figure 3.9 shows the paths of some of the rays originating from a point source, after they have been refracted by an astigmatic cornea. The surface of the cornea constitutes the interface between air, on the left, and the aqueous medium, on the right, in which those parts of the rays shown in the figure are all situated. The meridian of strongest curvature is *ma ma*, that of smallest curvature *mi mi*. (The figure has been drawn, purely as a matter of convenience, with the meridian *ma ma* in a horizontal plane.) If a point source of light is situated in the air, on the axis of this system, the cone of rays emitted by the source and striking the astigmatic cornea will become concentrated, first, into a vertical focal line $b_1 b_1$, and then further away from the cornea into a horizontal focal line $b_2 b_2$, this second focal line being longer than the first one. The astigmatic system is unable to focus the light from a point source into a point image. (Astigmatism comes from the Greek *a* not + *stigma* point.) As shown in Fig. 3.10 a vertical screen placed at

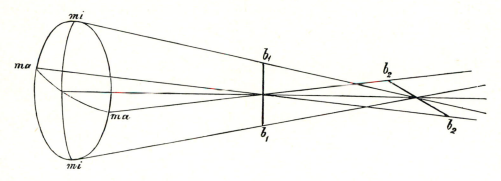

3.9 Effect of corneal astigmatism

The cornea is here assumed to be more strongly curved along *ma ma* than along *mi mi*. The light flux from a point situated on its axis is never re-united into a single focus point, but is concentrated into a vertical focal line $b_1 b_1$, and further back into another, horizontal, focal line $b_2 b_2$. (From Fick (1879), 'Dioptrik'. In Hermann's *Handbuch der Physiologie*, Vol. III, Pt I.)

increasing distances behind the cornea would intersect the refracted beam of light, first as ellipses having a vertical long axis, then as a straight vertical line (the focal line $b_1 b_1$ of Fig. 3.9), then again as ellipses, as a circle, as ellipses having a horizontal long axis, then as a straight horizontal line ($b_2 b_2$ of Fig. 3.9), and finally as ellipses of increasing size. In the case of a symmetrical system, all these sections, apart from the focus point, would be circles—it being taken for granted that the cone of the rays entering the eye is a cone of revolution.

Astigmatism is notoriously difficult to understand without the help of an experimental demonstration showing the actual path of the light rays illustrated in Fig. 3.9. This can be done using a large-scale model of an astigmatic eye filled with an aqueous solution of fluoresceine, whose fluorescence shows the path of the light. The strange shape of the light beam in Fig. 3.9 can then be seen in three dimensions, and the intersection of this beam by a screen placed in various positions presents successively the shapes shown in Fig. 3.10.

The presence of a symmetrical crystalline lens behind the asymmetrical cornea will bring the focal lines nearer to the cornea, without cancelling the astigmatism. If on the other hand the cornea is symmetrical while the lens is not so, astigmatism will again occur. Any lack of symmetry with regard to the axis of the eye will tend to cause astigmatism. The combined effect of all such causes of astigmatism, unless they happen to cancel each other exactly, will be similar to that illustrated in Figs. 3.9 and 3.10. The rays emitted by one object point will nowhere be brought together in one image point,

3.10   Images of an object point formed by an astigmatic eye

The figure represents the shape of the intersections by vertical planes positioned at increasing distances from the cornea, of the light flux produced inside the eye by an astigmatic system such as that of Fig. 3.9. The vertical line corresponds to $b_1\,b_1$, the horizontal line to $b_2\,b_2$ in Fig. 3.9. (From Fick (1879) 'Dioptrik'. In Hermann's *Handbuch der Physiologie*, Vol. III, Pt I.)

but instead will be concentrated into focal lines a certain distance apart. The orientation of these focal lines may be at any angle to the vertical—the two focal lines however always lying in planes at right angles to each other. This orientation of the focal lines, and the amount of astigmatism, vary from eye to eye, even in the same person. Few eyes are entirely free from astigmatism.

Regular astigmatism can be corrected by the use of suitable astigmatic or 'cylindrical' lenses, shaped so as to compensate for the different refraction of the visual system in different planes. Astigmatism may be combined with one of the symmetrical or 'spherical' errors of refraction, namely myopia and hypermetropia. The combined defect can again be corrected by suitable spectacles.[1]

Effects of astigmatism. The main effect of astigmatism on vision is that lines having certain orientations are more clearly seen than others. This can be illustrated by reference to Fig. 3.9. Suppose that the astigmatic eye is such that the second focal line $b_2\,b_2$ lies on the retina. In the drawing this line is horizontal. If the object point whose retinal image is this focal line belongs to a horizontal line outside the eye, the images of all the points of this line will be elongated in the same way. Accordingly all these focal lines will overlap

[1] *Irregular astigmatism* is caused by irregular defects of the corneal surface, having occurred for instance as a result of abrasion in an injury to the eye. It can be corrected only by the use of contact lenses. Water is used to fill the interspace between the corneal surface and the regularly shaped shell constituting the contact lens. This in effect 'repairs' the corneal surface as far as its optics is concerned.

and the horizontal line will be seen sharply (except at both ends). Conversely a vertical line at the same distance will appear blurred, because the image of each of its points will be elongated into a line lying across the direction of the vertical line. The first result of astigmatism therefore is a blurring of vision which varies with the orientation of the objects seen—whereas, for an eye out of focus but which does not suffer from astigmatism, the blurring is independent of this orientation.

The second effect of astigmatism is that it slightly deforms the shape of the retinal image of a whole object, relative to the image which would be formed if the eye were not astigmatic. It must be stressed that this deformation is only slight. For a case of strong astigmatism, Le Grand (1952, p. 145) has calculated that it will be only of the order of 1·5 per cent. Consequently, contrary to what is still being suggested from time to time, the presence of astigmatism in El Greco's eyes would in any case be incapable of explaining the lengthening of some of the human figures painted by this artist.

On the other hand, if a strongly astigmatic eye is corrected by a suitable lens, blurring will disappear, but the retinal image will now be deformed about five times as much as it was before correction, and in the other direction (Le Grand, 1952, p. 147). This is so because ordinary spectacles are necessarily worn at a certain distance from the cornea of the eye. If a normal observer, or an observer whose vision is corrected by spectacles, holds a pair of astigmatic spectacles at a distance of, say, a foot, in front of his eye, objects seen through these glasses will not as a rule look blurred, but their shape will be deformed; the effect usually is different for the two lenses of the pair of spectacles and the deformation of the objects changes as the spectacles are rotated.

This may have led to the wrong idea that the main effect of astigmatism in the eye is to deform the retinal image. An astigmatic lens used as has just been explained deforms rather like a distorting mirror. But, worn in the usual way close to the astigmatic eye for which it has been designed, it acts in a different way, its main function being to correct blurring. It is true that, in so doing, this correcting lens also causes a certain deformation of the retinal image, because it is not close enough to the cornea. But in the same astigmatic eye, uncorrected by the lens, this type of deformation is much smaller, and then of course there is strong directional blurring.

The El Greco fallacy. In any case an artist whose eyes would give him deformed retinal images could not be expected to make drawings showing this deformation, since his eye would deform his drawings in the same way as the objects drawn. The psychologist J. J. Gibson has called 'the El Greco fallacy' the belief that deformations in a picture must be the result of deformations in the vision of the artist who made the picture. Such a belief is clearly wrong in all cases where the deformation affects equally the vision of the picture and that of the objects depicted.

While an artist neither sees, nor depicts on the canvas, his retinal image, what he sees is dependent on the accuracy of his retinal image, or more precisely, the image which is projected on his fovea. If this image is blurred he will see external objects as blurred. Now an artist who is myopic sees near objects clearly, but he has only a blurred vision of distant objects. If he paints such distant objects, therefore, he is likely to paint them blurred, even though he sees his canvas sharply. The notion of the El Greco fallacy is not applicable in such a case; it applies only in cases where the object and its picture are altered in the same way.[1]

Accuracy of the retinal image. Visual acuity

The cones in the fovea are packed side by side so that they form a mosaic in which the distance between the axes of adjacent cones is about 2–$2 \cdot 5 \ \mu$. Now this is not much larger than the wave-length of visible light, $0 \cdot 4$–$0 \cdot 7 \ \mu$. Accordingly a good microscope is needed to observe this minute mosaic, but even so very small details of individual cones cannot be seen at all by visible light because of the limit set by diffraction to the resolving power of the microscope—the 'aperture' of which cannot be increased beyond a certain value.

Diffraction also sets a limit to the accuracy of the image which the eye itself can project on the mosaic of cones. Consider for instance the case of a grating consisting of alternate black and white bars, equal in width, of such dimensions that the grating can just be reliably distinguished from an evenly grey surface, under optimum conditions. It can be calculated that the retinal image of this grating must suffer from considerable blurring on account of the effect of diffraction, even if all the optical defects of the eye are taken to be of negligible importance. Again, on the basis of the construction illustrated in Figs. 1.2 and 3.5, it is easy to find out the distance separating the centres of adjacent 'bars' (in fact slightly darker and slightly brighter fringes) constituting the retinal image of this grating. It is about $2 \cdot 3 \ \mu$, in good agreement with the interaxial distance of the central foveal cones. It appears therefore that the eye can reach an accuracy which corresponds to the fineness of its receptor mosaic, and which at the same time comes close to the physical limit set by the wave properties of light. The latter point is illustrated by the fact that if a diaphragm with a small hole, as discussed in connection with Scheiner's experiment in Chapter 1, is placed in front of the eye pupil, the resolving power of the eye is decreased, as this decreases the aperture of the optical system of the eye.

What has just been said refers to high light intensities, when the pupil is contracted to a

[1] On the relationship of eye defects and eye disease to pictorial art, see Trevor-Roper (1959) and Wirth (1968). The possibility of falling into the El Greco fallacy presents a delicate problem, which should be discussed in each particular case. The present work deals only with normal vision, and, briefly, with current errors of refraction: it does not deal with pathological conditions or with anomalous colour vision. On the last problem, see Guillot (1967).

diameter of the order of 2 mm. The angle subtended at the eye by the intercentre distance of adjacent bars in the finest resolvable grating is a little less than half a minute of arc, which corresponds to a grating made up of bars 1 mm wide, placed 7 m away from the eye. Here the eye behaves almost as a 'perfect' optical instrument, the light intensity being such that only the wave properties of light are directly relevant.

At lower intensities, visual acuity, that is the ability of the eye to distinguish details, for instance in a grating, decreases, presumably because there is no longer enough light to stimulate the cones to a sufficient extent. Visual acuity decreases steadily with decreasing intensity. It is impossible to read a book in moonlight. At very low intensities, below moonlight level, the cones cease to function. The fovea now becomes blind, and vision is mediated entirely by the rods which are very numerous in the retinal periphery. As has been said in Chapter 2, under these conditions the reason why vision becomes very indistinct is that the light quanta stimulating the retina are relatively few and far between, so that the mosaic now formed by the *stimulated* receptors is a very loose one.

The eye still can recognize large shapes at intensities 10,000,000,000 times lower than that of sunlight. The accuracy and the sensitivity of the eye are here linked together and come close to the theoretical limit set by the quantum properties of light. The pupil is expanded at such low intensities, and the outer parts of the lens suffer from more defects than the central part, so that the optical system of the eye becomes a less accurate one, but this is immaterial since here the quantum properties of light itself preclude the formation of a sharp retinal image.[1] This high sensitivity is achieved only as a result of *dark adaptation*, that is, changes occurring in the retina and the visual nervous system, quite aside from the minor part played by the dilatation of the pupil. Dark-adaptation takes about half an hour to establish itself when one goes from daylight into a very dark place.

[1] On the vast subject briefly summarized here, see for example Pirenne (1967a) and Pirenne and Marriott (1962).

4 *The photographic camera and the eye*

Camera obscura with a lens

The well-known principle of the formation of the image of an object by a positive glass lens in air is illustrated by Fig. 4.1, which shows the paths of rays originating from three points *P*, *Q* and *R* of the object and striking the lens *AB*. The rays leaving any one of the object points form a divergent beam. The function of the lens is to render convergent that part of the divergent beam which strikes its surface. In the figure, which represents

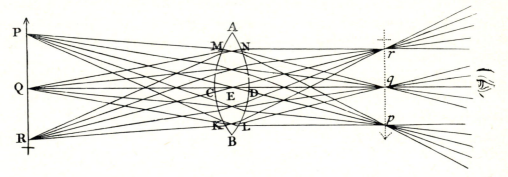

4.1   Formation of an image by a biconvex glass lens
(From Newton (1704), *Opticks*.)

an ideal case, the rays from *P* come exactly together at the image point *p*, those from *Q* at *q* and those from *R* at *r*. Thus *pqr* is the image of the object *PQR*; the image is inverted as in the pinhole camera.[1]

Figure 4.1 shows why the rays converge after having passed through the lens. The air is

[1] This is so assuming that the object is illuminated with monochromatic radiation, for a single glass lens suffers from *chromatic aberration*. It cannot make rays differing in wave-length converge onto the same focus. As Newton knew (*Opticks*, 1730, Bk I, Pt II, Prop. VIII), the human eye also suffers from chromatic aberration—although this is rarely noticeable under ordinary conditions. A combination of at least two lenses made of different kinds of glass is required to give an objective which is achromatic, or 'corrected for colour'. Helmholtz (1904) relates the intriguing comedy of errors which eventually led to the invention of achromatic optical systems.

less dense than the glass, and the paths of the rays are determined by the laws of refraction. The lens acts as if it consisted of an infinite number of glass prisms each of which would be defined by the two planes tangent to lens surface at the point of entry and at the point of exit of the ray considered (Fig. 4.2). Consider the rays diverging from the object point Q in Fig. 4.1. Except for the ray QEq, they are bent at the first and then at the second surface of the lens, that is at the two air–glass interfaces. Inside the lens the rays travel in straight lines because the glass is a medium of even density. The ray QEq, which

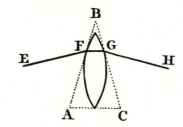

4.2   Refraction of a light ray by a biconvex glass lens
The lens bends the ray at F and G as if it were a glass prism ABC. (From R. Smith (1738), *A Compleat System of Opticks*.)

coincides with the axis of the lens, keeps a straight course because it falls on both lens surfaces under normal incidence, that is perpendicularly. The lens here leaves the direction of the ray unaffected, as if it were a sheet of plate glass struck perpendicularly by the ray QE.

In Fig. 4.1, the rays Pp and Rr are also drawn as straight lines and the three lines Pp, Qq and Rr cross each other at a single point E, called the *optical centre* of the lens. This is an approximation—valid only in the case of thin lenses. This approximation leads to a great simplification in the geometrical construction of the optical image, namely: the image of the object PQR is obtained by drawing straight lines through the optical centre E of the lens and producing them until they intersect, at pqr, the surface on which the image comes into focus. There is an obvious similarity between the rectilinear *main rays* PEp, QEq and REr of Fig. 4.1 and the straight lines AHa, BHb and CHc of Fig. 2.2, which define the shape of the image in the case of the pinhole camera.

Images in focus and out of focus. If the image of the object PQR in Fig. 4.1 is received on a screen, such as the ground glass screen used by photographers, it will be sharp only when the surface of the screen coincides with the plane pqr. If the screen is too near to the lens it will intersect the cones of rays which converge towards p, q and r, so that the images of the points P, Q and R will be round patches of light, or blur circles, corresponding in shape to the circular shape of the lens. The result will be similar if the screen is placed too far from the lens, since it will now intersect cones of rays diverging from the points p, q and r. Such out-of-focus images are similar to the images obtained with a pinhole camera the 'pinhole' of which is a fairly large circular aperture (Figs. 2.3 and 2.4).

We are all familiar with the fact that the position of the photographer's screen must be adjusted to the distance of the object from the lens. For instance, in order to photograph a near object the bellows of the camera may have to be considerably extended. This is because an object point placed nearer to the lens sends into it a more divergent cone of rays; consequently the cone emerging on the other side of the lens is less convergent, and its apex, the image point, is further from the lens. (If an object point is too close to the lens, the converging power of the lens is insufficient to render the refracted beam convergent, so that it becomes impossible to form an image in focus.)

Accordingly, when the screen is so placed that the image of objects at a certain distance is in sharp focus, nearer and farther objects as a rule form images out of focus, which are indistinct because the image of each of their constituent points is a blur circle. There is, however, a certain range of distances, extending on the far and on the near side of the distance for which the camera is focused, over which the sharpness of the image given by a lens is hardly decreased. This is called the *depth of field*. The use of a smaller diaphragm, which reduces the effective aperture of the lens, increases the depth of field.

Imperfections of lenses. The light-ray diagram of Fig. 4.1 shows the lens bringing together at one point the rays originating from each object point. The accuracy of the image formed by such an ideal lens would in fact be limited only by the diffraction of light. Most lenses fall far short of such an ideal. In any case, a single glass lens can form an image in sharp focus only for light of one wave-length, because of its chromatic aberration. Thus in the case of white light, the short wave-lengths will be brought to a focus slightly nearer the lens than the long wave-lengths, so that the image received on the screen will show coloured fringes and will be somewhat confused.

An achromatic system of lenses can be made which is almost completely free of this defect. Such lens systems are not necessarily suitable for photography, however, because the accuracy of the image tends to deteriorate, both with regard to its sharpness and to its geometrical shape, as one moves away from the axis of the lens. Photographic lenses are made to cover a much wider field than the lenses of telescopes, which Newton probably had in mind in connection with Fig. 4.1. The design of photographic lenses presents arduous technical problems (see e.g. Hardy and Perrin, 1932; Clerc, 1946 and Cox, 1956). It would be out of place to discuss these problems in this book, which tries rather to deal with the logic of the problem of the perception of pictures.

Pinhole versus lens in the photographic camera

For the practical purposes of photography, the lens camera presents over the pinhole camera two main advantages, both due to the large aperture presented by the lens. First, for objects in proper focus it is capable, potentially at any rate, of giving sharper images because of the greater spatial extent of the light flux entering the camera, which reduces the effects of diffraction. Secondly, the lens allows a greater quantity of light than the pinhole to enter the camera per unit time. Consequently the lens camera can give photographs in shorter exposure times than the pinhole camera. This is its great practical advantage. For the maximum degree of accuracy which can be given by a given lens, or by a given pinhole, can of course be achieved only if the sensitive plate has received a sufficient amount of light.

The main advantage of the pinhole camera, on the other hand, is that it automatically projects an image of which one can be certain that it is an accurate central projection of the objects photographed. For instance, on a flat photographic plate, a straight line belonging to the object is projected as a straight line (unless it is projected as one point). If the photographic plate shows a curved line, therefore, it is safe to conclude that the corresponding line in the object was also curved. Again the pinhole camera has a depth of field which in practice is almost unlimited, and it readily gives pictures covering a field extending to 90° or more. On the other hand, in order to obtain photographs having a good definition, much larger films or plates must be used than in, say, miniature cameras, and the times of exposures may be very protracted.[1]

A perfect lens camera should give photographs in accurate central projection, like the pinhole camera. Some of the compound lens systems used in cameras fall somewhat short of this ideal result. Photographic lens cameras giving pictures quite free from distortion, that is, in exact central projection, are not in common use simply because of the high cost of manufacture of their lens system.

Purpose of the photographic camera

While some paintings are made on cylindrical or other curved surfaces, this is rather exceptional. Most paintings, and, in general, most pictures, such as illustrations in books,

---

[1] Most of the pinhole photographs reproduced in this book were made with a Sanderson 'Tropical' half-plate camera fitted with an aperture 0·38 mm in diameter. The plates were 12 × 16·5 cm in size. For the photographs subtending the largest angles this 'pinhole' aperture was positioned 7·1 cm from the plate. For high obliquities the aperture in effect became much smaller, especially as it really was a short cylindrical hole drilled in a piece of brass. Accordingly the marginal parts of the wide-angle photographs are darker than their central region, especially as they are also more distant from the pinhole. Again definition decreases at high angles because of the increasing effect of diffraction at the 'pinhole' which becomes effectively smaller at these angles.

are made on plane surfaces. Flat pictures present considerable practical advantages. This is the reason why most camera lens systems are designed for the use of flat plates or films.

Thus most photographic cameras are specifically designed with a view to giving flat images in perspective, that is, central projections on a plane surface of the objects or scene photographed—which is achieved only as the result of the expenditure of considerable skill in the construction of their lens system.

As to the optical system of the human eye, it has been seen that it does not cast over the retina an exact central projection of the external world (although the central part of the retinal image closely approximates to such a projection). Moreover the retinal image is much sharper in its centre than in its periphery; it is in a state of continual motion over the surface of the retina; and of course the surface of the retina has a very strong curvature.

Retinal images occur as one link of the chain of events which constitutes the process of seeing. It is not this link that pictures, photographic or otherwise, are intended to duplicate: it is the external visible world itself. The purpose of photographs is to be seen. It is not the purpose of the photographic camera to see. Consequently there is no reason why photographs should mimic the peculiarities of the retinal image. In particular there is no reason why the surface on which photographs are made should be curved like the retina.

Clear detailed vision of an extended scene is obtained only as a result of eye movements that make the retinal image of every part of the scene of interest to the spectator fall, in turn, into the fovea which (in daylight) mediates the most accurate vision of details. Now a photograph is also viewed in this manner. Accordingly, if the photograph is to give a suitable representation of the scene, it must give a sharp, detailed, picture over its whole area. Again, the eye accommodates to bring into sharp focus the part of the scene which is being looked at, whether it be near or far. As this occurs without any conscious effort, at any rate in young emmetropic eyes, the spectator sees the whole scene clearly and distinctly. Accordingly the depth of field of the camera should be as great as possible in order to give a photograph which looks like the real scene.

It so happens that the human eye and the photographic camera both are built on the principle of the camera obscura (But this is not so for insect eyes.) One should not be misled by this similarity between them. Their purposes are different. While photographs are intended to be looked at, retinal images are not. The photographic camera is not an eye.

5 *Space and vision. Euclid's 'Optics'*

Space and light

From an empirical standpoint, the space of the land surveyor, the architect, the mechanical engineer, that is, the space of practical life, may be regarded as Euclidean space. This means that measurements made using rigid bodies, and on the assumption that the propagation of light is rectilinear in a medium of even density, give results which agree with those predicted on the basis of Euclidean geometry. Indeed, Euclid evidently composed his *Elements* as a treatise based at least in part on previous knowledge, including hard facts known from time immemorial to practical men.

Early in the nineteenth century, Gauss, who was one of the first mathematicians to consider the possibility of the existence of non-Euclidean geometries, set out to measure the angles of a triangle, defined by the tops of three mountains, and having sides measuring 69, 85 and 107 km. His aim was to find out whether the sum of the three angles was equal to two right angles, in accordance with Euclidian geometry, or whether this sum differed from $180°$ as should be the case if physical space were non-Euclidean (that is, if space were 'curved') to a measurable extent. The results of Gauss's triangulation measurements failed to indicate any significant deviation, outside the limits of experimental error, from $180°$ (Jammer, 1954).

Helmholtz in 1870, that is, before Einstein put forward his theory of relativity, wrote that in Euclidean geometry 'conclusion is deduced from conclusion, and yet no one of common sense doubts but that these geometrical principles must find their practical application in the real world around us' (Helmholtz, 1903).

All this does not mean that it is proved that physical space is Euclidean space. According to the theory of relativity, it is not, or at any rate it may be regarded as non-Euclidean. But deviations to be expected from Euclidean predictions are much too minute to be measured, say, in the laboratory. In the presence of a gravitational field, relativity theory states that one cannot, strictly speaking, use Euclidean geometry, because light does not travel in straight lines in such a field. Near the earth, however, the gravitational field is relatively so weak that the deviations of light rays from straight lines can, for all practical purposes, be neglected.

During total eclipses of the sun, measurements have been made of the apparent displacement of stars seen close to the periphery of the disc of the sun. The results are in good agreement with the displacement predicted by the theory of general relativity, namely 1·75 second of arc—a very small angle (Rosser, 1964). In fact, the wide acceptance of the theory of relativity nowadays is based on a whole range of arguments besides this bending of light passing near the sun. It may be worth pointing out that while theoretically it may be proved by experiments that real space is non-Euclidean, it would be impossible ever to demonstrate by physical measurements that space is strictly Euclidean, since measurements always suffer from accidental errors and thus necessarily fall short of the accuracy of theoretical geometry.

As explained by the wave theory, the rectilinear propagation of light is only an approximation. It has been seen that diffraction can 'bend the light into the shadow'. Yet, considering image-forming systems such as the telescope or the eye, the main effect of diffraction is to increase the size of the image of a luminous source, and diffraction does not cause systematic errors in any preferred direction.

When using an instrument such as a theodolite, the image of a reference point, formed by the telescope of the instrument, is brought into coincidence with a point of the graticule of the telescope. Diffraction in the instrument then merely limits the accuracy of the setting. As to diffraction (and optical defects) in the eye, as they influence in a similar way both images seen in coincidence in the theodolite, they can hardly introduce systematic errors. All this, besides their magnifying power, makes telescopes most suitable to the measurements of angles.

When we line up by eye a set of objects, on the other hand, it is often impossible to see near ones and far ones clearly in focus at the same time, as they require different degrees of accommodation of the eye. The lining up is then done on the basis of the centres of the objects, seen in a blurred or sharp manner. This is so when sighting with a rifle. In such cases the centres of the retinal images of the objects are made to coincide in the eye only. This is a theoretically more complex method, which of course is also less precise in practice, than sighting through a telescope. The problem must have been an important and difficult one in the case of those astronomical instruments, such as astrolabes, which were in use before the invention of the telescope. Tycho Brahe, who was one of the last astronomers to use such instruments, described them and discussed their use in 1598 (Raeder, Strömgren and Strömgren, 1946).[1]

Whereas the effects predicted by relativity theory are usually entirely negligible in practice, such is far from being the case for what is called *astronomical refraction*. This is

[1] On the dioptra used by the Greek astronomer Hipparchus (*fl.* 146–126 B.C.), see Hultsch (1899).

caused by the differences of density, and therefore of refractive index, in the various layers of the atmosphere. Since the outer layers are less dense than the inner ones, the light coming obliquely from a star, for instance, is progressively bent inwards in a vertical plane before it reaches the observer (Fig. 5.1). The effect becomes smaller and smaller as

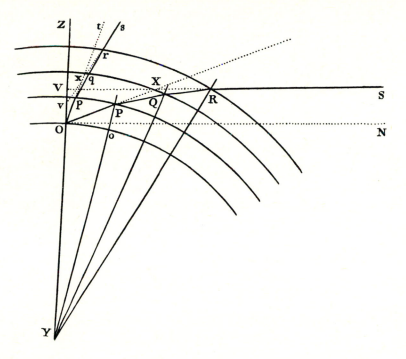

5.1 Astronomical refraction

A ray of light *SR* coming from a star and entering the atmosphere of the earth is progressively bent inwards as it passes successively through air layers of increasing density, until it reaches the eye *O* of the observer, who therefore sees the star in the direction *OX* instead of the true direction *ON*. This refraction is of smaller extent for rays such as *s r* coming from celestial bodies nearer the zenith, which is given by the direction of the line *YOZ*, *Y* being the centre of the earth. (The diagram is not to scale. Again, as the air density decreases continuously with increasing altitude, the path of such a ray as *SO* is of course a curve and not a broken line as in the diagram.) (From R. Smith (1738), *A Compleat System of Opticks*.)

one goes from the horizon to the zenith, for which position it is nil. But near the horizon it produces an apparent displacement of about half a degree. The angle subtended at the eye by the diameter of the sun or the moon is also equal to about half a degree. When we see the rim of the setting sun touching the horizon, therefore, the sun astronomically speaking has already set. That is to say, a straight line drawn from the upper part of the sun to the eye would just about be intercepted by the earth, so that the sun would be invisible if there were no atmosphere around the earth. The atmosphere bends the light of the setting sun to a marked extent.

Astronomical refraction affects the appearance of vertical, but not horizontal, dimensions. Accordingly, it explains the squat oval shape often assumed by the setting sun as it nears the horizon (Fig. 5.2). Another rare, but striking result of astronomical refraction

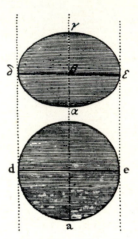

5.2   Oval figure of the horizontal sun or moon

Astronomical refraction causes an apparent raising of the whole disc above the horizon and distorts it into an asymmetrical oval $\alpha\delta\gamma\epsilon$. The horizontal diameter is unchanged by refraction. (From R. Smith (1738), *A Compleat System of Opticks.*)

is that several total eclipses of the moon have been seen near the horizon, when the sun was also seen on the opposite side of the sky. 'The ancient philosophers that knew nothing of the air's refractive power', Smith wrote, 'were very much perplexed with this strange phenomenon.'[1] For if the effects of the earth's atmosphere are disregarded, it would appear that a terrestrial observer should be unable to see at the same time the moon immersed in the geometrical umbra cast in the light of the sun by the earth, and the sun itself.[2]

The apex of visual angles: the 'point in the eye'

The angle subtended at the eye by the diameter of the sun, mentioned above, is an instance of a visual angle. The visual angle subtended by two points A and B is the angle AOB, where O is a certain point in the eye. In the case of celestial bodies, the eye is so small relative to the distances involved that the exact position of the point O in the eye

[1]   Smith (1738), Remark 372.
[2]   As to the dusky red colour assumed by the moon in a total eclipse, it is caused by light from the sun refracted in earth's atmosphere, which is thus able to reach the moon in the geometrical umbra cast by the earth. The reddish colour is due to the fact that the shorter wave-lengths of sunlight are lost by preferential scattering in the earth's atmosphere—so that the light scattered by a clear sky in sunlight is blue in colour. On these problems see for example Rudaux and Vaucouleurs (1959).

of course is of negligible importance. In the case of nearer objects, however, this is not necessarily so.

When the eye lines up objects situated at different distances, not simultaneously in focus on the retina, the points lined up are on a straight line with the centre of the *entrance pupil* of the eye, which is the natural pupil as it appears when seen through the cornea. Suppose that the pupil be reduced to a central aperture of the size of a small pinhole. The images of the object points, if out of focus on the retina, would then become small and sharp, and these small images would coincide with the centres of the corresponding blurred image as seen with the full pupil. Any set of object points, in line with the centre of the pupil, will therefore form images the centres of which are in coincidence on the retina. Consequently, for any given position of the eye, which is here supposed to be motionless, the apex O of the visual angles will be the centre of its entrance pupil. (Similarly, the apex of the corresponding angles for a photographic camera is the centre of the entrance pupil of the camera.)

For objects which are all in focus on the central retina, Fig. 1.2 shows that the apex of the visual angles should be at the crossing point of the thick straight lines Aa and Bb. In the approximate construction of Fig. 1.2 this point replaces the anterior and the posterior nodal points; to be quite exact one must take the anterior nodal point as the apex of visual angles. Now when the eye is in focus for very distant objects, it is found that nearer objects, down to a distance of about 6m, are also seen in sharp focus (presumably on account of the finite thickness of the receptor layer in the retina). Accordingly, for all objects at such distances, seen in foveal vision, the anterior nodal point will be the apex of the visual angles in the case of an eye which is supposed to be motionless in a fixed position.[1]

Now, not only are continual small motions of the eye necessary for normal vision, but when we want to see clearly any object which attracts our attention we shift our gaze onto it, the eye then rotating so that the object is imaged in the fovea. Thus, when our head is in a fixed position, we turn our eye rather as we would turn a telescope to look at different parts of the sky. Consequently, in natural vision the centre of rotation of the eye is the apex of the visual angles, in the same way as the centre of rotation of a telescope is the apex of the angles measured with this instrument.[2]

The centre of rotation, the anterior nodal point, and the centre of the entrance pupil

---

[1] It will be noted that the few millimetres distance between the nodal point and the centre of the pupil is very small in comparison with distances 6 m or more, so that little error will ensue if the centre of the entrance pupil is here also taken as the apex of the visual angles.

[2] The centre of rotation of the eye is near the centre of the eyeball. The fact that it does not coincide with the centre of the pupil can be demonstrated at once by holding a pencil vertically in front of our eye, touching the eyebrow and the cheek, in such a position as to hide a lamp a certain distance away. Turning then the eye towards the right or the left, the lamp again becomes visible—being seen 'out of the corner of the eye', by peripheral vision.

being all within less than half an inch of one another, however, their differences of position often are of negligible importance in practical problems relating to visual angles.

The rather intricate problem of the 'point in the eye' could not be clearly understood before the mode of functioning of the eye became known. It puzzled Leonardo da Vinci, and long before him, Archimedes (born *c*. 287 B.C., d. 212 B.C.). Archimedes obtained estimates of the angle subtended by the horizontal diameter of the rising sun by placing a vertical cylinder at such a distance that it was seen as just covering the sun's disc. He could at once have calculated the angle on the basis of the diameter of the cylinder and its distance from the eye if he had known the point in the eye relevant to his experiment—but this, precisely, he did not know. It appears that he therefore calculated two values of the angle, one taking the centre of the cornea as the apex of the angle, which gave him an upper value, and the other by drawing lines from the two sides of the cylinder to the two ends of a horizontal diameter of the pupil of the eye, which gave him a lower value for the angular diameter of the sun. The value obtained by modern astronomers (30′ 31″ to 32′ 35″ according to the distance from the earth to the sun) does lie between the upper and lower value calculated by Archimedes (Lejeune, 1947).

In what follows the phrase 'visual angle' or 'angle subtended at the eye' will as a rule mean an angle having its apex at the centre of rotation of the eye, which is about 13·5 mm behind the cornea. But it may be pointed out that when viewing objects through a pinhole smaller than the eye pupil, and displacing the eye to look along various directions through the pinhole, it is the centre of the pinhole which in effect becomes the centre of rotation of the eye, and thus the apex of the visual angles.

While they cannot always be determined with great precision, visual angles constitute objective data independent of the individual characteristics of the human observer involved. Indeed similar angles can be defined equally well in the case of an insect eye, or of a photographic camera, as in that of the human eye.

Natural perspective

As will be seen, Euclid's *Optics* is largely a treatise on the geometry of natural vision, dealing with the angles subtended at the eye by the objects considered. The straight lines defining this array of visual angles constitute the 'visual pyramid' or 'pyramid of sight' of Renaissance writers on perspective. A given position of the point in the eye defines one pyramid of sight, one single array of visual angles, for a given set of objects. The study of these visual angles may be called *natural perspective*.

Linear perspective as used by artists and architects, on the other hand, refers to the pattern of lines given by the central projection of the objects on a surface, the surface of the picture, the centre of projection being the relevant point in the eye. The perspective projection thus consists of the intersection of the pyramid of sight by the picture surface. Natural perspective is therefore more general in scope than linear perspective since each different surface gives a different section of the same pyramid of sight.

Parallel lines. Two parallel lines, in Euclidean geometry, are two straight lines, situated in a plane, which never meet when they are produced indefinitely. The distance separating them, that is, the length of the perpendicular drawn from one to the other, is always the same wherever it is measured. A straight railway line gives a concrete instance of parallel lines. Now it is a most familiar fact that standing on a long stretch of a straight railway line and looking in one of the two directions along the line, the two rails seem to tend to converge towards the horizon. It is important to note that this is so for *both* directions.

Similarly, a long wall of uniform height in front of which the observer stands may seem to get smaller towards the right as well as towards the left. But this is not always so, especially in the case of a short wall; thus an engineer may say that he sees such a wall as an accurate rectangle: the engineer is more interested in objective facts than in subjective appearances. Again, looking with one eye at a rectangular stone in a wall from a distance of a few inches, the stone thus being seen out of focus, the top and the bottom sides of the rectangle appear, to some observers, to be curved as if they tended to converge at each end. Such subjective appearances vary from observer to observer; their very existence has given rise to arguments. But this is not so of visual angles.

The height of the long wall in that part of it which is nearest to the eye subtends the greatest visual angle. The visual angle subtended by the height of the wall becomes progressively smaller and smaller as more distant parts are considered, either to the right or to the left. Thus in the case of a wall extending to a considerable length on both sides, the visual angle subtended by its height, considered from one end of the wall to the other, first increases, then reaches a maximum value, and again decreases.

The sunbeams we see in the sky when it is covered with broken clouds are nearly parallel to one another because the earth is very far from the sun and very small compared with it (Fig. 5.3). Their greatest divergence can amount only to about half a degree, the angular diameter of the sun. Yet such sunbeams often seem to diverge from the sun, in all directions around it (Fig. 5.3; Smith 98). This is an effect of perspective. The distance between the parallel sunbeams subtends a smaller and smaller angle as their distance from the eye increases. As we are unable to appreciate the enormous distance of the sun, which seems to be relatively near, the sunbeams seem to diverge from the sun itself—which is in the direction of the 'ancillary line' discussed below. In some cases, it is possible to see the same sunbeams with one's back turned towards the sun. They then seem to converge onto a point opposite to the sun (Fig. 5.3; Smith 99). This shows that the sunbeams are nearly parallel. They appear to converge in both directions like the two rails of a long straight railway line.

Similarly, the apparent divergence from a point in the sky of a shower of shooting stars is explained by an effect of perspective. The parallel luminous paths traced by a set

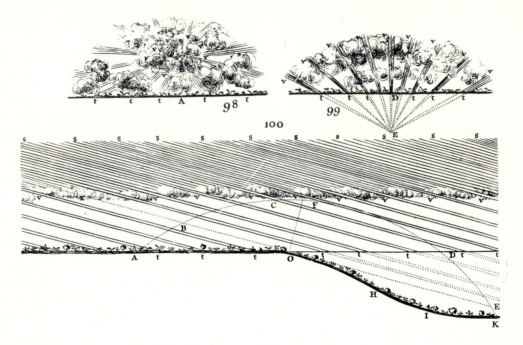

5.3   The appearance of sunbeams in the atmosphere

The light rays reaching us from the sun being nearly parallel, the sunbeams which pass through broken clouds and are made visible by light scattering in the atmosphere are also nearly parallel (100). But the observer at O sees them as diverging from the sun (98). Sometimes he can see them in the other direction converging towards the point E opposite to the sun (99). (From R. Smith (1738), *A Compleat System of Opticks*.)

of meteorites in the stratosphere must seem to diverge from a given position, precisely because they are parallel (Rudaux and Vaucouleurs, 1959). Natural perspective is of great importance in astronomy as we are quite unable to estimate visually the actual distance of the celestial bodies—which all seem to be on the 'vault of the heavens'. Their angular positions are often referred to a celestial globe, on which the arc of a great circle joining two given points has the same measure as the angle subtended by these points at the centre of the sphere.

Ancillary parallel passing through the eye. When considering any set of parallel lines, an ancillary straight line, parallel to the others, may be imagined as passing through the centre of the entrance pupil of the eye. This ancillary line would be seen as one point, in accordance with what has been said of sighting earlier in this chapter. The distance from this line to any other line in the set of parallels subtends a smaller and smaller angle as the distance from the eye increases. All the lines in the set of parallels will therefore seem to converge towards the point corresponding to the line passing through the eye. It should be clearly realized that this will be so whatever the position of the eye. For each different position, a different ancillary line, belonging to the set of parallels, will pass through the eye, and will give a different point of convergence for the parallels. This explains why when walking past a ploughed field, the parallel furrows seem to orient themselves towards a point in the distance, which moves with the observer. This point corresponds to a line parallel to the furrows, passing through the middle of the pupil, and which, as it were, remains 'attached' to the eye in all its displacements.

On the other hand, when the eye is in any given position, each different set of parallel lines will of course have its own different ancillary line passing through the eye, and giving a different point of convergence.

The problem of the ancillary line may be illustrated by a simple experiment. Suppose we are standing, say, in our bedroom and looking into a wardrobe mirror, in which we see the reflection of the room and its contents, ourselves included. Shutting one eye and using a taut string, it is then easy to verify that all the straight lines of the room or of the furniture contained in it, which are perpendicular to the plane of the mirror, would if produced meet on the surface of the mirror at a point which corresponds to the centre of the reflection of the pupil of the eye being used. This is so, first, because the reflection in the mirror is an undistorted image of the room, and secondly, because the line joining the eye to its reflection in the mirror is the ancillary line parallel to all the lines which are perpendicular to the mirror (private communication from Mr B. A. R. Carter; see Carter, 1970).

Apparent diminution with increasing distance. A given object, placed at increasing distances from the eye, subtends smaller and smaller visual angles. It is true that a man walking away from us in a room does not seem to become smaller, in the sense that he becomes a smaller man. This is an instance of psychological 'constancy'. But very distant objects do look small to everyone. This probably has been noticed from time immemorial. Cuneiform tablets from the library of the Assyrian King Assurbanipal, who reigned from 668 to 628 B.C., contain fragments of the legend of Etana, who was carried by an eagle towards the throne of the goddess Ishtar (H. Schäfer, 1963). In the course of his ascension, the legend says that Etana saw the earth become smaller and smaller. Finally, before it disappeared altogether, it looked to him as a flat cake on a wickerwork tray. This corresponds to Mesopotamian cosmology, according to which the earth was flat and everywhere surrounded by water, the wickerwork in the story corresponding to the waves of the ocean. This text proves that at least since the seventh century B.C. the apparent diminution of distant objects was a familiar phenomenon—even though at these times the corresponding effect of linear perspective was not used in pictorial representation.

The *Optics* of Euclid

Euclid's *Optics* (*c*. 300 B.C.) consists of a series of Theorems relating to natural perspective, which are demonstrated on the basis of the following definitions or assumptions: (1) Let it be assumed that lines drawn directly from the eye pass through a space of great extent; (2) and that the form of the space included within our vision is a cone, with its apex in the eye and its base at the limits of our vision; (3) and that those things upon which the vision falls are seen and that those things upon which the vision does not fall are not seen; (4) and that those things seen within a larger angle appear larger, and those seen within a smaller angle appear smaller, and those seen within equal angles appear to be of the same size; (5) and that things seen within the higher visual range appear higher, while those within the lower range appear lower; (6) and, similarly, that those seen within the visual range on the right appear on the right, while those within that on the left appear on the left; (7) but that things seen within several angles appear to be more clear.[1]

The geometrical background of Euclid's demonstrations was of course given by his *Elements*. The first thing to be noted in the *Optics* is that 'visual magnitude' in effect means 'visual angle', as shown by definition 4. In order to demonstrate that an object appears larger than another, what Euclid proves is that the visual angle it subtends is larger. The facts of psychological 'constancy' were not discussed by Euclid. Neither did he discuss the problem of the visual estimation of the actual size of an object, on the basis both of its visual angle and its distance from the eye. Yet it is unlikely that he and his contemporaries were quite unaware of such problems, while on the other hand it is even harder to accept that Euclid believed in the existence of a definite psychological quantity, the 'visual magnitude' of an object, which always was equal to the visual angle subtended by it. Clearly, Euclid chose to concentrate his attention on the study of visual angles, because they have objective magnitudes that can be measured or calculated. Indeed this was in any case the first task to be done for the scientific study of vision.

---

[1] From Burton's (1945) translation. A French translation has been published by Ver Eecke (1938); it is useful to refer to this work and to the additional material it contains to ascertain more accurately the meaning of Euclid's Definitions.

Euclid left undefined the exact position of the notorious 'point in the eye', the apex of the visual angles—a problem which could not have been unravelled in his times, and which in many cases is of greater theoretical than practical importance. He used the theory of the emission by the eye of straight visual rays, yet this theory enabled him to reach valid geometrical conclusions since they depend only on the rectilinearity of the rays, not on their direction either from the eye or to the eye.

Almost all the propositions of Euclid's *Optics* remain valid to this day. Among other things he studied the natural perspective, that is the 'appearance' purely in terms of visual angles, of parallel straight lines, circles, spheres, cylinders, cones—for one eye or for the two eyes. He also studied motion parallax, that is, the changes in visual angles which occur when the eye, or the objects viewed, are in motion: he proved, for instance, that when objects move at equal speed, those more remote seem to move more slowly. Effects of motion parallax are still used by pilots who land their aircraft by sight, as recently discussed by Gibson (1950).

Euclid went beyond the mere geometrical properties of vision. He dealt with the limits of visual acuity: 'Every object seen has a certain limit of distance, and when this is reached it is seen no longer.' This he explained on the assumption that the rays diverging from the eye are at some interval from one another, so that if the object is too small (in terms of visual angle) it falls in between the visual rays and is no longer seen. This led him to the explanation of the fact that 'rectangular objects, when seen from a distance, appear round': for the angular parts of the object then become too small to be seen. In general, as stated in Theorem 1, 'Nothing that is seen is seen at once in its entirety'.

Nowadays the theory of visual acuity is one of the most difficult parts of the physiology of vision, and is still the subject of arguments. Euclid was aware of the fact that the limits of the accuracy of our vision of details raises an important problem, and explained it on the basis of a single elegant hypothesis, which no doubt looked plausible to many of his contemporaries. In its literal form this hypothesis of visual rays separated by intervals is now unacceptable to us since it entails the emission of visual rays by the eye. Yet it seems to the present writer that it bears a resemblance to the modern concept of anatomical, and especially functional, mosaics of retinal receptors—even though this concept may never have entered Euclid's mind. At any rate, it is an intriguing coincidence that, according to the quantum theory of light, the reason why small black details silhouetted against a very dark night sky are invisible is essentially that their retinal images do fall *in between* the relatively few rods stimulated by light. (That is, their images would fall there if they could form images—the point precisely is that they cannot.) Euclid of course must have been thinking of maximum acuity and daylight vision. Now he does not refer to the lower accuracy of peripheral compared with foveal vision; but he mentions eye movements, in Theorem 1. What he means by his cone of vision is not quite clear;

it seems to mean simply the pyramid of sight relating to a given set of objects. In effect his theory may be taken as implicitly dealing, not with the visual field, but with the whole field of view, which is explored piecemeal by foveal vision. And this is the concept directly relevant to natural vision and to natural (and linear) perspective—so that Euclid's 'point in the eye' is the centre of rotation of the eye.

It is most likely that the *Optics*, like the *Elements*, was grounded on existing knowledge, which Euclid succeeded in accounting for on the basis of a few assumptions selected with astonishing insight and foresight. His *Optics* is not the work of a beginner. It is a synthesis achieved by a master, probably at the end of a long evolution.[1]

'Euclid alone has looked on beauty bare.'

[1] Zanetti (1968) explains that on optical grounds, Euclid was naturally led to base his *Elements* on the postulate of parallels, whereas it is non-Euclidean hyperbolical geometry which, on the same grounds, rests on 'arbitrary assumptions'. For to say that through a given point only one parallel can be drawn to a straight line is equivalent to saying that a straight line cannot be seen under a visual angle greater than 180°. Zanetti also shows that, for one eye in a fixed position, linear perspective as defined here is the only exact representation of the uniocular field of view.

6 *Experiments illustrating geometrical properties of the retinal image*

As the ordinary photographic camera produces flat pictures, it would be quite useless as a model to illustrate the properties of the very wide-angle images formed in the eye on the strongly-curved surface of the retina. Good models of the eye are difficult to set up, and all models have shortcomings. An actual eye, however, dissected out of a dead animal, can be used for such a demonstration without opening or cutting it, for the retinal images of intense light sources can be seen shining through the wall of the eyeball. The retinal images formed inside the eye are thus seen from the outside because the light diffuses through the sclera. As was first shown by the physiologist Magendie (1833) the eyes of albino animals are particularly suited to this purpose, since in them there is no lining of black or coloured pigment between the retina and the choroid. The translucent wall of such an eyeball transmits light rather like opal glass, so that bright retinal images can be observed in the same way as the image formed by a photographic camera can be seen on its ground glass screen, from the outside of the camera. Such an arrangement is similar to that first used by Scheiner and by Descartes (Fig. 1.1), but here the eyeball is left intact. The sharpness of the image observed in this way is very much reduced on account of the disturbing effect of thickness of the sclera, but it is sufficient to demonstrate geometrical properties of the retinal image produced by wide-angle arrays of small light sources.

The photographs reproduced in Figs. 6.1 to 6.5 show the retinal images, observed in this way, which were produced in albino rabbit eyes by sets of electric light bulbs. The eyes were removed from freshly killed animals and the surface of the eyeball was cleaned. The eyes were kept in a physiological saline solution (Ringer–Locke) when not actually used; the same solution was applied to prevent drying of the cornea during the experiments. In some experiments the bright image of a lamp, as seen through the sclera, was relatively sharp and small, in others it was very blurred; in some cases, the retinal image itself may have been badly out of focus, and there may also have been variations in the

[63]

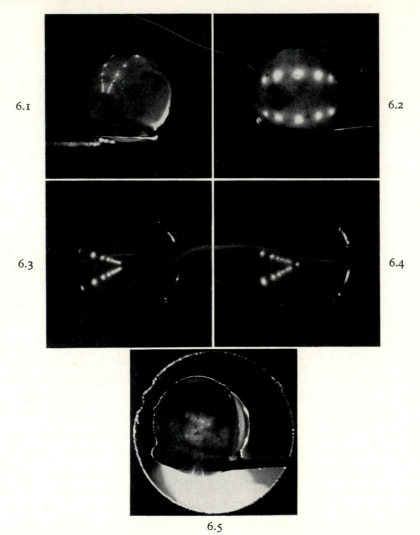

6.1

6.2

6.3

6.4

6.5

6.1 – 6.5 Retinal images of arrays of small electrical lamps, observed through the wall of the eyeball in an intact albino rabbit's eye.

In the photographs of Figs. 6.1 and 6.5 the eyeball can be seen, supported on a metal ring. In Fig. 6.5 the large circle around the eye is a hole cut in a cardboard screen. Figure 6.5 is the only photograph in which the cornea of the eye is visible, at the right; in the other photographs the cornea is on the side of the eye which is hidden from view. Figures 6.3 and 6.4 hardly show the outlines of the eyeball.

The bright spots visible in each case on the sclera of the eye are the images of the electric lamps formed on the retina inside the eye, and shining through the translucent wall of the eyeball. They are seen rather in the same way as the image on the ground glass screen of a photographic camera can be seen from outside the camera—but here the translucent surface is of course strongly convex in shape, since it is the surface of the eyeball.

The experimental arrangement for Fig. 6.1 is shown in Fig. 6.1 *a*, that for Fig. 6.2 in Fig. 6.2 *a*, and that for Figs. 6.3–6.5 in Fig. 6.3 *a*. Detailed explanation in the text. (Photos by A. Austin.)

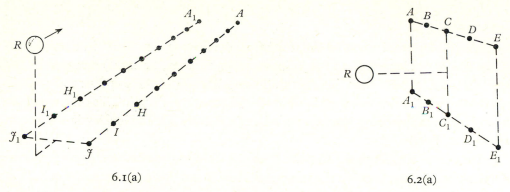

6.1(a)

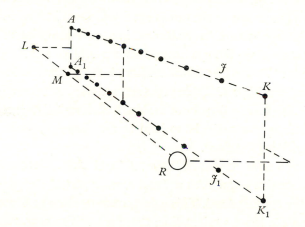

6.2(a)

6.1a Experimental arrangement relating to Fig. 6.1

The eye R formed the retinal image of the two parallel lines of lamps AJ and $A_1 J_1$ placed in front of it, at a lower level. The axis of the eye was parallel to these straight lines.

6.2a Experimental arrangement relating to Fig. 6.2

The eye R had its axis directed towards the centre of the array of lamps AEE_1A_1.

6.3a Experimental arrangement relating to Figs. 6.3–6.5

The array of lamps was AKK_1A_1. The eye R was placed with its axis parallel to AK for Figs. 6.3 and 6.4; its axis was turned by 70° for Fig. 6.5. The lamps L and M were used for Figs. 6.4 and 6.5 only.

amount of diffusion in the sclera. For the present purpose, however, it is the centres of the images of the lamps which are of importance. For, as explained above, when several points are situated on a straight line passing through the centre of the entrance pupil, the centres of their images, whether in focus or not, should coincide: this was found to be so in Experiments 4 and 5. The geometry of the retinal images of sets of lamps can thus be studied even when the images of individual lamps are not sharp.

Experiment 1

An albino rabbit eye R was held about 2 ft from the floor so as to 'look' in the direction of two sets of ten lamps AJ and A_1J_1 (pearl bulbs, 12 volts, 12 watts) arranged on the floor along two parallel lines (Fig. 6.1 a). The optical axis of the eye thus was roughly parallel to these lines, which were in front of it but at a lower level. This corresponds to the case of a man standing between the rails of a railway line and looking in a direction parallel to the rails.

In each set of ten lamps the distance from one lamp to the next was 40 cm; this was also the distance AA_1 between the two parallel sets. Thus the lamps formed a pattern of nine successive squares, JJ_1I_1I, II_1H_1H, etc.

The photographic camera was placed on a level with the rabbit's eye, slightly to the right behind it. The cornea was on the side of the eye which is hidden from view in Fig. 6.1 (in Fig. 6.5 the eye had been turned by an angle such that the cornea was seen, on the right of the picture). The lamps produced a highlight on the sclera, which is seen on the lower right side, and the metal ring supporting the eye is also visible in Fig. 6.1.

The pair of lamps JJ_1 nearest to the rabbit eye formed two images in the upper part of the retina. The following pairs of lamps formed images situated lower and lower on the retina as their distances from the eye became greater and greater. This corresponds to Euclid's Theorem 10: 'In the case of flat surfaces lying below the level of the eye, the more remote parts appear higher.' Taking into account the inversion of the retinal image, this means that with increasing distance of the lamps their retinal images move in the same direction, downwards, as that of a lamp held at a constant distance which would be raised progressively above the floor.

For each of the two straight sets of lamps, AJ and A_1J_1, the distance between the retinal images of successive lamps such as J and I, and I and H, decreased as the distance of the lamps from the eye increased. This corresponds to Euclid's Theorem 4: 'Of equal spaces located upon the same straight line, those seen from a greater distance appear shorter'—that is, the angles they subtend at the eye become smaller. As a result, the images of the more distant lamps, towards A and A_1, become crowded together in Fig. 6.1.

The distances measured on the sclera are not proportional to the corresponding angles subtended by the pairs of lamps, for their images do certainly not correspond to a central projection made from the centre of the (approximately) spherical retina. Nonetheless it is clear that in the present case greater visual angles correspond to greater distances on the retina, so that the experiment provides a qualitative illustration, at any rate, of Euclid's *Optics*.

The distances between the components of each pair of retinal images, each pair corresponding to two lamps equidistant from the eye such as J and J_1 and I and I_1 also, became smaller as the distance of the lamps increased. This corresponds to Euclid's Theorem 5: 'Objects of equal size unequally distant appear unequal and the ones lying nearer to the eye always appear larger', and to Theorem 6: 'Parallel lines, when seen from a distance, appear not to be equally distant from each other.'

This observation, and the preceding one, relate to the problem which will be examined in Experiments 4 and 5. In Fig. 6.1 the images of the two arcs of circle containing the images of the two parallel sets of lamps AJ and A_1J_1, which in this photograph appear in perspective as branches of ellipses, tend to converge. If produced, these two arcs would meet at a point which, as will be seen, is the image of the ancillary line parallel to AJ and A_1J_1, passing through the centre of the entrance pupil of the eye.

It is unlikely that the retinal image in the rabbit's eye, any more than in the human eye, is defined on the simple basis of a central projection of the objects through an optical centre in a fixed position inside the eye. Yet the images of each of the two straight sets of lamps must be expected to lie along the intersection of the sclera by the plane defined by the corresponding set of lamps and the centre of the pupil. For wide-angle images, deviation from central projection must affect the positions of the images along the intersection of this plane with the sclera but, on account of the symmetry of the eye's optical system, it should not be expected to produce lateral displacements of the images outside the plane. Experiments 3, 4 and 5 will show that, as far as can be ascertained here, such images do in fact lie in a plane. The curved images of the two parallels in Fig. 6.1 therefore must also be the intersection of the sclera by two planes.[1]

To summarize the results of Experiment 1: first, it is found of course that the retinal image of a straight line is always curved, since the surface of the retina is curved. Secondly, the images of the two parallel straight lines tend to converge, their separation

[1] In this first experiment where twenty lamps were used all together, the lining-up of these lamps was somewhat imperfect. To this probably must be ascribed some irregularities which can be detected in the photograph, though irregularities in the sclera may also have affected the image. In Experiments 2–5 a vertical pair of lamps was rigidly attached to the saddle of an optical bench. Thus, by moving the saddle along the bench into selected positions, it was possible to place the lamps in a number of pre-selected positions along two accurately parallel lines: AE and A_1E_1 in Experiment 2 (Fig. 6.2a); AK and A_1K_1 in Experiments 3–5 (Fig. 6.3a). In Experiments 4 and 5 a third lamp was attached to the saddle in order to define a third straight line LM parallel to the first two (Fig. 6.3a). Exposures for the successive positions of the lamps were superimposed on the same photographic plate, without moving the rabbit's eye or the camera.

As far as the present geometrical considerations are concerned, the result was of course the same as if, in Experiment 2, say, one single exposure had been made with two parallel sets of five lamps exactly lined-up and used simultaneously—instead of the actual five successive exposures with two lamps in five different positions.

The lamps used here were clear motor car headlight bulbs (12 v 48 w) with a straight filament. The shape of the filament could not be distinguished through the sclera in the retinal image. In some cases, particularly in Experiment 5, the times of photographic exposures were varied according to the distance of the bulbs from the rabbit's eye, which affected the brightness of the retinal image.

becoming smaller with increasing distance of the lamps from the eye. Finally the images of the squares formed by each set of four lamps tend to become markedly 'compressed', that is, narrower in height relative to their width, as they become increasingly distant from the eye.

Experiment 2

The rabbit's eye R was made to 'look' at two sets of 5 lamps, $ABCDE$ and $A_1B_1C_1D_1E_1$, arranged along two straight horizontal parallel lines in a vertical plane (Fig. 6.2a). The lamps formed a rectangle AEE_1A_1 of dimensions 40×20 cm. The eye R was placed 20 cm in front of the centre of this rectangle, with its optical axis directed towards this centre. This arrangement thus corresponds to the case of a man standing in front of a horizontal wall and looking straight at the middle of it.

The vertical distance between the sets of lamps $ABCDE$ and $A_1B_1C_1D_1E_1$ was equal to twice the horizontal separation of successive lamps, so that the lamps formed two squares ACC_1A_1 and CEE_1C_1, each 20×20 cm; the six lamps $BCDD_1C_1B_1$ also formed such a square. The camera was placed behind the eye, with its axis in line with the eye and the centre of the rectangle AEE_1A_1.

The photograph reproduced in Fig. 6.2 shows that the retinal images of the parallel straight lines $ABCDE$ and $A_1B_1C_1D_1E_1$ lay along two circles on the retina. These circles tended to converge both on the right and on the left. This convergence towards both ends is not an illusion due to the perspective of the photograph. For by adding further lamps along the lines AE and A_1E_1, beyond A and A_1 and E and E_1, the increasing convergence on both sides of the images of the two parallel lines was clearly seen; but this could hardly be shown on a single photograph such as that of Fig. 6.2 because of the strong curvature of the eyeball. Thus the image of a square such as $ABCC_1B_1A_1$ is of course not a square. Neither is it so for the square set of lamps $BCDD_1C_1B_1$, the image of which consists of the six light spots in the middle of Fig. 6.2.

In Experiment 1 this convergence of the retinal images of parallel lines could be clearly observed towards one side only, because the light of lamps placed along the parallel lines far behind the eye would have failed to enter the pupil. In Experiment 2, while the convergence was clearly seen on both sides, image formation became very poor in positions near the two points towards which the images of the two parallel lines do converge. These two points here would be the images of two lamps, on either side of the eye, placed on a line parallel with the lines AE and A_1E_1, and passing through the entrance pupil as defined for these conditions. These two lamps would be at $90°$ from the optical axis of the eye and thus subtend a visual angle of $180°$.

If peripheral vision extends as far in the rabbit as in man, the rabbit should just be able to see two lamps in this position. But in the present experiment, at any rate, the images of such lamps could not be seen through the wall of the eye. (Figure 6.5, however, does show the retinal image of one point of convergence when the plane containing the parallel lines is at an angle of about 70° with the optical axis of the eye, that is, at 20° from the 90° position.)

Experiment 3

The rabbit's eye R was held so that its optical axis was approximately parallel to two long horizontal parallel lines of lamps AK and A_1K_1 placed one above the other in a vertical plane on the right of the eye (Fig. 6.3a). Here each group of four lamps such as JKK_1J_1 formed a rectangle 25·5 cm high and 20 cm wide. The rabbit's eye was placed at a distance of 25·5 cm from the vertical plane containing the lamps. (The lamps L and M shown on Fig. 6a were not used in this experiment.) This case corresponds to that of a man standing at the end and on the side of a long horizontal wall and looking in a direction parallel to that of the top and bottom edges of the wall.

The conditions thus resembled those of Experiment 1, except that the parallel sets of lamps were in a vertical instead of a horizontal plane. But here the position of the photographic camera was chosen so as to obtain straight-line photographs of the curved retinal images of the sets of lamps. The camera was placed behind the eye, with its axis parallel to the two long straight lines of lamps, so that the two planes defined by these lines and the centre of the eye pupil intersected one another along the optical axis of the camera. If these two planes contain the images of the lamps which are formed along two arcs of circle on the rabbit's retina, the photographs of these arcs must be straight lines. The photograph of Fig. 6.3 shows that this is so, at least within the limits of the admittedly poor accuracy of this 'retinal' image.

Thus the retinal image here was essentially of the same kind as that in Experiment 1, but it was photographed from a special point of view. The two lamps K and K_1 nearest to the eye, to the right of it, formed their images on the extreme left, near the edge of the photograph of the eyeball; the pair of lamps A and A_1, farthest from the eye, formed the images nearest to the centre of the photograph. The photograph definitely shows that the retinal images of the two parallel lines AK and A_1K_1 do converge towards a meeting point.

Experiment 4

The conditions were similar to those of Experiment 3. No photograph was taken of the images of the lamps K and K_1, but otherwise the images of the two parallel lines of lamps AJ and A_1J_1 are the same as in Fig. 6.3. In the present experiment an additional lamp was attached to the saddle of the optical bench and adjusted in position so that, when it was moved along a straight line LM parallel to the two lines $A\mathcal{J}$ and $A_1\mathcal{J}_1$, its image no longer moved on the retina of the rabbit's eye. The single bright image seen in the middle of Fig. 6.4 was obtained by taking, on the same film as used for the lines $A\mathcal{J}$ and $A_1\mathcal{J}_1$, two exposures with the additional lamp in the positions L and M.

Thus this single image is the 'point' image on the retina of a third line parallel to the first two, which passes through the centre of the entrance pupil. It is the retinal image of the ancillary parallel line which is seen foreshortened as a single point, as discussed in the preceding chapter.

The visual angles subtended by opposite points on any two parallel lines become smaller and smaller as the distance of these points from the eye increases indefinitely. This applies to each parallel in turn considered in conjunction with the ancillary line. All the components of a system of parallel lines when extended indefinitely in a direction away from the eye must therefore form retinal images which tend to converge onto a single common point. Since the whole of the ancillary line forms a single point image on the retina, this point must be the convergence point of the retinal images of all the parallels.

In particular it must be the meeting point of the retinal images of the lines $A\mathcal{J}$ and $A_1\mathcal{J}_1$. It is easy to verify on Fig. 6.4, where the images of $A\mathcal{J}$ and $A_1\mathcal{J}_1$ appear as straight lines, that this is so.

Experiment 5

In this experiment all the conditions were the same as in Experiment 4, except that the axis of the eye was turned so as to make an angle of about 20° from the perpendicular to the plane containing the first two lines. That is, the eye was turned around the vertical by an angle of 70° towards the right in Fig. 6.3 a; accordingly the cornea is now visible on the right of the photograph of Fig. 6.5. Here again it was possible to adjust the position of an additional lamp so that, when moving along an ancillary line parallel to the first, it formed a single point image on the retina of the rabbit's eye, visible through the sclera (Fig. 6.5). This point image was again at the intersection of the retinal images of the first two parallel lines $A\mathcal{J}$ and $A_1\mathcal{J}_1$. The ancillary parallel line here had to be positioned somewhat differently, because the position of the pupil was altered due to the 70° rotation of the eye.

In Experiment 4 as in Experiment 1 the optical axis of the rabbit's eye was parallel to the lines of lamps, but this, of course, is by no means necessary to demonstrate the convergence of the retinal images of parallel lines. The convergence is still observed when the eye is rotated. Experiment 2 had shown, however, that in the extreme case where the axis of the eye becomes normal to the plane containing the parallel lines of lamps, image formation became poor near the points of convergence. A rotation of 70° instead of 90° was found to be about the largest rotation still giving images which it was possible to photograph.

Conclusions

These experiments, particularly Experiments 2 and 5, show that if any given set of parallel lines is extended indefinitely in both directions away from a motionless eye in any fixed position, the retinal images of the parallel lines do in general tend to converge in *both* directions. But convergence may be difficult or impossible to observe in more than one direction, simply because in the other direction images of the lines may not be formed on the retina. The readily observable point of convergence of the retinal images of parallel lines is the point image formed on the retina by the ancillary parallel passing through the centre of the entrance pupil. In the human eye the ancillary line of a set of parallels perpendicular to the axis of the eye should in principle form *two* point images on the retina, since image formation is just possible at 90° on both sides from the axis. This could not be actually demonstrated in the present experiments on the rabbit's eye, however.

If the eye rotates in its orbit, or is displaced bodily from one place to another, the retinal images of the members of any given set of parallel lines will change their disposition on the retina, but they will always keep converging towards at least one of the point images of the particular ancillary line which corresponds to each and every position of the eye. By suitably turning the eye or the head, convergence will always be readily observable in either one or the other direction, chosen at will.

All this refers to natural perspective. The main principle of linear perspective is illustrated by Experiments 4 and 5 in which it was found that straight lines passing through the centre of the entrance pupil of the eye were foreshortened, each as a single point image on the retina. Consequently, if straight lines are drawn from the centre of the entrance pupil to the various points of the object, the centre of the pupil remaining stationary, and if this pyramid of lines is sectioned outside the eye by a surface, then it follows that the picture defined by the intersection of the pyramid by the surface must form a retinal image coinciding, 'point' by 'point', with that of the object. The facts that the retina is curved, and that the retinal image is not an exact central projection of external objects, are irrelevant. What is relevant is that light travels in straight lines in the air, before entering the eye.

7 *The simple theory of linear perspective*

Theory

At the beginning of his treatise on linear perspective, Brook Taylor wrote: '...let the reader consider that a Picture drawn in the utmost Degree of Perfection, and placed in a proper Position, ought so to appear to the Spectator, that he should not be able to distinguish what is there represented, from the real original Objects actually placed where they are represented to be... In order to produce this Effect, it is necessary that the Rays of Light ought to come from the several Parts of the Picture to the Spectator's Eye, with all the same Circumstances of Direction, Strength of Light and Shadow, and Colour, as they would do from the corresponding Parts of the real Objects seen in their proper Places.' (Brook Taylor, 1811; reprint of the 1719 edition.)

Central projection

In order that the rays of light from each part of the picture reach the eye of the spectator (which must be in the right position, while he keeps his other eye shut), with the same direction as the rays which would come from the corresponding parts of the real objects, the picture must be drawn accurately in perspective. Linear perspective defines the size, shape and disposition of the objects as drawn in the picture, with their foreshortening and the apparent overlapping of some near objects upon far objects, for one eye in a given position—and for this position only.

Figure 7.1 from Brook Taylor's treatise shows that a drawing in exact perspective must consist of the central projection upon a surface, which is to be the surface of the picture, of the scene or objects to be presented. This surface of projection is, in Fig. 7.1, a plane, but the principle would be the same for a surface having a curved or irregular shape. The centre of projection O is the point in the spectator's eye which is the apex of the visual angles, that is, here, the centre of rotation of the eye. Straight lines are supposed to be drawn from each point of the scene or objects (which in Fig. 7.1 consist merely of one cube) to the projection centre O. The intersection of each of these straight lines with the surface of projection $FGHI$ is the projection of the corresponding object point. Thus the point A, one of the corners of the cube, is projected along the straight line AaO and a is its projection on the surface $FGHI$. Similarly the corners B, C and D are

7.1 The principle of linear perspective

The pyramid of sight defined by the object $ABCDE$ and the centre of rotation O of the eye of the spectator, who keeps his other eye shut, is intersected by the surface $FGHI$, thus forming on it the projection $abcde$ in linear perspective. If the surface $FGHI$ is a transparent Leonardo window, the eye sees this perspective covering the actual object exactly. (The whole figure here is of course shown in perspective including the picture $abcde$, which is seen foreshortened, and from the side opposite to the eye O. The spectator is depicted holding his hand to his eye presumably because in earlier illustrations of this period strings were used to materialize the lines constituting the pyramid of sight.) (From Brook Taylor (1811), *New Principles of Linear Perspective*.)

projected on b, c and d, so that the projection of the top face of the cube is $abcd$. This means that the visual angle subtended by any pair of points in the scene to be represented is, by construction, the same as the visual angle subtended by the projections of these points on the surface $FGHI$—thus an angle such as AOB is evidently the same as the angle aOb. Keeping always the point O as centre, or apex, all the visual angles subtended by components of the projection of the scene represented are the same as those subtended by the corresponding components of the scene itself.

In brief *the perspective projection is the section by a surface of the pyramid of sight* which is seen issuing out of the eye in Fig. 7.1. As the straight lines constituting the pyramid define the visual angles, these angles are automatically the same for the actual objects and for their perspective. Thus from the relevant centre, the *natural* perspective of the

7.2   Piero della Francesca's 'Flagellation'
Palazzo Ducale, Urbino. (Photo from the Istituto Centrale del Restauro, Rome.)

pattern constructed in linear perspective on the picture surface is exactly the same as the *natural* perspective of the scene represented. (Other things being equal, this of course will be so for *any* surface intersecting the pyramid.)

Consequently, if the projection surface *FGHI* is a transparent 'Leonardo window' and if the eye is accurately centred at *O*, the projection in linear perspective on this transparent surface will be seen to cover point by point the objects seen through the window. This is the main empirical, objective, basis of linear perspective.

The rules of linear perspective make it possible to draw the perspective of any scene

7.3 Plan and elevation of the scene represented in Piero della Francesca's 'Flagellation'

This is a reconstruction made by Mr B. A. R. Carter. The centre of projection is the point marked 'Eye', and the plane of projection is called 'Intersection'. The pyramid of sight is shown in plan and elevation. In the plan, the part of the scene which is included in the painting is shown in a darker shade. (From Wittkower and Carter (1953), *J. Warburg and Courtauld Institutes*, **16**, 292–302.)

or object defined by its plan and elevation, on a given surface, and for a given centre.[1] Both the surface and the centre of projection must be in an exactly defined position relative to the scene or objects (Figs. 7.2 and 7.3).

It is essential to remember always that a perspective projection is strictly valid only for one single eye placed at the right position with regard to the perspective or to the objects depicted in the perspective.

Retinal images

When the centre of rotation of the eye is at O, the retinal image of the picture projected on the transparent surface $FGHI$ will be superimposed onto the retinal image of the objects themselves (Fig. 7.1). The head is in a fixed position, but the eye is free to rotate in its orbit. The retinal image then shifts onto different parts of the retina and, as it does so, its shape becomes altered to some extent. But the crucial point is that for each and every position assumed by the eye, the retinal images of both objects and picture remain very nearly in coincidence, point by point. That is why the perspective is seen to cover the actual objects.

The experiments on the rabbit's eye have shown that a luminous point moved along such a straight line as AO forms a single point image on the retina, so that here the image of the point A and of its projection a will be in coincidence on the retina (Fig. 7.1). The same of course applies to any object point and its projection.[2]

As has been said when discussing the apex of visual angles, the precise position chosen for the 'point in the eye' is usually a matter more of scientific than of practical interest. In matters relating to linear perspective, this precise position is usually of minor importance. In the following, the phrase 'the eye' will often be used to mean the centre of projection, which is also called the point of view.

[1] See La Gournerie's (1859) treatise, written just before photography came into universal use, at a time when perspective was still an important subject of study for artists. Among recent treatises, Abbot's (1950) book, for instance, is a convenient and interesting one on the same subject.

[2] It is true that in the experiments on the rabbit's eye the straight lines passed through the centre of the pupil, not through the centre of rotation of the eye. These experiments involved strongly peripheral vision. Here it is assumed that the eye, while the head remains motionless, looks at each part of the scene in turn, using foveal vision. It has been seen that the apex of visual angles is then the centre of rotation of the eye. The above statement relating to the superposition of the retinal images then is true as far as those parts of the retinal images which are formed in the fovea are concerned. For any position of the rotating eye, that part of the retinal image of the actual object or scene which falls into the fovea is in coincidence with the corresponding part of the retinal image of the perspective drawn on the surface of projection. The coincidence will not be quite correct for images on the periphery of the retina, however, but the periphery mediates less distinct vision, and much less attention is normally given to it than to foveal vision. In any case, as most pictures are opaque to light, there is no opportunity to check that they are seen in exact superposition to the objects represented.

The effect of binocular vision

In his *Physiological Optics*, while discussing the difference between uniocular and binocular vision, Helmholtz described the following ideal experiment. Suppose that we find ourselves in a room well-known to us and brightly lit. Now if, while looking at the room, we close one eye, we may believe that we see the room just as clearly and precisely as when we were using both eyes. Yet, thus using one eye only, we would still receive exactly the same visual impressions if all points of the room were moved on their respective lines of sight, their distances from the eye being changed at will (Helmholtz, 1896, pp. 609–10).

Accordingly we may imagine that all the points of the room have been moved along their lines of sight until they reach a given surface. Now this surface will in effect be the surface of projection of the theory of linear perspective. We would therefore be unable to distinguish the picture in perspective from the room itself and the actual objects contained in it. The case discussed by Helmholtz is thus equivalent to that discussed by Brook Taylor. (It is a theoretical one largely because it again implicitly assumes a 'picture' made with the utmost degree of perfection.)

Now what Helmholtz had in mind in the above passage was that, using both eyes with normal stereoscopic vision, the picture in perspective could not and would not look the same as the actual room. With binocular vision the flatness of the picture would be noticed.

The centres of rotation of our two eyes being about 6 cm apart, the array of visual angles corresponding to the same objects is different for the two eyes. This can be seen if, looking out of a window, one closes one eye and then the other, and watches the resulting apparent displacements of near and far objects relative to each other and relative to the window pane. The Leonardo window gives for the two eyes, two perspectives which are not in coincidence, and which cannot be brought exactly into coincidence; there are between them *disparities* which depend on the distances from the objects to the eye.

In the case of binocular vision, therefore, pictorial representation strictly requires two different perspective projections, each having its centre at the centre of rotation of the respective eye. But the two perspectives must be presented separately, each to the corresponding eye. This is what is achieved by stereoscopic devices. Stereoscopic pictures give a sense of depth, or of the 'third dimension', which is lacking from each of the pictures viewed separately using the two eyes together (see the section on Anaglyphs in Chapter 11).

When we look binocularly at a flat picture, the visual angles involved are not quite the same for the two eyes, since the eyes are at different positions. This is clear for instance with regard to the frame of the picture; and it is this largely which enables us to locate the position of the picture with its frame. But, if the objects depicted are supposed to be at different distances, their single picture in perspective will not present for the two eyes the characteristic disparities of visual angles which they would present in reality.

In binocular vision the disparities between the arrays of angles corresponding to the two eyes are different for the projection on a surface and for the actual objects. As stereoscopic vision indicates depth, or lack of depth, mainly on the basis of such disparities, it will as a rule show that the picture is only a surface. It must be borne in mind, however, that stereoscopic vision becomes less and less precise as the distance of the objects considered increases, so that the surface of a distant picture may not always be recognized as a surface.[1]

The effect of accommodation

Now returning to the theoretical arrangement of Brook Taylor which uses one eye only while the head is motionless, but with the eye free to move in its orbit, the question will be asked: Why does not the degree of accommodation, that is the degree of focusing of the eye, give information about the distance of the objects, thus making it possible to distinguish between the real scene and its picture? The answer is that experiments show that the estimation of distance under such conditions is impossible for distant objects and very difficult for near ones. For example, experiments made by Wundt and reported by Helmholtz (1896, p. 778) show that a human observer is hardly able to give any indication of the absolute distance from his eye of a black thread presented to him against a white background. Again, for all distances larger than about 6 m, the accommodation of the eye remains practically the same independently of the distance; all objects at such distances are seen clearly at the same time.

In conclusion, for the case of vision with one single eye, free to rotate while the head is kept motionless, the central projection of linear perspective made for this particular position of the eye must give retinal images which are in effect the same as the retinal images which would be given by the objects themselves, for the reasons previously stated, and because the difference in the degree of accommodation of the eye required for picture and objects is an unimportant factor.

It will be borne in mind that, even if we shut one eye and do not move our head, we still see the external world as before in three dimensions. Two tentative conclusions may therefore be drawn. First it appears that a picture in perspective of a scene extended in depth, accurately drawn and painted, should give a very good illusion of this scene, in three dimensions, for one eye placed at the centre of projection. Secondly, when viewed

---

[1] It may be noted that, even when only one eye is used, moving the head sideways often makes it possible to detect whether one is faced with a flat picture or with actual objects in depth, again by virtue of characteristic alterations in the visual angles, that is, by the effect of motion parallax.

from a position away from the centre of projection, the picture should present a deformed view (still in three dimensions) of the scene depicted, since the linear perspective of the picture is no longer correct for the second position. It will be advisable to examine first an exceptional case in which, because *in this case* the simple theory of linear perspective does apply, these two expectations are found to be fulfilled.

Pozzo's painted ceiling

The very large ceiling, representing Saint Ignatius being received into Heaven, painted at the end of the seventeenth century by Fra Andrea Pozzo, S. J. (A. Putei, 1642–1709) in the church of St Ignazio in Rome, can be regarded as an exceptional and outstanding experiment the results of which are in accord with the simple theory of perspective outlined by Brook Taylor. Pozzo, in a book on Perspective, has himself explained how he executed his painting (Putei, 1693–1700; Pozzo, 1707).[1] Figure 7.4 is a photograph of the interior of the church. Figure 7.5 is a photograph of the painted ceiling.

Pozzo's method of projection. The surface of the ceiling of the nave, which reaches a height of about 30 m above the floor, is hemicylindrical in shape. Figure 7.6 shows the elevation of a longitudinal section of the church (the cupola in this engraving was not built, but Pozzo also painted a perspective of it). Figure 7.7 shows the plan and two elevations of the imaginary architectural structure which Pozzo painted on the curved ceiling of the nave. The three lower windows on this engraving are the actual top windows of the nave in Figs. 7.4, 7.5 and 7.6.

First, on the basis of the plan and elevation of the architecture he wished to represent in his painting, Pozzo drew on a horizontal plane a perspective view of this imaginary structure, using as a centre of projection a point O at eye level in the nave (see Fig. 7.9). This position is marked on the floor by a yellow marble disc. Figure 7.8 shows one quarter of his drawing; this projection was obtained according to the rules of perspective for a plane surface of projection. The real problem was to project it onto the hemispherical surface of the ceiling (Fig. 7.9). Pozzo squared his drawing in the manner usual to painters who want to obtain an enlargement of a preliminary drawing. He then fixed horizontally at a level $FEAB$ just below the hemicylindrical vault, a net M of thin cords or threads, containing as many squares as those he drew on his perspective. If the vault were supposed to be replaced by a flat ceiling at the level $FEAB$, it would thus have been a relatively simple matter to transfer, square by square, an enlarged drawing onto this flat ceiling, using the squares as a reference grid.

The squares in fact had to be projected on to the curved surface of the ceiling, from

---

[1] On Pozzo's life and works see Maffei (1966b) and Marini (1959).

7.4   The interior of the church of St Ignazio in Rome

Part of the painted ceiling of the nave is visible at the top of the photograph, and the painting of the tribune is seen above the altar. Both appear deformed because they are photographed from the wrong position. In between them, a dark veil covers the painting of the cupola, which had been damaged in a fire but is now restored. (Photo by O. Grassi, S. J.)

7.5   Pozzo's painting on the ceiling of the nave in St Ignazio

The photograph, taken from the relevant yellow marble disc, shows the painting as it is meant to be seen. It shows little of the real architecture of the church, except the windows. To the spectator standing on the marble disc, the painted architecture appears *in three dimensions* as an extension of the real architecture. This photograph fails to give the overwhelming impression thus produced in the spectator by this vast painting. (Photo by Brunner & Co., Como.)

7.6   Elevation of the interior of the church of St Ignazio

This is an elevation of the real architecture except that the cupola shown in this engraving was never actually built. (From Pozzo (1707), *Perspective*.)

7.7   Plan and elevations of the imaginary architecture painted by Pozzo on the ceiling of the nave of St Ignazio

The lower part of the two elevations shows real architectural elements, including the windows marked 1 (cf. Fig. 7.6). (From Pozzo (1707), *Perspective*.)

7.8   Part of the perspective drawing made by Pozzo for the nave ceiling in St Ignazio

This is a projection on a horizontal plane of the imaginary architecture of Fig. 7.7. (From Pozzo (1707), *Perspective*.)

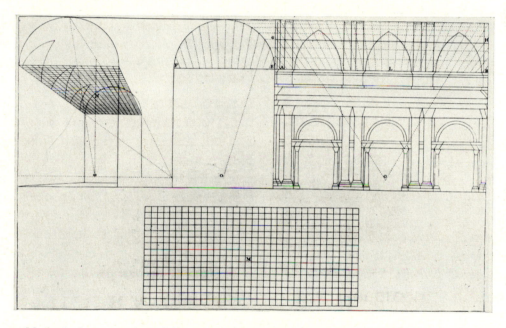

7.9   Method of construction of the perspective on the curved ceiling of St Ignazio

The net *M* was fixed horizontally at the level *FEAB*, just below the ceiling of the nave, and projected on this curved surface from the centre *O*, which is at eye height above the yellow marble disc. This gave Pozzo a reference grid for the transfer of the drawing of Fig. 7.8 on the hemicylindrical ceiling. See text. (From Pozzo (1707), *Perspective*.)

O as a centre. In principle this could be done by placing a lamp at O and tracing on the ceiling the shadows of the squares, projected as curved quadrilaterals of various shapes on this curved surface. Pozzo found, however, that this elegant method was unsatisfactory in practice. He obtained the projection of the net on the ceiling by drawing a taut thread from the centre O to the ceiling so that it touched each corner of each square in turn. Referring to his small squared drawing in perspective, he was then able to draw and paint his architectural view on the ceiling.

Besides the architectural elements, the painting contains a large number of figures, some of them floating in space in mid air and in the sky, which is visible through the opening in the middle of the architectural structure. Pozzo insists on the great care which must be taken to draw all such figures in exact central projection, as well as columns, cornices and other architectural features. This of course means that the preliminary drawing (Fig. 7.8) became strongly 'distorted' in many ways when projected on the ceiling, in the same general manner as the projections of the squares become irregular quadrilaterals on this curved surface (Fig. 7.15).

Thus the drawing finally made by Pozzo on the ceiling delineates accurately the section by this huge curved surface of the pyramid of sight which would correspond to the scene depicted if this scene were actually there in three dimensions, for the eye of a spectator standing on the yellow marble disc.

How the ceiling appears to the spectator. The result of all this work is striking. First, from the floor, the spectator is unable to see the painted surface, *qua* surface. It is impossible to determine where the ceiling surface actually is. From the position marked by the yellow marble disc, the arches supported by columns at both ends of the ceiling are seen to stand upright into space. They are seen in three dimensions, with a strength of illusion similar to that given by the stereoscope. It is impossible to see that in fact they are painted on a cylindrical surface. Again, among the architectural ornaments near the actual windows, it is impossible to distinguish those which are genuine from those which are merely painted. As the painted sky is much less bright than the sky seen through the actual windows, however, the illusion is far from complete. But it is well nigh complete as far as depth is concerned. The whole ceiling looks rather like a vast complicated piece of coloured sculpture. From an aesthetic point of view, it would appear that such a painted ceiling belongs to a species of art quite distinct from ordinary painting.

It may be noted that the small photograph of Fig. 7.5 fails to give the astonishing impression produced by the actual painting. Especially, it fails to give a genuine three-dimensional impression, either for the painting or for the actual architecture. The same remark applies to the other photographs of the paintings in St Ignazio reproduced here.

Secondly, if the spectator walks away from the yellow disc, thus departing from the centre of projection, the illusion of depth does remain, but the scene represented, still seen in 3D, becomes deformed. The columns, for instance, look no longer vertical, and they may look curved. This deformation continually varies as one walks about in the church. The impression one gets is that the whole structure, which no longer appears in line with the actual church as an extension of it upwards, would be about to collapse if it were real (Figs. 7.10, 7.11, 7.12, 7.13 and 7.14).

The explanation of all this must be that the ceiling is so high that even binocular vision is unable to detect the exact position and shape of its surface; the two eyes here function as one eye. As the drawing is an accurate central projection, and as the shading and colouring are very skilful, the illusion of solidity and depth asserts itself completely. For the complicated flux of light reaching the spectator's eyes, when he is at the right position, is very similar to what it would be if the painting were replaced by the actual scene the artist wished to represent, or rather, to be exact, by the complicated piece of coloured sculpture which corresponds to this scene. Again, when the spectator moves away from the yellow disc, the light flux now received by his eyes becomes very nearly the same for each new position as the light flux which his eyes would receive if the deformed scene he sees from this position were actually there in three dimensions.[1]

Disadvantages of this kind of painting. It may be noted that many 'illusionistic' painted ceilings fail to give such an overpowering illusion. (Pozzo's are the only ones the present writer has seen which do so.[2]) Pozzo also painted, on a flat circular surface above the middle of the transept, a perspective of the cupola (Fig. 7.16), the elevation of which is given in Fig. 7.6; this painting is seen in Fig. 7.10. The centre of projection of this picture is nearer to the high altar than that of the nave painting. While this painting of the cupola is rather less remarkable than that of the nave ceiling, it does also appear in

[1] There is in the National Gallery in London a cabinet containing two peep-shows painted by S. van Hoogstraaten (1627–78). One of these peep-shows represents a seventeenth century Dutch interior consisting of a hall with a black and white tiled pavement, opening on two furnished rooms with a view of a street and a canal. All this appears in three dimensions when viewed through the peep-hole. This peep-show looks very much like a real interior, extending far beyond the dimensions of the cabinet. The scene is painted in perspective on the inside surface of the box, from one single centre of projection, the centre of the peep-hole. The painting is carried over in a continuous fashion from one wall of the box to another. In the hall the tiles, two chairs and a dog are painted partly on the wall, and partly on the floor of the box. It is hardly possible to tell on which surface of the cabinet the various parts are painted. When something of the actual wall of the cabinet can be distinguished, the painted view is seen 'through' the wall. The principle involved here is similar to that of Pozzo's ceiling.

[2] On 'perspectivists', that is artists who made such illusionistic paintings, see Maffei (1966a). This interesting article, however, does not make a clear distinction between those paintings which appear in the same striking manner as Pozzo's ceilings in St. Ignazio, and those which fail to give such a strong illusion. Again, it does not refer to the works of perspectivists extant in Great Britain.

7.10 Photograph of part of the Pozzo ceiling, taken from the marble disc
This view of part of the ceiling, taken from its centre of projection, shows it as it is intended to be seen. The spectator sees the painted architecture in three dimensions, as an extension of the real architecture and in line with it. (From this position, the painting of the cupola appears also in 3 D, but deformed, because its centre of projection is different from that of the nave ceiling.) (Photo by Simonetta Calza-Bini, Rome.)

three dimensions and it is almost impossible for the spectator, even when he walks about, to convince himself that the cupola he sees is only a flat picture. It is only by climbing to the cornice which runs inside the church at a height of 20 m above the floor, that it becomes obvious that the cupola is a painting on a horizontal plane, and also that the

7.11   Photograph of the same part of the Pozzo ceiling as in Fig. 7.10 taken from a position away from the marble disc

The painted architecture still appears in three dimensions to the spectator, but as he is not at the centre of projection, he no longer sees it in line with the architecture of the church and some of the straight lines now look curved. (Photo by Simonetta Calza-Bini, Rome.)

roof of the nave is hemicylindrical. Both paintings then appear strongly deformed, but no longer in three dimensions (Fig. 7.15). The tribune of the church, that is, the curved ceiling above the main altar, is also painted, from yet another centre of projection, which is closer to the altar than the other two centres (Fig. 7.4).

7.12

At the end of Pozzo's book a section entitled 'An answer to the Objection made about the Point of Sight in Perspective' shows that he was aware of some of the difficulties raised by this mode of representation. Pozzo calls 'Point of Sight' the centre of projection. He defends his decision of using three different centres of projection for the three different paintings, on the grounds that the church is of great length compared with its height. The unescapable result of this, however, is that a spectator in the right position for one of the paintings does see the other two as deformed (see e.g. Fig. 7.10). The use

7.13

7.12, 7.13 Photographs of the other end of the Pozzo ceiling taken from a position away from the marble disc

The architecture, still seen in 3 D, appears at a strong angle to the real architecture of the church and seems about to collapse. (Photos by Simonetta Calza-Bini, Rome.)

of one single centre of projection for each of the three paintings, he defends, rightly, on the grounds that the illusion he wished to produce could not be produced otherwise. In the case of the nave ceiling, that is 'in a regular situation, and where the Work is all of a piece', he says that it is absolutely necessary to use one centre of projection only. In such

7.14   Photograph of the whole Pozzo ceiling taken from a point in the transept, well away from the marble disc

The painted architecture looks strongly deformed but is still seen in 3 D by the spectator. (Photo by Simonetta Calza-Bini, Rome.)

a case, 'if you assign several Points of Sight, you will find no place whence you may take a perfect View of the Whole, and at best you can only view each Part from its proper Point'. (Pozzo, 1707.)

Pozzo was aware of the deformations which appear in viewing the ceiling of the nave when the spectator is not at the centre of projection (Figs. 7.11–7.14). 'Since Perspective is but a Counterfeiting of the Truth', he wrote, 'the Painter is not oblig'd to make it appear real when seen from *Any* part, but from *One* determinate Point only' (Pozzo, 1707). Nonetheless, this evidently constitutes a considerable drawback. For it seems that not many more than three spectators in this immense church can at any one time see even one of the three paintings as it is intended to be seen. This whole scheme of painted

7.15 Photograph of the Pozzo ceiling taken at a position 20 m above the floor of the church

The photographer was standing on the cornice which runs around the church below the windows at a height of 20 m. He was at the corner near the choir of the church shown on the left of Fig. 7.4. From this position the spectator sees the painted ceiling as a strongly deformed picture on a curved surface. The scene depicted no longer appears in three dimensions. (Photo by A. S. Evett.)

decoration becomes, to a large extent, a very remarkable experiment in optics—which can hardly have been the principal aim of those who had the church built. It would appear that for this reason Baroque artists at later dates avoided the representation in painted ceilings of such vast regular architectural designs, and instead depicted, for instance, figures seated on clouds in the sky, seen through architectural frameworks of irregular shape, so that deformations were much less obvious to spectators standing in different positions.

7.16   Engraving by Pozzo of the perspective of the cupola he painted in St Ignazio

The painting here was made on a plane horizontal surface, so that the special problem relating to the construction of the perspective on the curved ceiling of the nave did not arise. The painted cupola is seen in 3 D by a spectator standing on the floor of the church, and has its own centre of projection marked on the floor. (From Pozzo (1707), *Perspective*.)

As far as the present problem of the relationship of optics to painting is concerned, the main point of interest in Pozzo's painting on the ceiling of the nave of St Ignazio, and also in his flat painting of the cupola, is that the spectator is quite unaware of the shape, position and other characteristics of the painted surface itself. It is this very unusual state of affairs which produces the irresistible illusion of three dimensions in the scene represented.[1]

The same illusion is not produced by ordinary painting or photographs viewed in the usual way. Here some at least of the characteristics of the picture surface can be perceived, as belonging to the surface. Even if the spectator is hardly aware of them, they must play an important role in his perception of the picture, as will be shown in the following chapters.

Finally, it may be noted that Pozzo's ceiling may be regarded as a trompe-l'oeil, on a colossal scale. Like most trompe-l'oeil, it fails to deceive the eye completely. It mainly deceives it with regard to depth or the third dimension, but falls short of 'the utmost degree of perfection'.[2]

[1] The late Professor Erwin Panofsky stated (in 1940) that 'perspective construction as practised in the Renaissance is, in fact, not "correct" from a purely naturalistic, that is, a physiological or psychological point of view'. Now Pozzo's painted ceiling is constructed strictly according to the laws of linear perspective. As far as it is concerned, it seems clear that (for the case of a spectator in the right position) the above statement, if taken at its face value, is invalid. But it would be rather unfair to suggest that Panofsky in this statement had in mind this special kind of painting—which incidentally is post-Renaissance. When he put forward his influential thesis on 'Perspective as a Symbolic Form' (1927)—a work which among other things contains a wealth of stimulating information on the historical evolution of the use of linear perspective—what Panofsky had predominantly in mind was the case of ordinary paintings, made on a plane surface, viewed in the usual manner. Here the situation is indeed complex; one has often overlooked how far the mode of perception of such painting differs from that of the Pozzo-type trompe-l'oeil. As has already been mentioned it seems to the present writer that it is this unrecognized complexity which indirectly made it possible for so many controversies to arise on the meaning and the use of perspective in the art of painting.

While the present writer has considerable misgivings with regard to a number of Panofsky's arguments and conclusions, it must be pointed out that he does not always find it easy to understand what, from an optical, physiological and psychological standpoint, Professor Panofsky, and the other art historians who have been influenced by his thesis, do exactly mean. (Panofsky's writings on perspective, and those of White (1949, 1951, 1956, 1957) have been discussed in particular by Gioseffi (1957, 1957–8, 1963, 1966a), Pedretti (1964), ten Doesschate (1964), and Zanetti (1951, 1959 and 1960). The present book does not refer specifically to every point of possible disagreement but is rather an attempt at a restatement of the whole problem and a systematic examination of its main points, largely for the sake of their intrinsic interest. Certain points which may appear obvious to some readers have none the less been insisted upon, precisely because of the misunderstandings to which they have given rise.

[2] A trompe-l'oeil is a painting which gives a genuine illusion of the third dimension. Thus it may be impossible to see a bas-relief painted in trompe-l'oeil otherwise than as a real three-dimensional relief—even though the spectator may feel that there is something odd about it. Trompe-l'oeil usually represent things having very little depth, like, say, a picture frame on which various objects are stuck. Then perspective, light and shade, and colour, all combine to produce an illusion of real relief which binocular vision and motion parallax are unable to destroy. The St Ignazio ceiling is a special case where a scene of great depth does really appear in three dimensions. The same is true of pictures seen with one eye only, as explained in the next chapter.

As shown especially by the latter example, in which, say, the texture of the half-tone print may be apparent even though the picture surface is not seen as a surface and the scene appears genuinely in 3 D, trompe-l'oeil usually fail to deceive the eye completely: this no doubt is part of their attractiveness.

Some reliefs painted in perspective, in the midst of actual reliefs forming part of the architecture of the building, may however give a complete illusion, especially if they are in a dim corner. There are examples of this in the Palazzo Barberini at Rome. But such instances may be regarded as cheap substitutes for sculpture rather than instances of the art of painting.

On the other hand there are trompe-l'oeil from the Italian Renaissance, representing cupboards with doors open, benches and chairs placed against the actual wall on which they are painted (as in the Vatican and in St Maria del Popolo at Rome), which fail to give a genuine illusion of the third dimension because the objects represented have too much depth. (When photographed from their centre of perspective, these trompe-l'oeil may look more genuine than when seen *in situ*, precisely because the photograph is not a trompe-l'oeil and fails to give a complete illusion of depth: for then the partial illusion given by photography may be as strong for the painted as for the actual objects.)

8   *The perception of ordinary pictures*

When viewed in the usual way with both eyes, ordinary pictures drawn in perspective—paintings in a gallery, posters, photographs, postcards, illustrations in books or newpapers—do not, whatever the sense of depth they may seem to give, appear in three dimensions like stereoscopic pictures.

Pictures seen with one eye only

Yet when they are viewed with one eye only, without moving the head, they may acquire this 'stereoscopic' appearance, even though the effect is unlikely to be as striking as in the case of Pozzo's ceiling.[1] A painting may then appear, through its frame, as a scene in three dimensions seen through a window. Even photographs in a newspaper may appear in the same way, as if seen through a hole cut in the paper. This effect takes a little while to establish itself, rather like that given by the stereoscope. Schlosberg (1941) discusses the main types of experimental arrangements which can produce it. He points out its 'all or none' character: either it 'works', or it does not. Thus there is a sharp distinction between the usual mode of appearance of pictures and this three-dimensional appearance given by a single picture viewed with one eye: the picture becomes a kind of trompe-l'oeil (see footnote 2, p. 93).

Assuming the eye to be at the centre of projection, the explanation is the same as for Pozzo's ceiling. As vision is uniocular, the flatness of the picture is no longer evident and the picture surface, *qua* surface, is no longer seen. So perspective, both linear and aerial, colour, light and shade, the factors specific to pictorial representation, come into full play. The complex flux of light received from the picture by the one eye used is similar to

---

[1] A painting by A. Wiertz (1806–65), 'The premature burial' (*L'inhumation précipitée*), showing a man trying to break out of his coffin inside a vault, used to be arranged in Brussels so that it only could be seen through a peep-hole in the wall of a room of the Museum. This macabre picture then made a much more startling impression than when simply hanging on the wall, partly because it acquired a strong three-dimensional appearance. Similar arrangements have been used to create trompe-l'oeil in experiments on visual perception (Piéron, 1952).

that which it would receive from the scene represented. Accordingly the picture appears as a scene in three dimensions.[1]

Thus there is a sharp difference between the ordinary appearance of a picture and the appearance of the same picture under the special conditions just described. There is an even more striking difference between the usual appearance of ordinary pictures and that of Pozzo's painted ceiling, as this painting looks strongly deformed, and yet in 3 D, when seen from a wrong position.

Ordinary pictures usually do not appear deformed

When, as is most often the case, ordinary pictures are seen binocularly from a position different from the centre of projection, they do not as a rule give a noticeably deformed view of the scene represented. This fact, usually taken for granted, is a most important one in practical life. If it were not so, the usefulness of pictures as representations might almost vanish.

The kind of deformation which might be expected to appear when the picture is seen from the wrong position is illustrated by Fig. 8.1. The portrait of 'Big Brother', which appears in a poster in the background of this photograph, looks deformed because the photograph has been taken with the plate at an angle to the plane of the poster containing the portrait. Now the point is that portraits which are *seen*, not photographed, from a position well away from the centre of perspective of the portrait, do not look deformed as that of Big Brother in Fig. 8.1. If they did, painted portraits and photographs in passports, for instance, would be of very limited use, as they could give a good likeness only to one person at a time.

[1] The same effect may be produced by colour transparency photographs seen with one eye through a positive lens, with the kind of viewer now in common use. As small transparencies require a lens in any case to be seen clearly, however, there is but little opportunity for comparison with the way they appear in binocular vision.

Javal, who was one of the translators of Helmholtz's Optics, invented an instrument he called an *iconoscope*, which gives an effect similar to that which occurs in the uniocular vision of ordinary pictures, even though binocular vision is used (Helmholtz (1867) *Optique physiologique*, pp. 822–3). Javal's iconoscope consists of a system of four mirrors, so arranged that the spectator sees with both eyes approximately the same view as he would see with one eye placed midway between his eyes. This eliminates the stereoscopic element in vision by suppressing the binocular disparities of the visual angles.

Leonardo da Vinci, on the basis of the fact that our two eyes give us two different views of the same scene, stated in his *Treatise on Painting* that it was impossible even for the most perfectly executed painting 'to seem in the same relief as the natural model, unless that natural model is looked at from a great distance with one eye' (McMahon (1956), Vol. I, p. 177). Yet he seems to have noticed the peculiar three-dimensional appearance which ordinary pictures can acquire when viewed with one eye only (Richter & Richter (1939), No. 29, see Italian text).

Leonardo's observations on binocular vision might conceivably have led him to invent the stereoscope. But in fact it was only invented in 1833, by Wheatstone; see Helmholtz (1866), p. 690; Asher (1961).

8.1 Deformation in a photograph of a photograph

The head of 'Big Brother' in the background looks deformed because it is a photograph, taken at a wrong angle, of another photograph. The head of the young man in front, on the other hand, does not look deformed when *seen* from a position away from the centre of projection of the photograph. See text. (From the Radio Times, 25 November 1965. 'The World of George Orwell: *Nineteen Eighty-four*'.)

8.2   Another photograph of a photograph
This appeared in *Time* Magazine on 29 March 1968 during President Nixon's electoral campaign. The portrait of President Nixon, in the background, looks deformed for the same reason as the portrait in Fig. 8.1.

In Fig. 8.1. itself, the picture of the young man in front of the poster hardly becomes deformed when viewed from a wrong position. The same would no doubt be true of the actual poster portrait of Big Brother, if the poster itself were seen in its own frame, whereas in Fig. 8.1 we only see a photograph of the poster, without its frame.

Similarly, in Fig. 8.2, the portrait in the background is deformed into something of a caricature, because it has been photographed at an angle. Yet, while most spectators attending the electoral meeting at which this large portrait was displayed were viewing it from a wrong position, they must hardly have noticed deformations of this kind—which would make the use of such portraits defeat its purpose.

When the shape and position of the picture surface can be seen, an unconscious intuitive process of psychological compensation takes place, which restores the correct view when the picture is looked at from the wrong position. In the case of Pozzo's ceilings, on the other hand, the painted surface is 'invisible' and striking deformations are seen. Again, striking deformations are seen in the case of anaglyphs, a stereoscopic device in which the scene represented is seen in three dimensions, and the picture surface again is 'invisible' (see Chapter 11).

The existence and importance of this concept of psychological compensation were conveyed to the present writer by a letter from Albert Einstein, dated 24 February 1955, in which he wrote:

'The perspective representation corresponds exactly to the optical impression given by the object for a certain position of the eye in front of the plane of projection (picture).

'When one views the picture on its own, but from a different centre, then one receives visual impressions which the object itself would not give. This will almost always be so, when one looks at a painted picture.

'Now it seems to me to be the case that the spectator will easily *compensate* intuitively for this deformation, when the angle α which defines the boundary of the object is small, so that all the visual rays strike the plane almost perpendicularly [Fig. 8.3]. When, however $\alpha/2$ is for instance equal to $45°$, then the picture will appear deformed, if it is viewed from a distance which is greater than the distance of the projection centre from the picture. Then the intuitive compensation is likely to fail, so that the picture appears deformed. It is not easy to say which compromise solution the painter must choose in such a case.'

'It is probable that the use of a sufficiently restricted angle α in combination with central projection, is the only reasonable solution.'[1]

---

[1] The whole passage of Einstein's letter which relates to perspective reads as follows in the original:
   'Die Frage betreffend der Perspektive im Zusammenhang mit der künstlerischen Darstellung erscheint mir doch noch problematisch. Die perspektivische Darstellung ist dem optischen Eindruck des Objektes genau entsprechend für eine bestimmte Lage des Auges gegenüber der Projektions-Ebene (Bild).
   'Wenn man das Bild allein betrachtet, aber von einem andern Zentrum aus, so erhält man

Einstein, does not state explicitly that the basis for this compensation must be the spectators' awareness of the characteristics of the surface of the picture. But it can hardly be anything else. Paradoxically this awareness must be helped by the use of binocular vision, even though the picture in perspective is a projection made for one eye only.

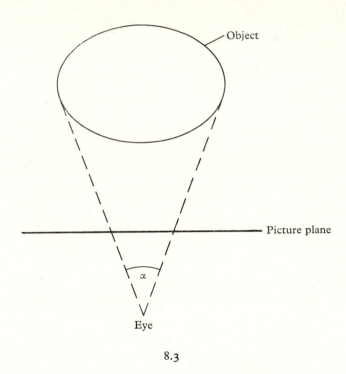

8.3

Gesichts-Wahrnehmungen wie sie das Objekt nicht vermittelt. So wird es nahezu immer sein, wenn man ein gemaltes Bild betrachtet.

'Es scheint nun so zu sein, dass diese Abweichung von dem Beschauer des Bildes leicht intuitiv *kompensiert* wird, wenn der die Objekt-Begrenzung charakterisierende Winkel α klein ist sodass alle Sehstrahlen die Platte nehezu senkrecht treffen. Wenn aber α/2 z. B. 45° ist, dann wird das Bild verzerrt aussehen, wenn man es von einer Distanz betrachtet, die z. B. wesentlich grösser ist als die Distanz des Projektions-Zentrums von Bilde. Dann wird wohl die intuitive Kompensation versagen, sodass das Bild verzerrt erscheint. Es ist nicht leicht zu sagen, was für ein Kompromiss der Maler in solchem Falle am besten wählen soll.

'Wahrscheinlich ist die Beschränkung auf hinreichend kleine α in Kombination mit der Zentralprojektion die einzig vernünftige Lösung. Dann ist Ihre Behauptung *im Wesentlichen* richtig.'

The first sentence ('The question concerning perspective with regard to representation in art does seem to me still unsettled') and the last sentence ('Then your thesis will *essentially* be correct') refer to a paper by the present writer published in 1952, now partly superseded, in which he failed to take into account the process of compensation which has just been discussed. A great deal of the present book consists of an examination of problems suggested by Einstein's letter. (The main thesis of the book was outlined by the author in 1963.)

8.4a   8.4b

8.4a, b   Two pinhole photographs of the same statuette taken from different distances

Photograph 8.4a was taken from a distance equal to half the height, photograph 8.4b from a distance equal to three times the height of the statuette. See text.

Bronze statuette stamped De Luca, Napoli. Reduced and restored copy of *Aphrodite*, No. 282, *British Museum Catalogue of Bronzes*; published in H. B. Walters (1915), *Select Bronzes, Greek, Roman and Etruscan, in the Department of Antiquities.* London: British Museum, Plate XXVIII. Said to have been found near Patras (perhaps at Olympia). Probably second century B.C. (Information kindly given by Mr R. A. Higgins.)

The influence of the choice of the angle α is illustrated by the two photographs of the same statuette reproduced in Figs. 8.4a and b. In Fig. 8.4a the distance of the projection centre to the statuette is equal to about one-half of the height of the statuette, so that α is about 90° (the distance of the projection centre to the photograph is too short to make it possible to see it clearly from this position). Artists and photographers have usually avoided the use of such a short distance for figures and portraits.

8.5a

8.5a   View of Venice by Canaletto 1697–1768
London: National Gallery.

In Fig. 8.4b the distance of the centre of perspective is three times the height of the statuette, the angle α being equal to about 20°. The classical proportions of the statuette here are retained, whereas they appear distorted in Fig. 8.4a. Moreover the picture gives a good representation of the statuette for any position in which the spectator is likely to place himself.

When on the other hand the angle α is very small, the picture approximates to an orthogonal projection—which may be regarded as a central projection from a centre so distant that the rays of the visual pyramid can be taken as being practically parallel. If

8.5 b

8.5 b   Enlargement of part of Canaletto's painting Fig. 8.4 a
This is a distant view covering a small visual angle. It corresponds to what would be seen with a telescope. See text.

the view is a distant scene, the objects depicted then appear 'squeezed' together, like the distant squares in the retinal image shown in Fig. 6.1. The picture then resembles what is seen in a telescope, or photographed by a telephoto lens (Figs. 8.5a and b).

Different projections of the same view

The two photographs of the Arch of Janus in Rome, Figs. 8.6a and b, were taken with a pinhole camera, both in the same manner, except that the plate of the camera was parallel to the plane of the façade for Fig. 8.6a, whereas for Fig. 8.6b it was placed at an angle of

25° to the façade. The camera was *not* displaced bodily from one position to another. Using a special arrangement, it was merely rotated by 25° around a vertical axis passing through its pinhole, the position of the centre of the pinhole thus remaining quite unaltered. Two accurate central projections of the view containing the Arch were therefore obtained from the same centre of projection *O* on two vertical planes, *AB* and *A'B'* (Fig. 8.6c), the only difference between the two being that the second vertical

8.6a

plane *A'B'* of projection was at an angle of 25° to the first plane *AB*, as shown in the diagram.

To make this quite clear imagine that a spectator places his eye so that its centre of rotation is at *O*, at the centre of projection, while keeping his head motionless (Fig. 8.6c). He then sees a certain view of the scene in front of him. Since he does not move about, his standpoint defines this view, which corresponds to the whole pyramid of sight relating to his eye's position. He can turn his eye and look in various directions, but what he sees is always part of the same view. Let the spectator now imagine in front of him a vertical sheet of glass, that is, a Leonardo window, placed in the position *AB*, on which glass pane he draws the Arch in such a manner that the drawing covers point by point the view he sees through the pane. This will give one section of part of his pyramid of sight, which will be like the photograph of Fig. 8.6a. Another drawing of the same view made in exactly the same way, again from O as a centre, but on a sheet of glass in the position $A'B'$, will give a different section of the same pyramid of sight, corresponding to the second photograph, Fig. 8.6 b.

By changing only the orientation of the surface of projection, any number of different photographs, or perspective drawings, can therefore be made of the same identical scene

8.6 b

8.6 a, b   Two pinhole photographs of the Arch of Janus in Rome

The photographs were taken from the same centre of projection O but on two different vertical planes of projection, AB for 8.6 a and $A'B'$ for 8.6 c as shown in Fig. 8.6 c. See text. This arch probably dates from the fourth century A.D.

from exactly the same centre of projection. Yet when the centre of rotation of the spectator's eye is kept fixed in this projection centre, what he sees is always the same view. As a rule, only trained artists and photographers clearly realize the different results which will be obtained if this same view is projected onto planes differing in their orientation.[1]

[1] This discussion strictly refers to vision with only one eye, the centre of rotation of which is in a fixed position. In effect, except when objects very close to the eyes are involved, it is also approximately valid when the spectator, standing in one position, looks around him with both eyes.

On account of the limited size of the photographic plate, Fig. 8.6a does of course show more of the view on the right of the Arch than Fig. 8.6b, and vice versa. The two photographs of the Arch itself, which is seen as a whole in both Figures, do, however, represent

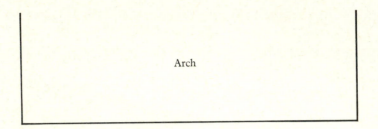

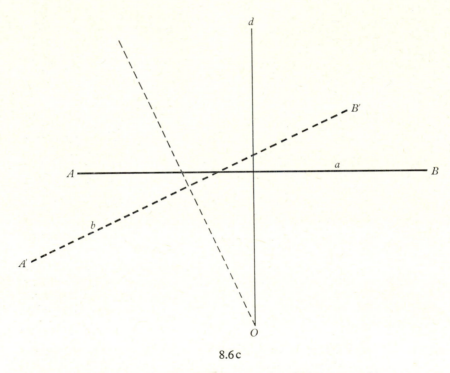

8.6c

8.6c Plan of the arrangement for taking the photographs of Fig. 8.6a and b.

exactly the same view of it. What is seen in one photograph is seen in the other. What is hidden in one photograph is hidden in the other. This is so for the architectural details just visible inside the right side of the passage through the Arch. It is only by bodily displacing the camera, or the eye, onto a new position towards the left, that more details

8.7a

8.7b

8.7a, b   Two pinhole photographs of the so-called Temple of Neptune at Paestum

The photographs were taken in the same way as Figs. 8.6a and b, but the angle of the planes of projection was 30° instead of 25°. This Greek Doric temple at Paestum, south of Naples, was probably built c. 460 B.C., in the same century as the Parthenon (447–438 B.C.). It is now believed to have been dedicated to Hera, not to Poseidon.

8.8a

8.8 b

8.8 a, b   Two pinhole photographs of the Temple of Neptune at Paestum, taken on a vertical and an inclined plate

The plate for 8.8 b was inclined at 20° from the vertical, the pinhole being in the same position for 8.8 a and b.

could be seen on this side of the interior of the Arch: this, of course, is simply due to the fact that 'we cannot see round corners'.

Yet the two photographs look very different. One is a frontal perspective. The other is a perspective taken at an angle, showing considerable foreshortening of the façade. Figure 8.6a, the façade appears like an architect's elevation; horizontal lines in it are horizontal, arcs of circle belonging to it are circular. In the other, Fig. 8.6b, the façade of the Arch is foreshortened; horizontal lines in the architecture all converge towards a point on the left; arcs of circles in the plane of the façade have become elliptical in shape. Indeed it may be said that Fig. 8.6a is composed like an Italian painting of the Quattro-cento, while Fig. 8.6b is more Baroque in style.

The two photographs, Figs. 8.7a and b, of the so-called Temple of Neptune at Paestum, were obtained in a similar way. The centre of projection is exactly the same for both. Only the orientation of the two vertical planes of projection differs, by an angle of 30°.

In the two photographs, Figs. 8.8a and b, of the same Greek temple, the centre of projection is again the same. The plane of projection is vertical in Fig. 8.8a. But in Fig. 8.8b it has been rotated by an angle of 20° around a horizontal axis. The result is that vertical lines now appear to converge upwards, whereas they are vertical in Fig. 8.8a. (In fact these two photographs were again taken from the same centre of projection as the preceding pair, so that Figs. 8.7a–8.8b give three different projections all of the same view—Figs. 8.7b and 8.8a give essentially the same projection.

Experiment

A similar pair of photographs (Figs. 8.9a and b) was made for a set of metal cubes and cylinders arranged as shown in the diagram of Fig. 8.9c. The set of metal objects is shown on the right of the diagram. The camera is shown on the left, its pinhole being at O. The photograph of Fig. 8.9a was taken with the plate ab parallel to the front of the set of objects; that of Fig. 8.9b was taken with the camera rotated by 20° around a vertical axis passing through O, the plate being moved to the position $a'b'$. The point O remained the centre of the pinhole of the camera for both pictures. Thus the two central projections of the same set of objects, Figures 8.9a and b, have the same centre of projection.

Enlargements of the two photographs of Fig. 8.9a and b were viewed, one at a time, through a hole 1 mm in diameter (Fig. 8.9d). Each photograph could be exactly positioned so that this small hole, or artificial pupil, was at the centre of projection O of the photograph. Furthermore, as shown in the diagram of Fig. 8.9d, the same vertical screen LM, pierced with a rectangular aperture, was interposed between the artificial pupil at O and the photograph, each photograph in turn being placed at the correct position. Under those conditions the observer viewing either photograph *AB* or photograph *A'B'* through the artificial pupil and through the aperture in the screen *LM* was unable to detect any significant difference between the appearance of one and the other. Both acquired a depth and relief similar to that given by stereoscopic pictures. The spectator

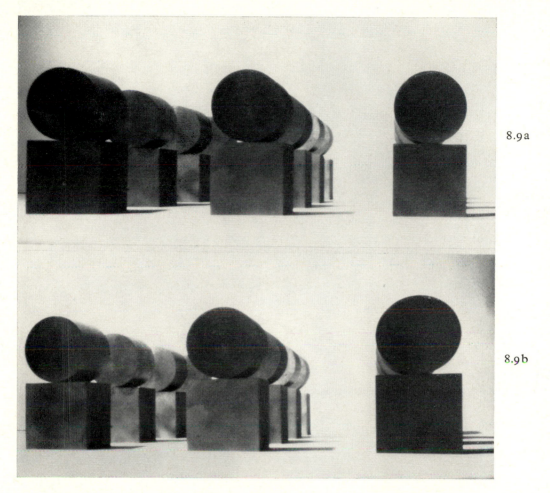

8.9 a

8.9 b

8.9 a, b Two pinhole photographs of the same set of cubes and cylinders
The photographs were made from the same centre, as shown in Fig. 8.9 c.

no longer saw the surface of the picture, *qua* surface, and had no inkling of its orientation relative to his eye. (The small artificial pupil was used in order to give to all observers a clear view of the photograph, as vision through such a small hole gives a very great depth of field to all eyes (see Scheiner's experiment in Chapter I).)

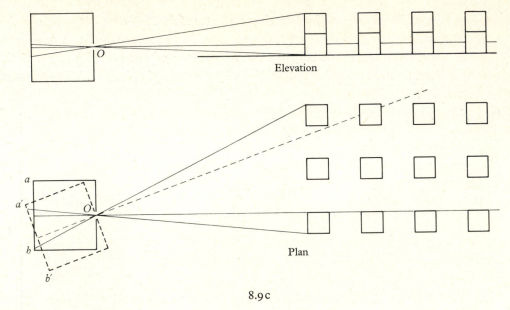

8.9c

8.9c   Arrangement for making the photographs of Figs. 8.9a and b.

The diameter and height of the cylinders, and the height of the cubes, were all equal to 2 in. The camera is shown on the left, in the two positions corresponding to Fig. 8.9a (plate at *ab*) and to Fig. 8.9b (plate at *a'b'*). See text.

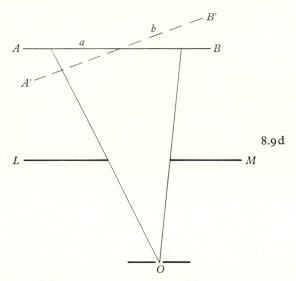

8.9d

8.9d   Plan of the arrangement for viewing Figs. 8.9a and b

Photograph 8.9a was positioned in the vertical plane *AB* and viewed through the artificial pupil at *O*, and through a rectangular aperture in the opaque screen *LM*. It was then replaced by photograph 8.9b, suitably positioned in the plane *A'B'* and viewed in exactly the same way. The observer could hardly tell any difference between the two, which were both seen in 3D.

In this experiment, therefore, the two photographs appeared in three dimensions (like Pozzo's ceiling) and they could hardly be distinguished from each other. The photographs had been positioned so that all the visual angles subtended by their various parts were the same as the angles which would be subtended by the corresponding parts of the objects themselves. This result again shows that pictures in perspective may, when viewed under special conditions, be seen as predicted by the simple theory of linear perspective. In agreement with this theory, different projections of the same objects, that is, different sections of the same visual pyramid, made and viewed from the same centre of projection, may appear the same to the eye when special arrangements are made. (The same result was obtained using two photographs of a set of objects consisting of 12 square pillars; Pirenne, 1967 *b*.)

Essentially the same experiment was made with Figs. 8.8 a and b, the plane of Fig. 8.8 b being inclined at 20° from the vertical. Both photographs gave the same view, in 3 D, of the temple. Held in the hand, on the other hand, Fig. 8.8 b rather looks like one of 'those crazy pictures of skyscrapers', and most observers agree that it cannot really be made to look like Fig. 8.8 a. In such a case, it will be noted that no mask is used and that the boundary of the photographs is seen, which gives clues as to the position of their surface.

The spectator's awareness of the surface pattern of ordinary pictures

It has often been taken for granted that using one eye only, and holding by hand in the right position pictures like the pairs of photographs just discussed, they can all be made to look the same without any special difficulty (the present writer used to think so, but had to change his mind once he had made the above-described experiments). In fact this is not so. The pairs of photographs, Figs. 8.6 a and b, and 8.8 a and b, cannot easily be made to look the same in this informal way. It is true that the architectural views are wide-angle photographs, the height of Fig. 8.8 a and b for instance subtending about 96° at the centre of projection, so that the centre of projection is usually too near the picture for clear vision. But even in the case of enlargements which can be seen clearly from their centre of projection, the two photographs of each pair do not look quite the same when held in the hand, even when they are viewed with one eye only.

Viewed with both eyes, in the usual manner, these photographs, as well as paintings in perspective, give a certain sensation of solidity and depth, even though not a 'stereoscopic' one. But, on the other hand, in Figs. 8.6 a and b and in Figs. 8.9 a and b, for instance, the spectator also recognizes either a frontal perspective or a perspective taken at an angle.

It may be concluded that under ordinary conditions the actual pattern *on the surface* of a representational picture must be perceived, as a surface pattern, even though the spectator may only be dimly aware of this, *at the same time* as the objects represented are seen as a scene in depth.

The main point of the above experiments is that they made the surface of the picture 'invisible', *qua* surface. The frame of the picture itself was no longer visible, being hidden by the new 'frame' given by the aperture in the screen placed between the artificial pupil and the picture. In ordinary vision the spectator's awareness of the surface pattern is obviously helped to a great extent by the frame or by the regular shape of the boundary of the picture.

The awareness of the surface pattern of a painting is clearly of great importance from an aesthetic point of view. The artist or the photographer must compose the scene he wishes to represent, by deciding from which standpoint he is going to depict it. But the choice of the surface of projection for this perspective of the scene and of the boundary or frame of this surface also are of decisive importance for the composition. For instance, in a frontal perspective of a façade the horizontal lines are parallel to the top and bottom of a rectangular frame. In a perspective taken at an angle, they are no longer so. This, from an artistic standpoint, is of major importance.

'There is a kind of emotion which is quite particular to painting,' wrote the painter Delacroix, 'and which results from such and such arrangement of colours, lights, etc. That is what one may call "the music of the painting". Even before knowing what the painting represents, being at too great distance to see what it represents, often you are taken in by this magical accord.' (Roger Marx, 1963.) Such an aesthetic effect can only be produced by the harmonious characteristics of the flat pattern of the surface of the painting, since it occurs before the scene represented can even be identified. The fact that this pattern is in fact also perceived to some extent at close range, when the scene represented is clearly seen, shows that representational painting does not differ as radically as is sometimes believed from non-representational, 'abstract', painting, in which only that flat painted pattern is often considered as being of importance.

An unsophisticated spectator may entirely fail to appreciate the artistic worth of a purely non-representational design. But in front of a representational painting by a great artist, he may be influenced, quite unwittingly, by the purely aesthetic character of the surface pattern of the picture, even while he may think he is only interested in the scene represented.

Our awareness of the characteristics of the surface of a picture may be called a 'sub-sidiary' awareness, in the sense in which Polanyi (1958, 1962) uses this term, in con-tradistinction with our 'focal' awareness of the subject represented. At the same time as we are attending to the scene in depth, we are also aware, in a much less positive way, of many clues relating to the surface and the frame of the picture.[1]

---

[1] This applies to the case of a spectator whose major interest lies in the scene represented. The connoisseur and the expert can transfer his focal awareness from the scene to the painted surface,

The crux of the argument of this chapter is that it is only in those exceptional cases where every precaution has been taken to make any awareness of the picture surface impossible, that the picture assumes a different, genuinely three-dimensional appearance, similar to that given by the stereoscope.

as a surface. As to the artist executing a painting, he must perforce become focally aware of the manner he disposes his pigments on his canvas, and thus of the surface pattern of his picture. Therein lies the main difficulty of the craft of representational painting or drawing.

Further discussion of the problems of focal and subsidiary awareness in the perception of pictures will be found in the Foreword and in Polanyi (1970).

9 *Objects with curved surfaces*

Spheres and human figures

The outline of a sphere always appears circular to the eye, for the cone tangent to the sphere and having its apex at the point in the eye always is a right circular cone. Now the section of such a cone by a plane is a circle only when the axis of the cone, which passes through the eye O and through the centre of the sphere, is perpendicular to the intersecting plane AB (Fig. 9.1). When the cone is cut by a plane $A'B'$ oblique to its axis, the angle of the axis to the plane being smaller than the angle of the cone, the resulting section is an ellipse.[1] Thus in a picture in exact central perspective, the projection of a sphere should in most cases be an ellipse. An instance of this is given by the pinhole photograph of a stone sphere on the right of Fig. 9.2. It may be emphasized that when the centre of rotation of the eye is at the centre of projection, then for each and every position of the eye the retinal image of the ellipse, assumed to be drawn on a Leonardo window, will coincide exactly with the retinal image formed by the actual sphere—whereas a circular image on the window would not do so. The spectator, without moving the head, is free to look at each part of the sphere or of its elliptical image in turn. When his eye thus rotates in its orbit, both retinal images may become altered; yet they always remain in coincidence.

The axes of all ellipses such as those in Fig. 9.2, when produced, pass through the point (the 'principal point') where the perpendicular from the centre of projection intersects the plane of projection. The eccentricity and the orientation of the elliptical projection of a sphere vary with the position of the sphere in the picture. This is shown in Figs. 9.3 and 9.4 which are pinhole photographs, and therefore accurate central projections, of a set of five and a set of fifteen spherical objects (see Fig. 9.5). In each figure, the central sphere, which has its centre on the perpendicular from the eye to the picture plane, is the only sphere which is projected as a circle.

When an enlargement of the photograph of Fig. 9.3 is viewed through a small artificial pupil placed at the centre of projection of the picture, and through an oval aperture in a

---

[1] This is the usual case in the practice of perspective. For angles of intersection equal to or greater than the angle of the cone, the section is a parabola or a hyperbola.

screen which hides the edges of the picture, most observers report that it looks like a set of equal spheres, and cylinders, seen in three dimensions. Such an arrangement is similar to that of the experiment described above for the set of cubes and cylinders in Fig. 8.9 d. Here again the simple theory of perspective works as predicted; for under

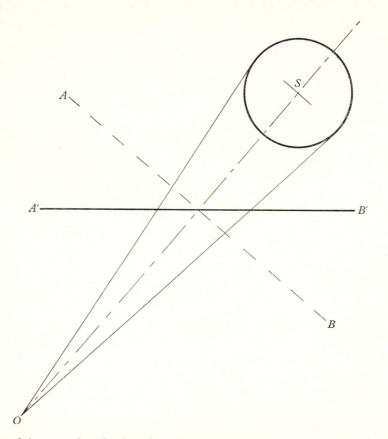

9.1   Diagram of the central projection of a sphere upon a plane
In the usual case, the projection of the sphere S on the plane $A'B'$ is an ellipse. It is only in the case of a plane such as AB, perpendicular to the line joining the projection centre O to the centre of the sphere, that the projection is a circle.

these conditions the cones defined by the centre of perspective and the elliptical projections in the photograph are all right circular cones, and the visual angles are all the same as those which would correspond to actual spheres (Fig. 9.5). In this experiment the observer is not aware of the precise position and shape of the picture surface.

Looking at a photograph such as Fig. 9.3 with the naked eye, without the interposition of a screen with an aperture, however, it is very difficult or impossible to find a position

9.2   Pinhole photograph of spherical architectural ornaments

The projection of the large sphere is elliptical in shape and the great axis of the ellipse is directed towards the principal point of the perspective. Picture taken on the roof of the Church of St Ignazio in Rome.

9.3 Pinhole photograph of a set of five spheres on top of five cylinders

The objects photographed were aluminium cylinders and steel balls, all one inch in diameter. The picture was taken as explained in Fig. 9.5. (From Pirenne (1967 a), *Vision and the Eye.*)

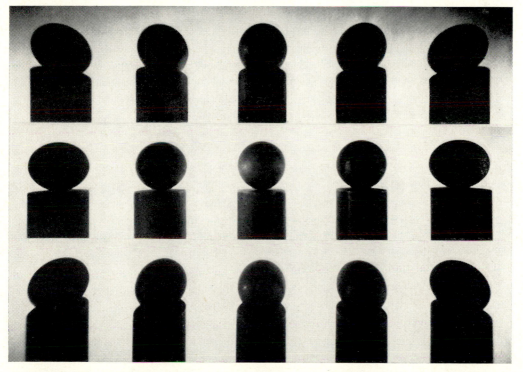

9.4 Composite pinhole photograph of fifteen spheres on top of cylinders

The objects were the same as for Fig. 9.3. The arrangement is explained in Fig. 9.5. (From Pirenne (1967 a) *Vision and the Eye.*)

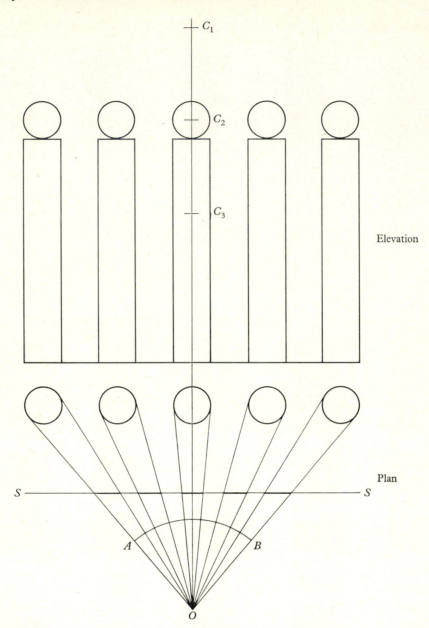

9.5   Diagram of the arrangement for making Figs. 9.3 and 9.4

The surface of projection was a vertical plane SS parallel to the plane of the axis of the cylinders. For Fig. 9.3 the arrangement was as shown. For Fig. 9.4, the photographs were taken, in effect, with two additional rows of spheres placed at the levels C_1 and C_3, besides the row shown at the level C_2 in the diagram.

If the surface of projection were replaced by a spherical surface AB having its centre at the centre of projection O, the projections of all the spheres would be circular in outline. (From Pirenne (1967 a) *Vision and the Eye*.)

from which it is seen as a set of true spheres. Using binocular vision, this is impossible. The so-called marginal distortions in the photograph then always remain very conspicuous—these 'distortions' of course are in fact exact central projections.

Now, most artists have always depicted spheres as circles, not as ellipses. Italian

9.6　Raphael's School of Athens
(Vatican. Photo by Alinari.)

artists of the Renaissance thus 'corrected' the 'distortions' shown in Figs. 9.3 and 9.4. It is true that Leonardo da Vinci (McMahon, 1956, Vol. I, p. 92, Vol. II, p. 49v) knew that the projection of a sphere in most cases is an ellipse; but, according to La Gournerie (1859), he never depicted a sphere in any of his paintings. In his *School of Athens*, Raphael (1483–1520) depicted two spheres at the right side of his painting (Figs. 9.6 and 9.7). But he drew their outlines as circles. The architecture which extends over most of the painting is drawn in perspective as one whole, from one main centre of projection. But the spheres (and the numerous human figures) are not drawn as projections from this centre. They are drawn from a number of subsidiary centres of projection, each in front of the position which the respective sphere or figure would occupy in the painting.

This is an instance of the modifications made to the strict theory of central projection, even by artists who paid great attention to linear perspective. In the case of Raphael's spheres, La Gournerie relates in his treatise (1859, p. 170) that he made the following experiment. In an engraved reproduction of the *School of Athens*, he replaced the circular

9.7   Detail of Raphael's School of Athens
The two spheres at the right are depicted as circles whereas their exact central perspectives should be elliptical. (Vatican. Photo by Alinari.)

pictures of the two spheres by ellipses having the correct, rather elongated, shapes which correspond to the position of the spheres relative to the main centre of projection. (The distance of this projection centre to the picture plane, in this painting, is about equal to the width of the painting.) These correct central projections, producing the same retinal images as would be given by actual spheres, were found to be quite unacceptable. They did not at all look like spherical objects—whereas Raphael's circles do so.

Thus it appears that the spectator looking at Raphael's picture of the spheres must make a complicated intuitive compensation. On account of natural perspective, the circles appear foreshortened to him. They do not form in his eyes the retinal images which would be formed by actual spheres. But, on the basis of his knowledge of the shape and position of the surface of the painting, he recognizes them as circles drawn on a flat surface. Since real spheres always look circular, he concludes that these circles represent spheres. It will be noted that all this, which must somehow occur unconsciously, can be done as well when the spectator uses both eyes, and is in the wrong position. To most spectators, the *School of Athens*, in which the perspective is in parts inaccurate, appears as an outstanding example of the use of perspective. Indeed it is wide-angle photographs, in which the perspective is accurate in all particulars, which on the contrary strike many as containing 'distortions'.[1]

Human figures are usually depicted in the same manner as Raphael's spheres, from different subsidiary centres of projection placed each in front of the position in the painting of the figure concerned. This is so in the *School of Athens*. The artist has painted the various figures rather as if he had done their portraits, each portrait being placed in a separate part of the painting. It will be noted that for the artist this is the most natural and easy way of painting such figures. It is again in the case of wide-angle photographs that human figures, near the edge of the picture, often appear 'distorted'. The heads of the figures appear elongated along various directions which depend on their position relative to the point where the perpendicular from the centre of projection strikes the picture plane, as in the case of the spheres of Fig. 9.4. Artists whose aim is a good likeness do not draw figures as shown in the photograph of the Greek statuette, Fig. 8.4a, which gives an exact projection. (Pozzo drew accurate central projections, but his paintings were of a very special kind.)

---

[1] The camera obscura, fitted with a lens, and with a plane mirror, which gives an upright image on a horizontal surface, was used by artists in the eighteenth century. Several types of these 'optical machines for forming the pictures of objects, with their use in drawing' are described by R. Smith in his *Compleat System of Opticks* (1738), Bk III, Ch. 15. Gioseffi (1959) has built and experimented with yet another type of camera obscura, known to have been used in the eighteenth century, and which was large enough for the artist to work with the upper part of his body inside the camera, stray light from outside being excluded by the use of a curtain. Such cameras project on a sheet of paper a luminous image of external objects, similar to the image cast by a photographic camera on its ground glass screen. The artist is thus able to trace on the paper the outlines of objects in the image produced by the camera, which is a central projection of the external scene. There are very strong reasons to believe that Canaletto (1697–1768) made at least some of his townscape drawings with the help of such a camera. According to Gioseffi, the dome of a church in one of Canaletto's drawings is asymmetrical with regard to the vertical, a kind of 'distortion' which is typical of photography and of perspectives drawn with rigorous accuracy, but which, he says, would be 'inconceivable' in the case of a free-hand drawing executed by eye direct from the real object. (Yet in the background of Mantegna's (1431–1506) painting of 'Christ in the Garden of Olives', which is in the Musée des Beaux Arts of Tours, there is a round building the dome of which is drawn in such an asymmetrical manner.)

9.8   Pinhole photograph of columns of the so-called Basilica at Paestum
Frontal perspective. The 'Basilica' is a Greek Doric temple of the sixth century B.C.

9.9   Another pinhole photograph of the Basilica at Paestum
Perspective at an angle. The centre of projection was the same as for Fig. 9.8.

Rows of columns

Figure 9.3 shows that in a row of cylindrical objects parallel to the plane of projection, the cylinders further away from the centre of projection give projections which become, not thinner, but wider. The diagram of Fig. 9.5 explains this apparent paradox. The

9.10   Engraving of the cloister of the Charterhouse at Rome
From Letarouilly (1840–57), *Edifices de Rome Moderne.*

angle subtended at the centre of projection by the width of the cylinders does become smaller for more peripherally placed cylinders, but the section by the plane *SS* becomes wider because of the increasing obliquity of this plane. In the experiment with the artificial pupil described above with regard to the spheres on top of the cylinders, the cylinders also look like true cylinders all equal in size.

In Fig. 9.8 it will be noticed that the projections of the Doric columns become thicker towards the right and the left, for the same reason.

When representing such a row of columns, artists have usually avoided this effect and

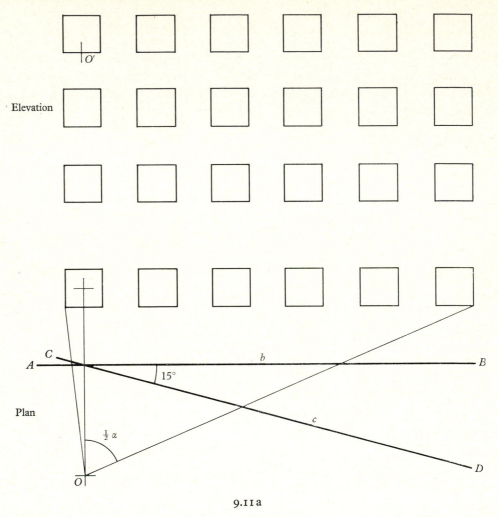

9.11a

9.11a Elevation and plan of the set of eighteen cubes, two perspectives of which are given in Figs. 9.11b and c.

Both perspectives are made from the centre of projection O, the first on a vertical plane AB parallel to the faces of the cubes, the second on a vertical plane CD at an angle of 15° to AB.

The angle $\alpha/2$ is about $66\frac{1}{2}°$, so that if the set of cubes were extended to the left to cover the same angle as to the right, Einstein's angle α would be 133°. This leads to strong 'marginal distortions' in the two central projections of Figs. 9.11b and c.

given equal width to all the columns. Similarly they have deviated from exact central projection when depicting a row of columns at an angle to the picture plane, thus avoiding the rather puzzling effect shown in Fig. 9.9, where the more distant columns on the left seem to become thicker, relative to their height, than those in the middle of the photograph. Thus in the architectural drawing of Fig. 9.10 by Letarouilly, the last column on

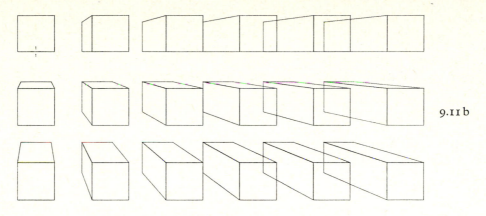

9.11 b

9.11 b   Central projection of the set of eighteen cubes

The projection was made from O onto the plane AB. The projected faces of the cubes are square, as in the elevation of Fig. 9.11 a.

This figure, as well as Figs. 9.11 c, 9.12 b, c and 9.13 b, were produced at the Computing Laboratory of Oxford University by Dr M. D. McIlroy and Mr J. E. Stoy using an English Electric KDF 9 computer and a Calcomp plotter. (Most of the work was programmed in FORTRAN; the basic graphic routines were adapted from a Culham Laboratories package. See F. M. Larkin, *A User's Guide to the Culham Graphical Output System*, H.M. Stationery Office, Code 91/3/21/75.)

9.11 c

9.11 c   Another central projection of the set of eighteen cubes of Fig. 9.11 a

The projection here was made from the same centre of projection as for Fig. 9.11 b, but on a vertical plane inclined at 15° to the plane containing the faces of the cubes. (Picture made by computer as Fig. 9.11 b.)

the right is the thinnest, and the second from the right is thinner than the other two on the left.

A row of square pillars does not give rise to the same problem. When projected on a plane parallel to the plane in which they lie, the rectangular fronts of the pillars all give

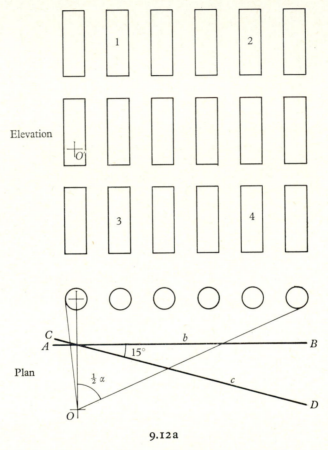

9.12 a

9.12 a   Elevation and plan of a set of eighteen cylinders, two perspectives of which are given in Fig. 9.12 b and c
The arrangement was similar to that explained in the legend of Fig. 9.11 a.

projections of the same shape and size. This is because the projection of a plane figure on-to a plane parallel to it gives a figure which is geometrically similar to the original. The problem arises for columns because their surfaces are curved.

Figures 9.11 b–9.13 b show the difference between the central projections of sets of cubes, which may be taken as representing square pillars, and sets of cylinders repre-senting columns. These figures show the strange perspective effects given by columns

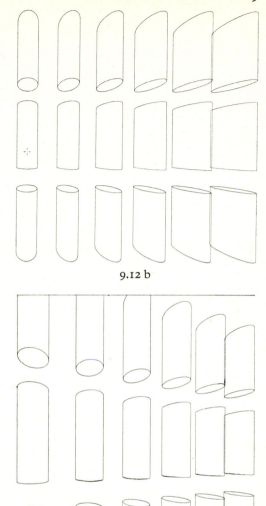

9.12 b   Central projection of the set of eighteen cylinders of Fig. 9.12 a

The projection was made from *O* on the plane *AB*, parallel to the plane of the axes of the cylinders (Fig. 9.12 a). Note the increasing widening of the projections of these 'columns' towards the right, in contrast with the faces of the cubes in Fig. 9.11 b. (Picture made by computer as Fig. 9.11 b.)

9.12 b

9.12 c   Another central projection of the set of eighteen cylinders of Fig. 9.12 a

This projection was made from *O* on the vertical plane *CD*, inclined to the plane of the axes of the cylinders (Fig. 9.12 a). (Picture made by computer as Fig. 9.11 b.)

9.12 c

placed at large angles from the principal point, that is the point of intersection of the perpendicular from the centre of projection to the picture plane. The effects shown here are extreme cases of those 'distortions' which many artists have either 'corrected', or avoided altogether.

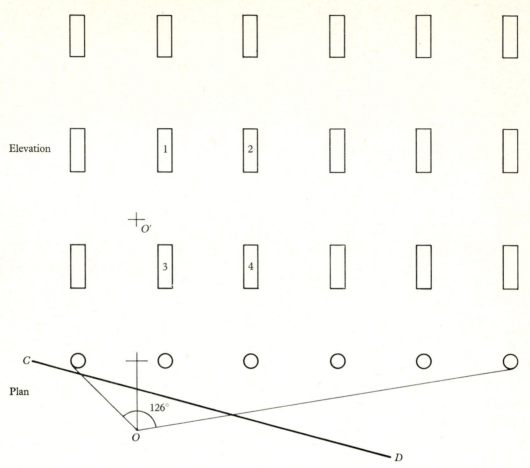

9.13 a   Elevation and plan of another set of eighteen cylinders, the perspective of which is given in Fig. 9.13 b.

The cylinders here are more widely spaced than in Fig. 9.12 a, but the cylinders marked 1–4 are common to both sets. The total angle subtended by the projection from O is about 126°, which leads to very strong marginal 'distortions' in the central projection on the vertical plane CD.

Balusters and similar objects

The surface of the curved part of a baluster is a surface of revolution, having a vertical axis. Accordingly it always appears to the eye as symmetrical relative to a vertical plane passing through the axis and through the eye. Apart from exceptional cases, there is no such symmetry in the central projection of a baluster on a vertical plane. Figure 9.14 shows this clearly for the balusters distant from the centre of the picture; the deviation from symmetry is small for the two central ones.

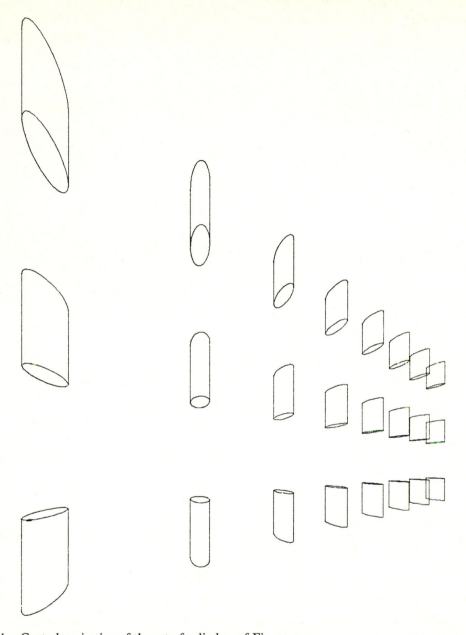

9.13 b   Central projection of the set of cylinders of Fig. 9.13 a

The widths of the projected cylinders pass from a very large value on the left through a local minimum, then a local maximum, and would finally tend to zero towards the right if the number of 'columns' were extended indefinitely. Measured on an arbitrary scale, the 8 projected widths in the Figure are about 2·41; 1·00; 1·15; 1·30; 1·34; 1·35; 1·31 and 1·22. (Picture made by computer as Fig. 9.11 b.)

Artists have again avoided this effect in their painting, departing from exact perspective in order to draw symmetrical outlines of the balusters. The same applies to vases, lamps, cups and other solids of revolution (Figs. 9.15 and 9.16).

9.14   Pinhole photograph of a balustrade on the roof of the Church of St Ignazio in Rome
Note the 'distortions' of the shape of the balusters away from the centre of the picture. The perspective construction of the straight lines in this photograph is analysed in Fig. 10.2 of next chapter.

Conclusion

In the case of almost all objects with curved surfaces the shape of which is well-known to the spectator, artists have usually modified the exact rules of perspective which of course imply the use of a single projection centre. This is in contrast to the warning given by Pozzo with regard to the construction of his ceiling in perspective, namely that figures and architectural features there must all be drawn in accurate central projection from the centre of projection indicated by the marble disc in the floor of the church. While Pozzo aimed at and achieved a grandiose trompe-l'oeil effect, however, artists making ordinary paintings did not aim at such an effect, and must have expected their pictures to be viewed from various positions—under which conditions the spectators are aware of the position, shape, and other characteristics of the surface of the picture.

9.15 Banqueting scene. Painting from Pompei

The tops of the small table and of the cups placed upon it are drawn more or less as ellipses, but the great axes of these ellipses are nearly horizontal, not showing the inclinations which appear in Fig. 9.16. (Another painting at the Naples Museum, Inv. No. 9015, shows a similar depiction of a number of round objects, but is seriously damaged.) (Museo Nazionale, Naples. Inventory No. 9024.)

The above modifications to central projection are not always easy to harmonize with the perspective of the straight parts of the objects, drawn in accurate projection from the main centre of projection. Difficulties arise notably with regard to curved mouldings in the bases and capitals of columns. Figures 9.8 and 9.9 show the strange shapes which may be assumed by the circular tops of Doric columns in central projections.

9.16 Pinhole photograph of small cups and other solids of revolution

The elliptical projection of the circular edges of the cups have axes which vary in their inclination to the horizontal according to their position. The width of the picture subtends an angle of roughly 90°. (Photo by A. S. Evett.)

9.17 Saenredam: Interior of S. Bavo, Haarlem

The bases of the near columns, especially the middle one, show features typical of an exact central projection. See text. (Photo by The National Gallery, London.)

It would appear, in fact, that many Italian painters of the Renaissance avoided such architectural features, or at any rate did not make them play a major role in their composition. The engravings in treatises on perspective also contain but few such instances, no doubt because exact perspective in such cases leads to results which experience taught artists to avoid as odd and displeasing. La Gournerie (1859) deals in detail with this problem. He points out that most treatises in perspective published before his own fail to discuss or even mention the modifications which experience led artists to make to the rules of exact perspective.

The Dutch painter Saenredam (1597–1665), however, did put to artistic use some of the perspective effects which have just been discussed. In Fig. 9.17, some of them appear in the base of the central column of the painting. The principal point is far to the left (as in Figs. 9.11 b and 9.12 b) and $\alpha/2$ is also a large angle in this picture. It appears that Saenredam increased the height of the near column, thus changing the architecture of the church, so as to avoid still stranger effects which otherwise would have occurred with regard to the tops of the columns. It will be noted that these effects only occur in the perspective, that is, in the section of the visual pyramid. They are not seen when one looks at the real architecture (see Carter, 1967).

10 *Central projection of straight lines. Subjective curvatures*

The central projection of a straight line is reduced to a single point if the line passes through the centre of projection, that is, through the centre of rotation of the eye. Then the straight line is a line of sight, all the points of which have projections in coincidence with one another—and have coinciding retinal images, as shown in the experiments on the rabbit's eye. This applies to surfaces of projection having any shape.[1]

When the surface of projection is a plane, a straight line which does not pass through the centre of projection is projected as a straight line. For its projection is the intersection of the plane defined by the line itself and the centre of projection, with the projection plane: this intersection of two planes is, of course, a straight line.

Advantage of a plane surface of projection

Thus in a plane picture, all lines which in the scene depicted are objectively straight are projected as straight lines, except when they are foreshortened into single points. Consequently, when the picture is seen from a position different from the centre of projection, the straight lines belonging to the objects represented will still be seen as straight lines, even if the shape of the objects then take up a deformed appearance.

This is one of the main advantages of pictures having a plane surface. The position is different in the case of central projection on a curved surface, when it becomes much more important to keep the eye at the right position.

Suppose an architectural view is projected on the inside of a spherical surface, the centre of the sphere being the centre of projection. Then all straight lines of the objects (except those passing through the centre, which are projected as single points) are projected as segments of great circles on the sphere. Seen with one eye placed at the centre

---

[1] It would not be true, however, if the straight line forming through the eye were entirely contained in the surface of projection, in which case the line would be its own projection. But this is a case of theoretical interest only, since the surface of projection itself would then pass through the eye.

of the sphere, these great circles will appear as straight lines, at any rate in the sense that it will be possible to cover them exactly by a taut thread held in the right position in front of the eye. From positions away from the centre of the sphere, on the other hand, the segments of great circles will as a rule look curved, and it will be impossible to bring a taut thread in coincidence with them.

Again, it is because Pozzo's nave ceiling is painted on a curved surface, namely a hemi-cylindrical one, that some of the straight parts of the architecture depicted in it look curved when viewed from the wrong position. This vast ceiling is so distant from the spectator that, when he is standing at the right place, he sees straight architectural features as straight even when he uses binocular vision. This would not be so for perspectives on curved surfaces placed close to the eyes. Then even if one eye is at the centre of projection, the other eye will be at a position significantly different from it. The surface itself will probably be seen as a curved surface, so that all lines in it may look curved, even if they can be covered by a taut thread, by virtue of the curvature of the surface to which they belong.

Parallel lines which are parallel to the projection plane

The central projections on a plane of a set of straight parallel lines which are parallel to the plane, are straight parallel lines. Thus, for instance, on a vertical plane of projection, all vertical lines are projected as verticals. In most of the pinhole photographs reproduced in this book, the camera was positioned with the help of a spirit level so that the photographic plate was in a vertical position. Vertical lines belonging to the architectural scene photographed are then all represented by vertical lines in the picture. (In Fig. 8.8b, on the other hand, where the camera was tilted by an angle of 20° from the vertical, the verticals in the architecture are no longer vertical in the photograph.)

Consider now the case of two horizontal lines situated in a vertical plane. Such a pair of parallels may be illustrated by the lines at the top and at the base of a long horizontal wall. In the section on Natural Perspective, it has been seen that the visual angle subtended by the height of the wall, for different positions along its length, is largest for that part of the wall which is nearest to the eye. This angle becomes smaller and smaller towards *both* ends of the wall: it would become smaller than any small value chosen at will if the length of the wall were supposed to be extended indefinitely. Again, it has also been seen in Chapter 6 that the curved retinal images of two such horizontal lines tend to converge in *both* directions. If we consider a plane of projection vertical and parallel to the wall, however, the central projection of the horizontal top and bottom lines of the wall is a pair of parallel, horizontal, straight lines.

This simple geometrical result has repeatedly proved a stumbling block. It has caused a considerable amount of controversy, and it has even led to various suggestions according to which straight lines should be depicted as curved on a plane surface of projection. Jopling in 1835 made the following comments:

'The fact, however, has puzzled several; for many good draughtsmen are neither mathematicians nor geometricians; and they have asked, Will not the two horizontal and parallel right lines, for example, forming the top and base of a long wall, appear, to a person who may stand in front of the middle of it, to get nearer and nearer to each other the further they extend both to the right and to the left of the centre? Have not such lines, therefore, the appearance of curves? And ought not their representation, when drawn on a plane, as thus viewed, to be curved lines, as there is no appearance of angle in the middle?

'The answer to these questions is, that straight parallel lines on the plane of projection, when viewed from the point of sight, will appear to approach each other; and also appear as much curved, in proportion to their length, as the long lines of the top and base of the wall would so appear from the point, at a proportional distance, from which they were viewed.'

In other words, the height of the wall in positions more distant from the eye subtends smaller visual angles than in nearer positions—simply because of the increasing distance from the eye, the height of the wall being a constant. When the eye is at the centre of projection, the angles subtended by the height of the projection of the wall in corresponding positions become smaller, to exactly the same extent, for the same reason. This might be expressed by saying that, while the wall is *seen* foreshortened both towards the right and towards the left, the projection is also seen foreshortened in exactly the same manner—the word 'foreshortened' here referring to the visual angles of natural perspective, not to the shape of the projection. The projection of the object on the plane is itself an object, our vision of which obeys the laws of natural perspective. Whereas Jopling's remark to some extent introduces the controversial notion of the subjective curvature of straight lines (an appearance which some claim to be aware of, whereas others deny it) the present problem can be solved purely as the objective basis of natural perspective and visual angles.

The perspective of the wall is not a replica of appearances or subjective impressions. It is not a replica of the retinal image. Neither is it a direct recording of the relevant visual angles.

The picture in perspective is a substitute for the actual objects, so constructed that, when the eye is at the centre of projection, the corresponding visual angles are always the same for the objects and all their component parts, on the one hand, and for the corresponding projection of these objects and all their parts, on the other. Under such conditions, the eye being at the centre of projection, both the top and the base lines of the wall, and their projections as two straight parallel lines on a transparent Leonardo window, form on the retina images which are in coincidence with each other, superimposed point by point. The exact shape of the retinal images is irrelevant, as well as the fact that when the eye rotates in its orbit from one position to the other, the retinal images of the objects and of their projection shift onto different parts of the retina: thereby they alter their shapes to some extent, but both in the same way so that they remain in coincidence with each other.

Parallel lines at an angle to the projection plane

In Fig. 8.6a the horizontal lines in the façade of the Arch are parallel to the vertical plane of projection. This corresponds to the case which has just been discussed. In Fig. 8.6b, taken from exactly the same centre of projection, these lines make an angle of 25° with the projection plane. Here all the horizontal lines of the façade are projected as straight lines which converge towards a point on the left of the picture, which is called their vanishing point. This is the point where an ancillary line, parallel to the horizontals of the façade and passing through the centre of projection, pierces the plane of the photograph.

This follows from what has been said in the section on Natural Perspective in Chapter 5 with regard to sets of parallel lines considered together with the ancillary parallel passing through the centre of rotation of the eye. As one considers positions on the parallels which are further and further removed from the eye, the visual angles subtended by the distances between the parallels become smaller and smaller. This applies to the distances of any one of the parallels to the ancillary line. Now the perspective image of the whole of the ancillary line is the single point where it pierces the plane of projection. Since the visual angles subtended by the distances of the projections of all the other parallels to the ancillary line must, like the angles subtended by the distances between these parallel themselves, become smaller and smaller with increasing distance, these straight projected lines must necessarily converge towards the point image of the ancillary line. Except when parallels are parallel to the projection plane, any given set of parallel straight lines will have its own vanishing point defined by the direction of the parallels, which determines where their ancillary line intersects the plane of projection.[1]

In both Figs. 8.6a and b the part of the actual Arch nearest to the centre of projection was close to the right inside vertical edge of the passage through the Arch; it was at a distance from the right end of the Arch equal to about one-third of the width of the whole Arch. This is the position where the height of the actual Arch subtended the

---

[1] If we call *distance of the picture* the length of the perpendicular to the plane of projection from the centre of projection, and *principal point* the point where this perpendicular intersects the plane, then the distance of the vanishing point to the principal point is equal to the distance of the picture multiplied by the tangent of the angle of the parallels with the perpendicular to the plane of projection. In Fig. 8.6b this angle is $90 - 25 = 65°$ and its tangent is equal to 2.14.

largest visual angle from the centre of projection. (This is so, of course, regardless of which projection surface may be chosen.) Now the preceding reasoning relating to Fig. 8.6b is clear as far as the parts of the horizontal lines situated on the left of the nearest position are concerned. There the angles subtended by the height of the building do decrease towards the left. From this nearest position towards the right, these visual angles must also begin to decrease, however. Yet the straight projections of the top and bottom lines of the Arch still diverge; they do not converge. The explanation is that the distance from the eye to the projection plane increases, but in such a fashion that the angles subtended by the projected height of the building do in fact *decrease* towards the right, even though the projected height does increase in size.

In such a case as that of Fig. 8.6a it has been seen that the angles subtended by the horizontal projections of the distance between the top and the base line do decrease both towards the right and towards the left, being largest at the position nearest to the eye. In Fig. 8.6b the angles vary in exactly the same manner, as indeed must be the case since, with the eye at the right position, that is at the centre of projection, both photographs when held in the right position would be seen exactly to cover each other and to cover the actual Arch.

The reason why there is no vanishing point on the right in Fig. 8.6b is that the surface of projection is a plane, so that the ancillary line intersects the picture in one point only. If a spherical surface of projection were used instead of a plane, however, with the centre of the sphere as centre of projection, then there would be for each set of parallels two vanishing points, at the two ends of the diameter of the sphere parallel to the set. The set of parallel straight lines would then be projected as great circles, and would meet at both vanishing points, in the same way as all meridians on a terrestial globe meet at the North and at the South pole. In such a case, and in this case only, visual angles would be proportional to the corresponding segments of great circles they subtend on the surface of the sphere.

Importance of the orientation of the projection plane. For a plane surface of projection there is one vanishing point for all the parallels of a given set, when they are not parallel to the projection plane. The position of the vanishing point of a given set, for a fixed centre of projection, varies with the orientation of the projection plane. A third photograph of the Arch made from the same centre of projection on a vertical plane with the camera pointing towards the right, instead of the left as Fig. 8.6b, would show the same horizontal lines now converging towards the right instead of the left. A third, different projection of the same view from the same centre would thus be obtained. In the special case where the parallels are parallel to the projection plane, as in Fig. 8.6a, their projections are parallel in the picture.

These instances show that, all other things being equal, the pattern formed by the projections of sets of parallel lines is strongly dependent on the choice of the plane of projection. Strictly speaking perspectives such as Figs. 8.6a and b are not different aspects of the same view. They are the same view projected on different surfaces, the view and all its projections producing retinal images in coincidence for any given position of the eye in its (fixed) orbit. If we are aware of different aspects when we look at an object such as the Arch without changing our standpoint, this is so probably because we remember pictures in perspective of similar objects, and imagine how the Arch could be depicted on different planes.

Orthogonals to the plane of projection

Principal point. In the case of a set of straight lines which all are perpendicular to the plane of projection, the vanishing point is called the *principal point* of the perspective. It is of course the projection of the ancillary line perpendicular to the plane and passing through the eye, that is the centre of projection. The distance from the projection centre to the principal point is called the *distance* of the picture or of the projection plane; it is the shortest line joining the 'point in the eye' to the plane.

It should be stressed that the principal point is not a characteristic point relating to the eye or the vision of the spectator. In all this the eye is always free to move around its centre of rotation. For a given position of the centre of rotation of the eye, any number of projection planes can be chosen, and each will have its own principal point. In Fig. 8.6a the principal point is the vanishing point of the orthogonals to the façade which are seen within the passage through the Arch. In Fig. 8.6b these lines are no longer orthogonals to the plane of projection; their vanishing point is now to the right of the principal point relating to the new surface of projection.[1]

Horizon. All the ancillary lines relating to sets of horizontal parallels are horizontal. As they all pass through the centre of projection, they define a horizontal plane which cuts the vertical plane of projection as a horizontal line, which is called the *horizon*. The horizon, so defined, therefore contains the vanishing points of all horizontal lines, including the principal point.

Frontal projections. Many paintings containing architectural elements have been made on a plane of projection parallel to the façade of the building represented, as in

---

[1] In the case of a spherical surface of projection, when the centre of the sphere is the centre of projection, there is no such 'principal' point. Because of the symmetry of the sphere, all straight lines passing through the centre intersect the surface of the sphere under normal incidence; and it is obvious that here there is only one possible 'orientation' of the surface of projection relative to the objects to be projected.

Fig. 8.6a. This is so in Piero della Francesca's Flagellation (Figs. 7.2 and 7.3). The orthogonals to the façade are then also orthogonals to the plane of projection, so that their vanishing point is the principal point of the perspective. In such cases the projection of the plane of the façade is geometrically similar to the façade itself. Objectively horizontal and vertical lines belonging to the façade are depicted as horizontal and vertical lines. A circle in the plane of the façade is projected as a circle.

Bearing in mind the example of Figs. 8.6a and b, it is important to realize that this is essentially due to the particular choice which has been made of the plane of projection. For the same projection centre, that is from the same position of the rotation centre of the eye, a vertical plane at an angle to the façade would change the pattern of lines considerably. The classical pattern of parallel horizontal lines in Fig. 7.2 would be entirely altered. Although the new picture would be another representation of the same view of the same scene, it would be a different painting. It could be made to appear the same as the original painting only by using the special arrangements of the experiment of Chapter 8, which do not correspond to the usual way of viewing paintings.

Parallel lines at 45° to the projection plane

Distance points. All sets of parallel lines at an angle of 45° to the plane of projection have a vanishing point whose distance from the principal point is equal to the distance of the latter point to the centre of projection. Consider those horizontal parallel lines at 45°

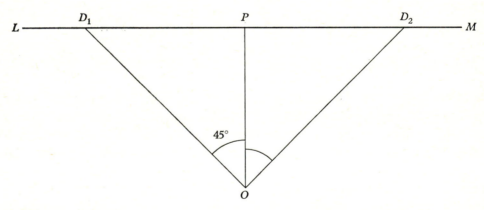

10.1 Distance points

The plane of the paper is a horizontal plane containing the centre of projection O and intersecting the vertical plane of projection along the horizon LM. The line OP is perpendicular to the projection plane; its length is the distance of the centre to the plane. The two lines OD_1 and OD_2 form an angle of 45° with OP; consequently D_1P and PD_2 are equal to OP. The points D_1 and D_2 are the distance points, that is, the vanishing points of the horizontal parallels at 45° to the projection plane. See Fig. 10.2.

to the projection plane, which are inclined to the left. Their vanishing point will be at D_1 in Fig. 10.1, where O is the centre of projection, LM the trace of the plane of projection, and P the principal point. The angle POD_1 is equal to 45°, the line OD_1 being the ancillary parallel of this set. Similarly horizontal parallels inclined to the right will have their vanishing point at D_2, the angle POD_2 being equal to 45°. The points D_1 and D_2 are called *distance points*. The principal point being at P, the angles OPD_1 and OPD_2 are right angles. Since the angles POD_1 and POD_2 are both equal to 45°, the angles OD_1P and OD_2P are also equal to 45°, so that the two triangles OPD_1 and OPD_2 are isosceles. Therefore PD_1 and PD_2 are both equal to OP, the distance of the projection centre to the plane of projection; and the distance OP is of course equal to half the distance between D_1 and D_2.

Reconstruction of a scene depicted in perspective

Accordingly, in a picture in perspective containing a horizontal square which has one side parallel to the picture plane, the distance of the picture from the projection centre can in principle be determined by producing the diagonals of this square until they meet the horizon of the picture. These diagonals, being at 45° to the picture plane, have perspectives which intersect the horizon of the picture at the distance points. This is of great help in reconstructing the plan and elevation of the architecture depicted in a painting, as was done by Carter in Fig. 7.3 for the 'Flagellation' by Piero della Francesca. The principal point is the vanishing point of the orthogonals to the picture plane. Together the position of this point, and the distance, define the position of the projection centre chosen by the artist, that is, the position of his eye relative to the picture plane. In practice the problem is not always an easy one to solve, however, because it is usually difficult to produce the relevant lines with sufficient accuracy—even in the case of a photograph. It is advisable to use as many lines, or sets of lines, as possible to be able to check the results against one another.

All this may become clearer by referring to the photograph of Fig. 10.2, where the plane of projection was parallel to the balustrade represented. The distance points D_1 and D_2 have been obtained by producing the diagonals of the square bases of the balusters. The diagonals inclined towards the left all meet at D_1; those inclined towards the right all meet at D_2. The principal point P was obtained by producing these sides of the square bases and tops of the balusters which are perpendicular to the picture plane. The three points D_1, P and D_2 are on the horizon of the picture, that is on the trace of the horizontal plane passing through the centre of projection. Thus, the centre O, that is the pinhole of the camera, was on the line perpendicular to the picture at P, at a distance equal to PD_1 or PD_2.

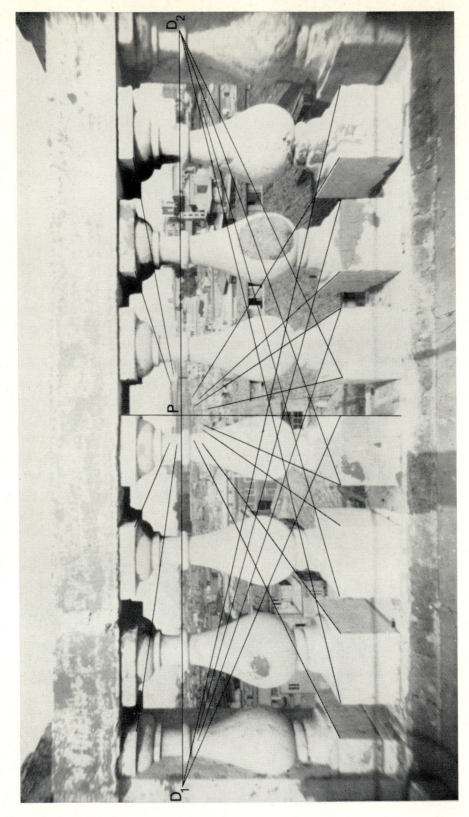

10.2 Principal point and distance points

Pinhole photograph of a balustrade on the roof of the church of St Ignazio in Rome. The photographic plate was parallel to the vertical plane of the balustrade. The principal point P is the vanishing point of the orthogonals to the plane of projection. The distance points D_1 and D_2 are the vanishing points of horizontals at $45°$ to the same plane. The horizontal line D_1PD_2 is the horizon of the perspective. The distance of the pinhole (that is, of the centre of projection O of Fig. 10.1) to the photographic plate was equal to D_1P or to PD_2.

The angle D_1OD_2 was therefore equal to 90°. The large size of the angle subtended by this photograph accounts for the marginal 'distortions' which appear in it. It will be noted that Piero della Francesca's painting, Fig. 7.2, on the other hand, subtends an angle considerably smaller than 90°.

Subjective curvatures

Many observers find that when they direct their gaze to the side of a long straight line, for instance a searchlight beam in the night sky, the line appears curved to them, presenting its concavity towards the point to which their gaze is directed. The straight line looks straight when looked at directly, however. Thus the apparent curvature changes, or disappears altogether, according to the direction of the gaze. A straight horizontal line, as the gaze is moved progressively upwards, will in turn look concave downwards, straight, and then concave upwards. These subjective curvatures are apparent only in indirect, peripheral vision. This probably explains why some observers report that they cannot see them. Normally, of course, we look directly at any object which attracts our interest, in which case a straight line looks straight, so that in everyday life such subjective phenomena are rarely noticed.

When an enlargement of the pattern of Fig. 10.3 is viewed with one eye placed at the distance indicated by the length of the line A, the observer keeping his gaze fixed upon the centre of the pattern, the figure appears to many observers as an ordinary checkerboard made up of black and white squares equal in size and arranged in straight lines. The curvatures of the lines used in the construction of this pattern have been chosen so as to compensate for the subjective curvatures of straight lines which would be seen at the corresponding degrees of peripheral vision.

From the standpoint of linear perspective, it must first be pointed out that if the line of a searchlight beam, for instance, is covered by a taut thread, both beam and thread undergo the same changes of apparent curvature according to the direction of the observer's gaze. Consequently, to argue that an objectively straight line should be depicted in a perspective drawing as curved appears to be instance of the El Greco fallacy. Whatever the straight line looks like subjectively, there is *prima facie* evidence that a straight line depicting it in the drawing will have the same subjective appearance (whatever this might be) when the viewing conditions are the same. The subjective deformations of the one must be expected to be the same as the deformations of the other. This, however, assumes that we can examine both lines at leisure.

Now the case of the path of a shooting star or a meteor is an exception to this, for there is not time to move the eye to examine such a transient phenomenon. Hence it may well be justified to draw the straight path of a shooting star as a curve, if it appears curved

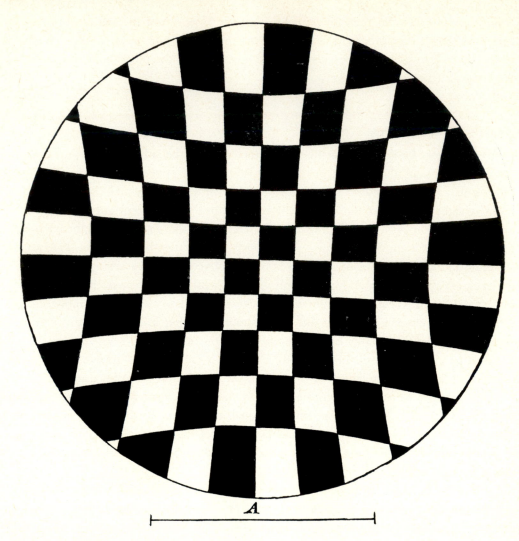

10.3 Demonstration of subjective curvatures

Looking at the centre of an enlargement of this picture, with one eye only, placed in front of the centre of the picture at a distance corresponding to the length of the line *A*, the observer sees it as an ordinary checkerboard made up of black and white squares. It is essential to fix one's gaze steadily on the centre of the pattern. (From Helmholtz (1896), *Handbuch der Physiologischen Optik*.)

when actually seen by peripheral vision. Apart from such exceptional cases, in which the viewing conditions are significantly different for the thing represented and for its representation, it is hard to see any reason why, in *uniocular* vision, objectively straight lines should be depicted as curved on a plane surface. (The case of the projection of parallel lines such as those forming the top and the base of a long straight wall has been discussed above.)

But the special subjective curvatures which are observed in binocular vision must be examined before turning to a discussion of the systems of 'curvilinear perspective' which have lately been put forward.

Luneburg's theory of binocular vision. Luneburg (1947) and his followers (Blank, 1959) have put forward a mathematical theory of binocular visual space perception according to which 'visual space' would be a non-Euclidean (hyperbolic) space. Luneburg's 'visual space' is a mathematical concept introduced to account for the observer's *subjective* estimation of distances, either between observer and object, or between object and object. These 'subjective distances' usually differ from the actual distances measured

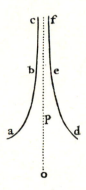

10.4   Straight parallel alleys may look curved

Robert Smith comments as follows: 'He' (i.e. 'my highly esteemed friend *Martin Folkes* Esquire') 'also informed me, that the parallel sides of a very long and broad walk, avenue, road, or the like, do not appear to converge like two straight lines tending to a very distant point; but rather like the legs of two hyperbola's *abc, def* converging towards each side of an assymptote *op* drawn from the eye at *O* parallel to the sides of the walk, as represented in the figure'. (From R. Smith (1738) *A Compleat System of Opticks*.)

in physical space. This leads to particular illusions. The theory refers to binocular, stereoscopic vision, studied under special conditions, chosen precisely to eliminate clues which are not specific to binocular vision (Blank, 1959). The main experimental evidence is given by the 'alley experiments', to which Blumenfeld drew attention in 1913. In such experiments, the observer is as a rule asked to adjust in a dark room the positions of pairs of small light-sources so as to form an alley, either with sides which appear parallel to him, or in which the lamps of all the pairs appear to have equal separations. The main experimental difference is, however, that for the 'parallel alley' the intermediate lights are left on, whereas for the 'distance alley' they are put out. Objectively the alleys so obtained are found to have sides which are curved, and furthermore the two tasks lead to different alleys, the 'parallel alley' lying inside the 'distance alley'. It seems that most experiments so far have been made with all the lamps situated in the horizontal plane passing through the two eyes of the observer (Ogle, 1962). It is a rather old observation, on the other hand, that the parallel sides of a straight road, for instance, may appear curved to some observers (Fig. 10.4).

As far as the theory of linear perspective is concerned Luneburg's mathematical theory (which refers to subjective observation, not to the physical space of optics) is less fundamental than the illusions it seeks to explain. It may be noted that psychologists such as Graham (1951) and Ogle (1962) feel that the theory may lack sufficient experimental foundation. The illusions it seeks to explain relate specifically to binocular vision. Now, while binocular vision enters into the perception of pictures with regard to the spectator's awareness of the picture surface, the illusion or suggestion of depth produced by a picture depends on the use of clues and elements which are *not* those of binocular vision. Under ordinary conditions of binocular vision the illusions occurring under special dark-room conditions often fail to take place, no doubt because many other perceptual factors then come into play beside those of 'pure' binocular vision. Even in the dark-room experiments made on the perception of parallel lines by ten Doesschate and Kylstra (1956), in which the 'lines' were luminous straight tubes, no subjective curvature of the lines was observed.

The main fact is that in ordinary vision, for most observers, there are no obvious subjective curvatures which are present only when both eyes are used, and which disappear when one shuts one of the eyes. (The curvatures discussed at the beginning of this section are seen with one as well as with two eyes.) None the less, it is advisable to keep an open mind with regard to subtle differences between binocular and uniocular vision, which may explain certain special features in the works of some representational painters.

Systems of 'curvilinear perspective'. Various systems of perspective have been proposed, by Hauck (1875) and Panofsky (1927) among a number of others, according to which the representation on a plane of objectively straight lines should, for most of the lines, be curved. Now according to the argument developed in the present book the *Optics* of Euclid does not lead to such a conclusion. The theory of central perspective which has been discussed rests upon the principles contained in Euclid's *Optics* and *Elements*—which, contrary to what Panofsky argued, are definitely *not* in disagreement with the perspective theory of the Renaissance. (The 'curvature of space' of the theory of relativity, which is sometimes appealed to, is of course quite irrelevant.)

It would appear that it is the fact that the retina, and perforce the retinal image, are curved, which has led some authors to the idea that a truly 'physiological' perspective should consist of some kind of pseudo-development upon the picture plane of an image curved in shape like the retinal image, which allegedly would lead to systems of 'curvilinear perspective'. But, first, the retinal image is not what we see: what we see is the external world. Secondly, the geometrical construction of such a pseudo-development remains obscure—unless it leads back to central, 'rectilinear', perspective. It would be pointless to reiterate the argument that central perspective, in which straight lines are never projected as curves on a plane, is the only method which is capable of producing a retinal image having the same shape as the retinal image of the actual objects depicted.

The fact remains that a certain number of paintings, discussed for instance by White (1957), contain curved lines which apparently are meant to represent straight lines in the objects depicted. First it may be pointed out that in the world around us relatively few objects have outlines which are exactly straight. And exactly straight lines are often found unpleasing. Artists therefore may have copied, sometimes with some exaggeration of the curvatures, lines which were not exactly straight; or they may even have introduced non-existent curvatures for aesthetic purposes. Secondly the composition of some of the paintings may have been influenced by the appearance of the reflection given by a convex mirror, where most straight lines look curved (see Schwarz, 1959). This mode of depiction has the advantages of squeezing into a small compass the peripheral parts of the scene represented (rather like 'fish-eye' photograph cameras which cover a very wide angle) but at the cost of not giving an exact central projection.[1]

The possibility can by no means be ruled out, however, that some of these curvatures may have their origin in the fact that the artist may have noticed subjective curvatures due to the use of binocular vision, and introduced them in his work. Painting and drawing although essentially uniocular modes of representation, may thus have been made to reproduce effects belonging specifically to binocular vision. This, however, is a possibility which seems to have been little studied.[2]

Curvatures in Doric temples. Many of the ancient Greek temples in the Doric style, for instance the Parthenon at Athens and the so-called Temple of Neptune at Paestum (both of the fifth century B.C.) show subtleties of curvature and inclination, commonly called 'refinements', which greatly contribute to the impressive harmony of these masterpieces of architecture. The stylobate, that is, the main floor of the temples, is slightly curved, forming a convex surface. The columns also have a convex profile

---

[1] 'Curvilinear' systems of perspective have been discussed and criticized for instance by Gioseffi (1957, 1957–8, 1966a), ten Doesschate (1964) and Zanetti (1951).

A book by Barre and Flocon (1968) again advocates the use of 'curvilinear perspective', and is illustrated by many drawings based on the authors' method. This rests on a peculiar way of using an axiom put forward by Bouligand, Flocon and Barre (1964) according to which 'The same magnitude appears the smaller as it is more distant from the observer'. Now this axiom is in full agreement with Euclid, *if* magnitude is taken to mean visual angle. But, for the present writer, the way the authors apply it for instance to the depiction of a long wall seems impossible to understand. For, according to the authors, if the plane of the projection were in coincidence with the plane of the wall, the wall should be depicted, 'full size', as two curved lines converging at either end. So the picture of the wall, full size, would utterly differ from the wall itself.

[2] As Mr B. A. R. Carter pointed out to me, if the artist 'measures' with a pencil or ruler held at arm's length, and if he simply transfers these measurements onto his canvas, he will obtain curved representations of straight lines. In some cases such representations may thus be due merely to the use of this procedure.

(entasis), strongly marked at Paestum, rather less so in the Parthenon. Some of these curvatures probably played a practical role: the convexity of the stylobate is useful for drainage. Yet these refinements must also have had 'beauty' as their object (Dinsmoor, 1950; Robertson, 1964). In the Parthenon the columns at the corners are thicker than the others: it seems clear that the purpose of this was to avoid their looking too thin against the bright sky, since a bright background seems to 'eat' into the outline of dark objects in front of it. Apart from this, it is hard to give any convincing explanation of the refinements, at any rate of the curvatures, on the basis of optical facts or theories—even though the Greek are said to have had such theories. It is sometimes argued that these objective curvatures were used to compensate for effects of subjective curvature. But there is no reason to believe that the architects did wish to make the relevant lines look quite straight in any case. Consideration of these curvatures of the Doric style mainly suggests the rather obvious conclusion that slightly curved outlines, when suitably chosen, can help to produce a most extraordinary artistic impression. Choisy (1904) and Gioseffi (1966b) have examined in more detail possible optical explanations of the Doric refinements.[1]

These curvatures have been mentioned here largely because they often are discussed in connection with the theory of linear perspective. The link between the two subjects seems tenuous, however, since perspective deals with the problem of the accurate representation of given objects, whereas architecture is not a representational art.

[1] On a further visit to Paestum it was pointed out to me by my wife—as Mr A. S. Evett had done on a former occasion—that when standing in front of the narrow end of the temple of Neptune, at a distance such that the building subtended some 90° at the eye, then both the stylobate and the 'steps' looked rather strongly curved, this apparent convexity being *upwards*: that is, in the same direction as their slight objective convexity. This objective curvature therefore cannot have been intended to compensate for subjective curvatures: it only reinforces them. Furthermore Mr S. A. Medd pointed out that objectively straight steps, as those of S. Maria Maggiore in Rome, also look markedly convex upwards. No simple optical principle seems able to account for these subjective effects—which, it may perhaps be stressed, were noticed by several persons independently of one another.

11 *How pictures look when*
viewed from the wrong position

Influence of preconceived ideas

Theoretical ambiguity of perspective. Any given picture in perspective seen with one eye placed at its centre of projection corresponds to an infinite number of possibilities, for the central projection of an object on a surface is also the projection of any number of other possible objects—which, for the projection centre considered, would all give the same projection on the same surface. Thus the well-known rooms built by Ames have shapes which are central projections of ordinary rooms, but are in fact completely distorted in comparison with the rooms we are used to in daily life. Ames's rooms look like ordinary rooms. Human figures in them, however, appear much too small or much too large, according to the position they occupy, because the figures appear in a general perceptual framework which has been accepted as a room of familiar shape (Ittelson, 1952).

The manner in which the scene depicted in a picture is seen also depends very strongly on the spectator's preconceived ideas, these ideas becoming reinforced into a whole framework of consistent relationships in the case of a whole scene consisting of objects with which the spectator is familiar—especially when light, shade and colour have been skilfully used by the artist.

In theory, a picture in perspective might be expected to be thoroughly ambiguous, even when viewed from the right position. In practice, most pictures representing scenes made up of elements of a kind with which the spectator is familiar are far from being ambiguous. In the case of Pozzo's nave ceiling, all spectators, when at the right position, see the painted architecture as a continuation of the real architecture of the church, and when they are at the wrong position they see it undergo the same strange deformations. This absence of ambiguity must be explained by the spectator's preconceptions concerning the objects and figures depicted.

[151]

Perspective illusions in architecture. Perspective illusions in architecture also rely on the spectator's preconceived ideas concerning the building he sees. Thus the arcade of Fig. 11.1a looks, in reality as in the photograph, like a long arcade of constant width and height. Yet it was built by Borromini (1599–1667) on the plan of Fig. 11.1c. The actual arcade is the solid perspective, in three dimensions, of an imaginary arcade of normal shape. It is built so that each of its parts, each of its columns, for instance, would cover accurately the relevant part of the imaginary arcade of constant width and height, for a spectator placed at the right position at the entrance of the arcade. From this position, the arcade looks much longer than it is, the decrease in its actual height and width with increasing distance from the spectator is not noticed, and the statue at the end of it looks much larger than its real size (Fig. 11.1d). A man standing at the end of the arcade looks like a giant, an effect similar to that produced in Ames's rooms. Conversely, viewed from the end opposite to the entrance in the other direction, the arcade appears much shorter than it does from its entrance (Fig. 11.1b).

A more subtle effect has been realized by Michelangelo (1475–1564) in his design of the Piazza of the Capitol at Rome. As shown in the plan of Fig. 11.2c the façades of the two palaces on either side of the Piazza are not parallel. The space separating them is larger at the back of the Piazza, near the Palazzo dei Senatori, than near its entrance, at the top of the ramp which leads up to the Piazza. The result is that, when the spectator stands near the Palazzo dei Senatori, the Piazza gives the impression of being deeper than it is (Fig. 11.2b) because he tends to take it for granted that the buildings are arranged on a rectangular plan (Fig. 11.2e). The actual convergence of the actual façades is mistaken for the increased perspective convergence which would be given by longer parallel façades. The design of the pavement of the Piazza contains no straight lines, which might counteract this effect, but consists of intercrossing curved lines which rather help the illusion.

To the spectator entering the Piazza from the top of the ramp, on the other hand, the Piazza appears less deep than it is (Figs. 11.2a and 11.2d) and looks rather square in shape. It seems possible that this indeed was the main effect that Michelangelo intended to achieve on this historical site, where limitations of space curtailed his freedom.

Nevile's Court in Trinity College, Cambridge, is built on a plan similar to that of the Capitol Piazza. It was completed by Sir Christopher Wren (1632–1723), who built the College Library which closes the far end of the Court. From the opposite side, which gives an imposing view of Wren's Library, most spectators agree that the Court looks square. The spectator's position is then similar to position S_1 in Fig. 11.2d. Now Wren was of course influenced by Italian architecture: it seems possible that he was inspired by the arrangement of the famous Capitol Piazza at Rome and chose the position of his Library, relative to the existing three sides of the Court, so as to achieve the same effect as Michelangelo.

11.1 b

11.1 a

11.1 a,b   The perspective arcade by Borromini in the Palazzo Spada, Rome
Pinhole photographs taken (a) from the entrance and (b) from the other end of the arcade. See the plan in Fig. 11.1 c and the diagram of
Fig. 11.1 d showing why the arcade seen from its entrance looks longer than it actually is.

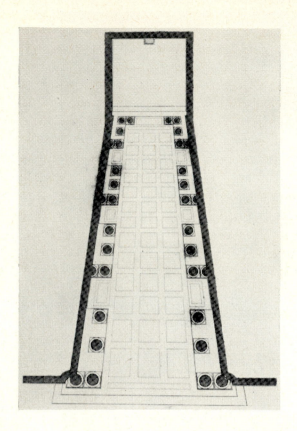

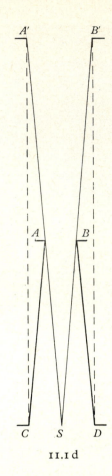

11.1 c

11.1 d

11.1 c Plan of the Borromini arcade in the Palazzo Spada
(From Letarouilly (1840–57), *Edifices de Rome Moderne*.)

11.1 d Diagram of the perspective effect produced by the arcade in the Palazzo Spada

On the implicit assumption that the sides AC and BD are parallel, as they would be in an ordinary arcade, the spectator S at the entrance thinks he sees a longer arcade the sides of which are $A'C$ and $B'D$.

Theoretical deformation of pictures viewed from the wrong position

Returning to the case of flat pictures in perspective, drawing 98 of Fig. 11.3 is the perspective of an arcade, made from the centre of projection marked by the point O in drawing 97 which gives the plan of the arcade. Exactly the same central projection (drawing 98) would be obtained for the arcades the plans of which are given in drawings 95 and 96, using the respective projection centres marked O on these plans. The projection of the picture on the ground plane is the line ab in each of the three plans. The

11.2 a

11.2 b

11.2 a, b   The Piazza of the Capitol in Rome

Pinhole photographs of the Piazza taken (*a*) from the top of the ramp leading to it, and (*b*) from a position near the Palazzo dei Senatori, which is visible in the background of (*a*). The plan of the Piazza is given in Fig. 11.2 c. The diagrams of Fig. 11.2 d and e show why the Piazza looks deeper from the second than from the first position.

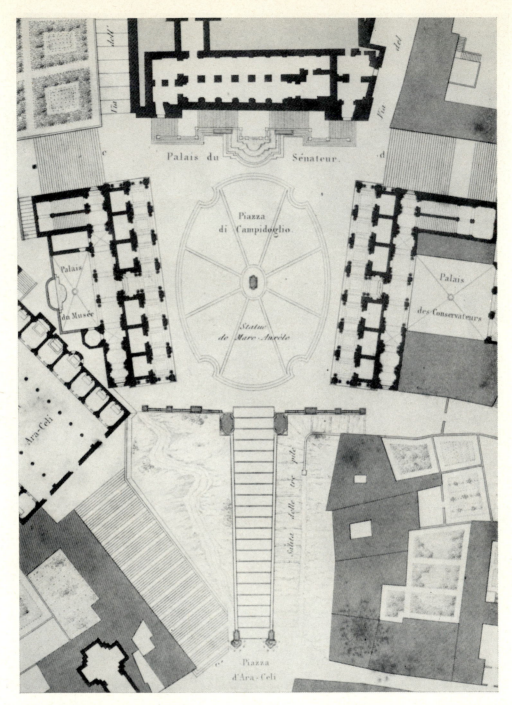

11.2c   General plan of the Capitol

The plan of the Piazza del Campidoglio shows the disposition of the palaces which form three of its sides. (From Letarouilly (1840–57), *Edifices de Rome Moderne*.)

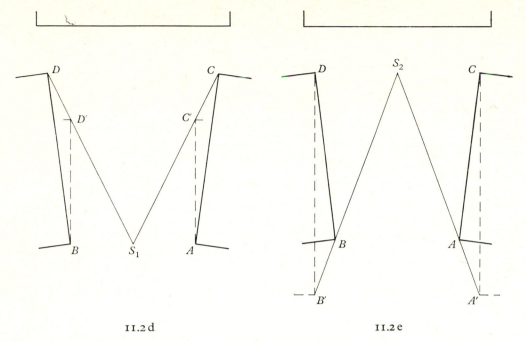

11.2 d   11.2 e

11.2 d, e   Diagrams of the perspective effects of the Piazza of the Capitol

In 11.2 d the spectator S_1 at the top of the ramp sees the façades AC and BD as AC' and BD'.
In 11.2 e the spectator S_2 near the Palazzo dei Senatori sees these façades as $A'C$ and $B'D$ and the
Piazza appears deeper than it is, whereas in 11.2 d, from S_1 it appears shorter.

centre of projection always remains at the height above the floor, indicated by the line of
the horizon passing through the point P in drawing 98. Accordingly, if the perspective
of drawing 98 is viewed with the eye placed relative to it not at the point O of drawing
97, but at the point O of drawings 95 or 96, the perspective now should appear to
represent one of the oblique arcades of drawings 95 or 96. Thus when the eye moves to
the left of the right position, the arcade should appear oblique towards the right. When the
eye moves at the same time to a position more distant from the drawing, the arcade
should also appear to become more elongated, as in drawing 95.

  For most observers deformations of this kind are neither obvious nor striking. Many
people only notice such deformations when their attention has been drawn to them, and
then only after some practice, even if they use one eye only. The apparent deepening of
the view when the eye moves farther from the picture, and its apparent flattening when it
moves nearer, are the deformations least difficult to detect. No doubt, besides the spectator's subsidiary awareness of the picture surface, the spectator's preconceived idea
that the perspective cannot be meant to represent arcades with such unusual shapes as

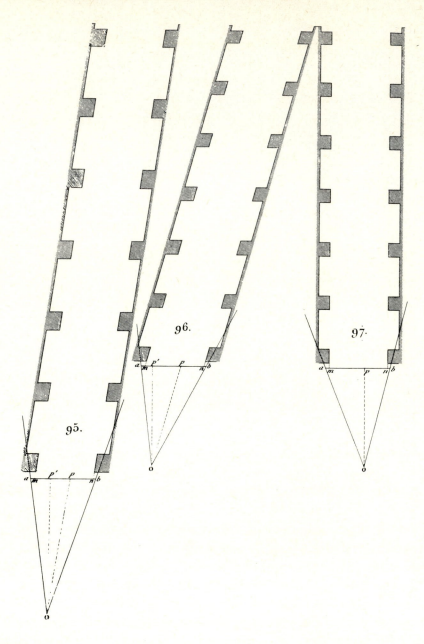

98.

11.3   Theoretical effect of displacements of the eye on the appearance of a perspective

Drawing 98 refers to the arcade the plan of which is given in 97, for the eye position marked *O* in 97. It is also the perspective of the arcades the plans of which are given in 95 and 96, when the eye's position is moved to the corresponding positions marked *O* in 95 and 96. Theoretically, therefore, the drawing should appear to represent arcades 95 or 96 when the eye is displaced from the position *O* in 97 to the relevant positions for 95 or 96. In practice, for most observers, such alterations are rather difficult to notice. (From La Gournerie (1859), *Traité de Perspective Linéaire*.)

those of drawings 95 and 96 hinders their seeing the oblique deformations. (How inconspicuous these deformations are is shown by comparison with the deformations shown by anaglyphs (pages 163–4) in which the scene is really seen in 3 D and the surface of the pictures is 'invisible'.)

Stable elements in pictures. Taking it for granted that the scene represented is of a kind with which the spectator is familiar, the theory of perspective predicts that some elements of the picture must remain unchanged when the spectator moves away from the right position. Thus a straight line foreshortened to one point in the picture seems directed towards the eye of the spectator, wherever he may stand. Each and every spectator sees it directed towards himself. This is so, first, because only lines of sight, passing through the spectator's eye, are represented in this way, and, secondly, because this representation does of course remain unchanged in the picture when the spectator changes his position. Accordingly, a rifle depicted so that its muzzle hides entirely the barrel will appear to threaten the head of every spectator. If part of the barrel is depicted above the muzzle, in strong foreshortening, every spectator will see the rifle pointing towards his body.

The sighting eye of the rifleman will also appear to look at the spectator, wherever he may be. The apparent direction in which the rifleman seems to be looking depends upon the depiction of the various parts of his eye. In spite of the effects of natural perspective, the drawing of the eye hardly changes its aspect when one moves relatively to it, whereas the aspect of an actual eye would definitely be altered. Thus if, from one position, the eye of a real person looking steadily in one direction shows, say, the pupil in between two equal triangular areas of the white of the eye, then from another position the two areas of white may become unequal, and one of them may even become invisible. As no such change occurs in the eye depicted on a surface, a portrait either 'looks' at all the spectators, or 'looks' at none of them.

What has just been said applies to perspectives on curved as well as on plane surfaces, and to vision with two as well as one eye. Again it is valid for ordinary pictures and for special cases such as Pozzo's painted ceiling.

In the case of a picture in central projection on a plane, all objectively straight lines always remain straight lines whatever the spectator's position—except of course for the lines of sight, projected as single points. If the plane of projection is vertical, vertical lines are verticals in the picture. Consequently a building will appear to stand upright even when its picture is viewed from the wrong position.

Relatively stable elements under special conditions. If now the eye of the spectator remains in the plane of the horizon of the plane picture, that is in the horizontal plane passing through the centre of projection and the principal point of the perspective, then from a position away from the projection centre, the depiction of lines which are objectively horizontal and parallel will still give the impression of horizontal and parallel lines—because their vanishing point is on the horizon. It can also be shown that the ratios of the parts into which a horizontal line is divided appear to remain unchanged under those conditions. Thus if the pediment of a building depicted in perspective is an isosceles triangle, it will continue to appear as a triangle having two equal sides; similarly a gothic arch will still appear symmetrical relative to its vertical axis. Again the disposition of the windows in a façade in perspective remains unchanged when the eye is at the wrong position, provided always it remains within the plane of the horizon of the picture (La Gournerie (1859) p. 223). If, say, a painting is hung at the right height in a gallery, this condition will be fulfilled, at least approximately. (If a painting has to be placed too high on the wall, it can be inclined forward, so that the eye of the spectator still can come within the plane of its horizon.)

When the eye moves out of the plane of the horizon, the deformation of the picture should become much more important, but La Gournerie points out that even then the deformation will occur in a regular manner if the picture is accurately drawn in perspective. On a flat surface the composition thus retains a considerable degree of harmony.[1]

It must also be noted that the arrangement of cast shadows depicted in perspective is not upset when the eye views the picture from a wrong position.

Ordinary pictures viewed with both eyes

The preceding paragraphs summarize some of the conclusions reached by La Gournerie (1859) who made a special study of the deformations which theoretically should occur in the appearance of a perspective on a plane when it is viewed with one eye from a position other than the projection centre. (The general discussion of the problem is related to the theory of mathematical homology.)

It is interesting to note that on this basis, in the case of objects bounded by straight lines, there are important elements in pictures in perspective which remain stable, even though La Gournerie's discussion does not take into account the spectator's subsidiary awareness of the picture surface in the perception of ordinary pictures. It is the case of objects having curved surfaces of known shape, discussed in Chapter 9, which shows most

---

[1] On the other hand, La Gournerie (1859) wrote that he was able to detect how accurately a picture was drawn in perspective by the fact that the deformations which occur when the eye is in the wrong position become more conspicuous when the perspective is correct.

Conversely, therefore, it may perhaps be surmised that paintings such as Cézanne's, which are not drawn in exact central perspective, are able better to retain their own peculiar harmony for all positions of the spectator, precisely because they are not drawn in exact perspective.

definitely the complex and considerable role played by this awareness, especially when, as is normally the case, binocular vision is being used. It is clear that this must apply to the picture as a whole, including both straight and curved lines and surfaces. In general, therefore, the fact that many find it difficult to see the deformations theoretically predicted for a spectator who is not at the correct position, must be explained by an intuitive process of psychological compensation which is based both on the spectator's awareness of the surface of the picture, and on his preconceived ideas regarding the components of the scene presented.

It is the existence of these processes which must largely explain that pictures in perspective can be used as widely as they are as *representations* of complicated scenes or objects, even for purely practical purposes. On theoretical grounds alone, and on the basis of our present knowledge of vision, it might have been thought that the only pictures which could be of real use would be stereoscopic pictures, or at any rate pictures set up in a special way to be viewed through a peep-hole. It has of course always been taken for granted, on the basis of experience, that this is not so. Perspective views are found to be most useful for instance to engineers and architects. Again, pictorial advertisements seen from a moving staircase (as commonly displayed, for instance, in the London Underground) do not, while one is carried by the side of them, show the strange deformations which might theoretically be expected to occur. As this work has attempted to show, however, the reason why this is so is not an obvious one.

Whereas in some very special cases, like Pozzo's ceiling, the illusory space of the picture is undistinguishable from the physical space of daily life (as is also the case of Borromini's architectural illusion) one is driven to the conclusion that this cannot be so for ordinary pictures. Such pictures produce an illusion of a very particular kind, to which we become accustomed as part of our education. This probably explains why it has often been reported that when a photograph is shown to people in whose civilization photographs and similar pictures in perspective are unknown, they fail to perceive what the photograph means to represent, at least until it has been explained to them.[1]

---

[1] This is largely based on anecdotes, most of which seem hard to trace. In a private communication, however, Dr A. W. Exell (formerly Deputy Keeper of the Botany Dept. of the British Museum (National History)) told me that he found that members of the Chokwe tribe in Lunda in North-East Angola 30 years ago (in 1936) failed to understand the meaning of photographic pictures. But, as Dr Exell points out, one cannot exclude the possibility that they might have regarded the photos as 'unlucky' and refused to become involved. Segall, Campbell and Herskovits (1966) discuss this matter, and give a first-hand report of a Bush Negro woman who, when shown a photograph of her own son, was able to perceive the subject only after the details of the photograph had been pointed out to her.

Yet some primitive people, at any rate, while very skilled in the use of their eyes, are subject to the same perspective illusions as 'civilized' people, even in the case of an object unfamiliar to them. Allport and Pettigrew (1957) made visual tests on Zulu children in Natal, South Africa, using the rotating trapezoidal window illusion described in 1951 by A. Ames, Jun. The illusion

A plane mirror—or, better, a system consisting of two such mirrors—does, on the other hand, give a complete illusion of ordinary physical space. The mirror, apart from a general alteration of the direction, sends to the spectator's eye the very same light which would be sent by the real objects seen reflected in it. This applies to both eyes, and remains true when the spectator alters his position. What we see in the mirror in fact is reality itself. The plane mirror, when its surface is invisible, is the only optical instrument which functions in this way. (On these grounds, some even deny that the word 'illusion' should be used to describe the effect produced by a mirror.) In any case, the illusion produced by the stereoscope, trompe-l'oeil pictures, and ordinary paintings belong to other categories, since their aim is the *re*-presentation of reality.

Deformation in anaglyphs. The stereoscopic devices known as anaglyphs readily show the deformations predicted by the theory of perspective. Two central projections of the same scene or object are made from centres separated by a distance equal to the distance between the pupils of the two eyes. These two projections are drawn or printed on top of each other, in the same way as if the projections of a scene viewed through a Leonardo window were drawn in superimposition on the window, for each eye in turn—without moving the head. A different colour is used for the two projections. They are viewed through glasses having different colours for the two eyes, chosen so that the right eye only sees the projection corresponding to it, and the left eye only the projection corresponding to it. The object represented is then seen in three dimensions.

Now whereas in the case of an ordinary stereoscope the position of the eyes is fixed, in the case of anaglyphs the spectator wearing the colour filters can move about relative to the double picture. It is then found that the object seen undergoes strong deformations, of the kind forecast for instance for the arcade of Fig. 11.3 when the eye moves away from the centre of projection. In the case of anaglyphs, the observer is hardly aware of the

is that instead of steadily rotating, as it actually does, the window is seen to sway back and forth in an arc of 90–180 degrees. The trapezoidal window is in fact the perspective projection of an ordinary rectangular window, and can be mistaken for such a window. Primitive Zulus, however, live in round huts devoid of windows and use hardly any rectangular objects; but they must be used to the sense of the vertical and the horizontal.

The authors report as their most striking finding that under conditions optimally chosen to produce the illusion (uniocularly at 20 ft) virtually as many primitive Zulus report the trapezoidal illusion as do urban Zulus or 'Europeans'.

The illusion really is one of uniocular perspective, so that under particular sub-optimal conditions, when binocular vision is used, the illusion may not occur. The window is then seen to rotate as it actually does because the true information mediated by stereoscopic vision supersedes the illusion caused by perspective. Under these conditions the authors found that experience with, and identification with, western culture make it more likely for the illusion to occur: the subjects then are familiar with windows. 'In this particular case, therefore', Allport and Pettigrew write, 'one may say that the primitive children see things "as they are" more often than do the children of civilization.'

surface of the picture, as a surface. Again, the sense of the third dimension given by the discrepancies between the two projections overcomes the possible effect of preconceived notions concerning the object represented. The deformations occur because, when the observer's eyes are in the wrong place, they are in fact presented with the two projections which would be given, for the positions of his eyes, by the deformed object which he sees. In the case of such stereoscopic devices, the theoretical ambiguity of a picture in perspective no longer exists, since there are now two projections of the same object made from two different centres. Observation of such deformations, shows, by contrast, how weak are the similar deformations in the case of ordinary pictures.

12 *Imitation in painting*

Imitation or representation evidently is not, in itself, the aim of representational art. It is only one of the artist's means of expression, like the composition of the subject of his painting, and of course the choice of the point of view and of the projection surface on which the painting is made. None the less, some painters are generally included among the most original artists, who precisely seem to have sought to imitate nature as closely as possible: the brothers Van Eyck, Leonardo da Vinci, Vermeer, Seurat.

Leonardo's writings on painting, for instance, show explicitly that he strove to represent what he saw. The question then arises: how can such an attitude be compatible with the creation of original work?

Nowadays this problem may appear to be an insoluble riddle, unless the question be brushed aside as utterly simple-minded. For the belief has become widespread that an exact, complete and objective representation of the visible world could be made by an artist, but that this 'mere imitation' would not be Art. Furthermore, it is believed that such a representation can be obtained 'scientifically' by the use of photography. Now, of course, if this were really so, the artist's task could only be a task of selection and transformation, which in effect would use as a basis and starting point a perfect objective representation, itself devoid of artistic interest.

But, in fact, such a perfect, objective, representation can be obtained neither in painting nor in photography. So, the striving of an artist after the (unattainable) ideal of 'copying nature' does not necessarily entail any loss of originality.

It may be noticed that, in connection with the art of acting, the fallacy concerning 'mere imitation' probably would not arise. It seems likely that most theatre-goers, even today, would disagree with Partridge's opinion of such an actor as Garrick. In his novel *Tom Jones*, Fielding (1707–54) tells us how Tom Jones took his friend Partridge to the theatre to see Garrick in the role of Hamlet. Tom Jones 'expected to enjoy much entertainment in the criticisms of Partridge, from whom he expected the simple dictates of nature, unimproved indeed, but likewise unadulterated by art'. '...At the end of the play, Jones asked him, "which of the players he liked best?" To this he answered, with some appearance of indignation at the question, "The king, without doubt". "Indeed,

Mr Partridge", says Mrs Miller, "you are not of the same opinion with the town; for they are all agreed that Hamlet is acted by the best player who ever was on the stage". "He the best player"! cries Partridge, with a contemptuous sneer, "why, I could act as well as he myself. I am sure, if I had seen a ghost, I should have looked in the very same manner, and done just as he did. And then, to be sure, in that scene, as you called it, between him and his mother, where you told me he acted so fine, why, lord help me, any man, that is, any good man, that had such a mother, would have done exactly the same. I know you are only joking with me; but indeed, madam, though I was never at a play in London, yet I have seen acting before in the country; and the king for my money: he speaks all his words distinctly, half as loud again as the other—Anybody may see he is an actor."'

Limitations of pictorial representation

Leaving aside such exceptional cases as Pozzo's ceiling, peep-shows, and ordinary trompe-l'oeil paintings (in which invariably the subject matter has very little extension in depth) ordinary pictures viewed binocularly in the usual manner do not give a genuine three-dimensional representation of their subject matter. This point has been discussed at length in previous chapters. In spite of the fact that it may give a very strong *suggestion* of depth, the representation given by ordinary pictures is of a *sui generis* nature, and depends on the spectator's subsidiary awareness of the characteristics of the picture surface. This at once shows that ordinary photographs do not, any more than paintings, give a perfect imitation of the scene they represent.

Furthermore, it is more difficult for the photographer than for the painter to compensate for some other limitations of his technique, precisely because of the partly automatic nature of photography.

The range of luminances in a photographic print or in a painting is often much more limited than the range actually existing in nature, as for instance in the case of an interior inside which the sunshine penetrates by small windows, through which the sky is also visible. Such scenes, which have been most successfully painted by Dutch artists of the seventeenth century, are notoriously difficult to photograph.

Again the general level of luminance may be much higher, for instance in a sunny landscape, or much lower, for instance in a moonlit scene, in reality than in the picture hanging in a gallery. Now visual acuity, colour, contrast, do vary with this level of luminance. The painter can compensate in part for such differences of luminance between his canvas and the actual scene he wishes to represent. Seurat's pointilliste technique imitates the effect of shimmering sunlight, even though the physical luminance of his canvas is much lower than that of the sunlit scene.[1]

[1] The main principles of Seurat's technique, known as 'pointillisme', 'divisionisme' or 'néo-impressionisme', had been expounded by Brücke in 1877 and 1878 *before* Seurat painted his

Helmholtz (1871–3) and Brücke (1877) have discussed in detail such limitations of pictorial representation and the techniques used by artists to circumvent them. Far from giving a scientific recipe for making perfect pictorial imitations, their writings do in effect prove that in many cases it is impossible to achieve a perfect pictorial imitation with regard to light, shade and colour. Thus the 'utmost degree of perfection' postulated by Brook Taylor in his discussion of perspective is impossible to reach. It is for this reason that Pozzo's ceiling, even though it gives a real three-dimensional impression, does not produce a total illusion. Stereoscopic pictures similarly do give a 3 D impression, but not a complete illusion: indeed the almost perfect impression of relief given by the stereoscope tends rather to emphasize, by contrast, the limitations of the photographic representation in other respects.

The case of moonlit scenes may provide a simple instance of the dependence of visual physiological effects upon the general luminance level. In recent years it has become well-established that colour vision is mediated only by the cone receptors of the retina, whereas the rod receptors only mediate colourless, or at any rate monochrome, vision. Now in a dark moonless night the light is too weak to stimulate the cones—the centre of the fovea, which contains cones only, then is blind. The rods alone are functioning, and colours cannot be distinguished; only differences of light and shade are perceived. In moonlight cones are functioning to a certain extent, as well as the rods, so that some colours can be recognized. Now as moonlight is roughly one million times dimmer than sunlight, a man wearing light-tight very dark goggles with a transmission only about one part in one million will see (after he has become adapted to this low level of illumination) the sunlit scene around him as a moonlit scene, with pale colours, dark shadows, and blurred outlines.

Of course an artist would directly paint a moonlit scene with pale colours, dark shadows and blurred outlines, but his canvas is meant to be viewed at a luminance level much higher than that of the actual scene. The canvas then sends to the eye much more light than an actual moonlit scene, yet it does at least strongly suggest moonlight. It would be theoretically possible to paint a moonlit scene in bright colours and arrange to see it only in very dim light of the correct intensity, but, needless to say, such experiments are foreign to the art of painting.

The proof that the physical basis of colour, that is, the varying spectral composition

---

main pointilliste works. Brücke traced the elements of this technique back to Rubens and Murillo, discussing also textiles and mosaics. His book appeared in 1878 in a French translation, published together with a translation of Helmholtz's (1871–3) Lectures on Optics and Painting. It is most probable that Seurat read this book (which is still to be found in Continental Public Libraries). Brücke (1878) explains Seurat's aim and method more clearly than most later writings dealing specifically with Neo-impressionism: for instance the book by the painter Signac (1899), Seurat's discipline, fails to explain all this adequately.

of the light emitted or reflected by objects, is present at night as well as in daytime, is given by the fact that, using long exposures, colour photographs can be made of objects the colour of which cannot be seen because the light they send to the eye is too weak. Thus brightly coloured photographs have been made of nebulae which are so dim that their colours cannot be seen even with the help of the most powerful telescopes (see Pirenne and Marriott, 1962).

The example of moonlit scenes shows that artists can readily compensate for the difference in illumination between their canvas and the scene they wish to depict. This is much more difficult in the case of photography. An ordinary colour film used to photograph a moonlit scene will produce a picture if the exposure is made long enough; but this brightly-coloured photograph will not correspond to what is seen.

Yet the idea that photography automatically gives an exact and complete representation of the world we see around us seems to have become embedded in people's mind at an early stage. Töppfer in 1865 was already worried by 'Daguerre's machine', which he seemed to have put on the same footing as a mirror. The 'Artists' Almanack' published by *Punch* in 1849 contains a remark which must have been current at the time: 'That he who only paints what he sees degrades himself into a daguerreotype'. In principle, it should have been sufficient to compare with reality (or with what we see in a mirror) the results given by photography to realize its deficiencies. The scientific prestige of photography must have prevented this conclusion from being drawn, a preconceived idea thus overruling the testimony of the sense of sight.[1] This is an instance of how difficult it is to *see*.

Some psychological problems of the artist

Our visual perception is to a large part based on elements of which we are hardly aware and is influenced by previous experience and by preconceived notions of all kinds. A great part of some scientific studies necessarily consists in learning to see. Mrs Johnson Abercrombie (1960) has made a special study of this problem. She writes that 'students know how difficult it is to look with profit at, say, a skull, or down the microscope at a section of skin, until they have had some kind of instruction in what to look for and preferably have a diagram beside them'. But on the other hand 'teachers know that if students have such aids to observation they...tend to see what they expect to see whether it is there or not. Many a student's drawing resembles a textbook figure more than the specimen in front of him; and the more complicated the specimen is or the more unfamiliar, the more its picture looks like the book. How to tell students what to look for without telling them what to see is the dilemma of teaching.'

[1] 'Les arts "d'imitation" se meuvent entre l'idée bien définie de représenter "exactement" la "réalité", de chercher à égaler ce qu'on obtient d'une bonne photographie ou d'un moulage, et les effets de l'intervention du système vivant qui doit exécuter cette représentation.' (Valéry, 1939.)

Two illustrations may be of interest here. In the engraving by Hogarth (1697–1764) part of which is reproduced in Fig. 12.1, the bottle on the right shows a bright reflection of a window in spite of the fact that in the room where this 'Modern Midnight Conversation'

12.1 Detail from Hogarth's engraving 'A Modern Midnight Conversation'
Note the reflections on the two bottles.

was held the windows must have been quite dark. Furthermore the reflection of the window is at the wrong angle, for the vertical sides of the window should remain vertical even when the bottle is tilted. Again, in another part of the same engraving, not reproduced here, the flame of a candle held almost horizontally is depicted as burning almost

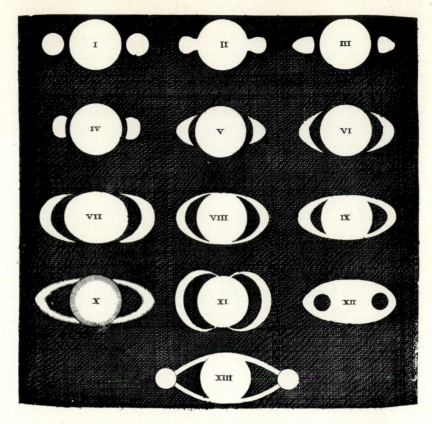

12.2   Drawings of the planet Saturn made by astronomers previous to Huygens

I represents an observation of Saturn by Galileo in 1610. Galileo saw Saturn triple, as two smaller circles on either side of a large circle. Huygens also saw this, in the same phase of Saturn, when using a small telescope. II is an observation of the same planet by Scheiner in 1614. Huygens again saw something similar using a relatively poor telescope. I and II are thus accounted for by the defects of the telescopes, and by the fact that bright objects of any shape appear round when they are seen indistinctly. III is an observation by Riccioli in 1641 or 1643. IV–VII represent forms of the planet suggested by Hevelius on the basis on a theory of his own. VIII and IX are forms observed by Riccioli in 1648–50. Riccioli thought the two 'handles' of the planet were unequal in size—and consistently saw them so. Huygens remarks that 'when someone has worked out a hypothesis which leads to such a consequence, he easily deceives himself and believes in the reality of what he hopes to see'. X is the reproduction of a figure by Divini drawn on the basis of his observations in 1646–8. XI represents observations by Fontana in 1636. XII represents observations by Gassendi in 1646. XIII represents observations made by Fontana in Naples and by others in Rome, 1644 and 1645. The plate does not reproduce observations of Saturn made when the ring is invisible. (From Huygens (1659), *Systema Saturnium*.)

in line with the axis of the candle, instead of rising vertically. There is little doubt that lapses of this kind (which are not uncommon in realistic paintings or drawings) are based on preconceived ideas of how things should be, instead of on direct observation of how they are.[1]

Perhaps a more interesting case is given by Fig. 12.2 in which Huygens in 1659 reproduced the drawings of the planet Saturn made by earlier astronomers, including Galileo in 1610. Saturn had faced astronomers with a puzzle until Huygens, having built a better telescope than his predecessors, saw Saturn's ring and was able to explain the phases of this planet (Figs. 12.3 and 12.4). The drawings in Fig. 12.2 were made on the basis of

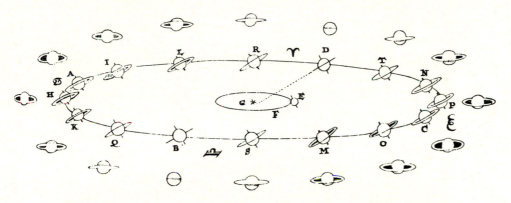

12.3   The phases of Saturn according to Huygens

Saturn in 16 equidistant positions of its orbit—which it describes in about 30 years. Around the orbit Huygens has drawn the various phases under which the planet presents itself to us. There are two points of the orbit where the ring appears at its widest, the planet shining most brightly; and there are two positions where the ring becomes invisible. (From Huygens (1659) *Systema Saturnium*.)

---

[1] Anyone who attempts to draw accurately will have noticed in his drawings errors which were caused by false preconceptions, especially when vision was not quite distinct. Thus, to take a minor instance, in a landscape made in the Basses Pyrénées, I drew the silhouette of a distant isolated chapel, built on the top of a smooth bare hill, as a rectangular nave flanked by a large square-topped tower. In fact this chapel simply consists of a large rectangular hall, but there is next to it a clump of very large trees. It is this round clump which I mistook for a square tower—having also underestimated the actual size on account of the distance.

Euclid said that a rectangular object at a distance looks round. Five centuries later Sextus Empiricus (A.D. *c.* 200) referred with some insistence to this illusion: 'The same tower appears round from a distance, but square from close at hand' (*Outlines of Pyrrhonism*, Bk I, §§ 32, 118; Bk II, § 55). What this sceptical philosopher apparently failed to notice, however, is that round objects may also look square.

The results of some dark-room experiments have a bearing on this. A large luminous circle, or half this circle, was flashed on a screen at an intensity near the absolute limit of visibility. The observer often mistook the half circle for the full circle, whereas the original expectation had been that sometimes he would merely tend to mistake the barely seen full circle for one of its component halves (Pirenne, 1948).

observations with poorer telescopes of lower magnification. They show the uncertainty of interpretations made by scientific observers on the basis of insufficient information, when the true shape of the object is unknown.

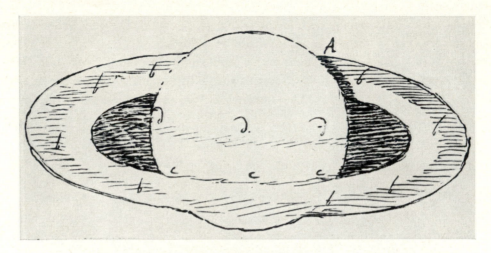

12.4 Sketches of two phases of Saturn by Huygens
The pen drawing was made on 8 December 1675; the date of the wash drawing is unknown. (From C. Huygens (1925) *Oeuvres Complètes*, Vol. xv, pp. 119 and 365.)

In everyday perception there is a tendency to ignore or reject what does not fit in with the expected pattern—as well as to see expected things even if they are not there. G. H. Lewes (1879), quoted by Mrs Johnson Abercrombie (1960), expressed this in saying 'And the new object presented to Senses, or the new idea presented to Thought, must also be *soluble in old experiences*, be *re*-cognized as like them, otherwise it will be unperceived, uncomprehended.'

In the exceptional cases of great artists taking reality as their theme, however, this vicious circle can be broken. 'Originality', wrote Hazlitt (1778–1830), 'is the seeing nature differently from others, and yet as it is in itself.' Rembrandt, he said, 'lived in and revealed to others a world of his own, and might be said to have invented a new view of nature. He did not discover things *out of* nature, in fiction or fairyland, or make a voyage to the moon "to descry new lands, rivers or mountains in her spotty globe", but saw things *in* nature that everyone had missed before him, and gave others eyes to see them with. This is the test and triumph of originality, not to shew us what has never been, and what we may therefore very easily never have dreamt of, but to point out to us what is before our eyes and under our feet, though we had no suspicion of its existence, for want of sufficient strength of intuition, or determined grasp of mind to seize and retain it.' (Hazlitt, 1936.)

This may be contrasted with Pascal's (1623–66) remark: 'What vanity is painting, which attracts admiration by the resemblance of things the originals of which are not admired.' (Pascal, 1939.) While Pascal did not admire the original objects depicted, however, the artist probably admired them. Laymen are often astonished by the kind of things which arouse the wonder of original artists. A great artist expresses his sense of wonder in his works; but there are persons, even most intelligent ones, like Pascal, apparently, who fail to perceive it even in the paintings of great masters.

While *my* perception of the visual world is limited, yet reality does potentially present us all with an 'infinite variety'. An original artist therefore may become aware of certain visual elements or certain aspects of reality which had not been clearly perceived, or at any rate which had not been represented, by his predecessors. If he succeeds in making use of them in his paintings, he will have made an 'artistic discovery'. What the physicist and astronomer Biot (1774–1862) said of science is applicable to painting: 'Nothing is so easy to see than what has been found yesterday, and nothing more difficult than what will be found tomorrow.' Needless to say, in the art of painting, things have not evolved in a simple manner. Among other things, on account of the limitations of pictorial representation, the utilization of new visual elements may come into a conflict, even from the mere standpoint of realism, with that of elements already in use.

On account of these limitations and of those of our visual perception, a variable period of time is required before the new visual elements which the artist has introduced in his work become understood and accepted by the public. For the artist's contemporaries, such a work may present a character at the same time of strangeness and of truth which captivates their attention. Those who will come later will not be impressed in the same way; on the contrary, what may strike them may be the lack of other elements, more recently introduced by later artists. It is because we have seen the works of Giotto's successors, that those of Giotto himself no longer appear as realistic to us as to his contemporaries.

At different times in history, painters have used an immense variety of visual elements taken from reality, which elements have been combined together in any number of ways. The extreme diversity facing us in the whole of all representational works as art should therefore not surprise us. It is unnecessary to turn to subjectivism, or to invoke the alleged 'essential relativity of truth and reality', to explain it.

It is true that many artists seem to have purposely transformed reality in painting it. 'Le peintre pour imiter transforme' as Töppfer (1865) liked to repeat. Yet it is hardly possible to transform what one has not seen, or what one has not yet succeeded in representing. Many of these transformations or distortions are not transformations of the real visible world, always elusive and imperfectly known, but transformations of pictorial representations already done. The artist always tends to see reality through paintings already done, or even through photographs.

In a passage on the evolution of painting, Leonardo da Vinci wrote that Giotto's (1267–1337) and Masaccio's (c. 1401–29) greatness was due in part to their ceaselessly seeking their inspiration in nature. He says 'That painting declines and deteriorates from age to age when painters have no other standard than painting already done.' 'Oh how great is the folly of those who blame those who learn from nature, setting aside the authorities who were disciples of nature.' (Richter and Richter, 1939, No. 60.)

The external world presents the artist, like the scientist, with a 'continual upsurge of unpredictable novelty'.[1]

A painting can fix an aspect of reality

The artist's aim is to communicate something well-defined—even if it is the 'expression of vagueness'. His wish, therefore, must be to facilitate the spectator's perception and to reduce its arbitrariness. It might be questioned whether it is really possible to reach such a result. For, since it is so difficult to see the real world, must not the spectator's perception of the painting itself be submitted to the same degree of uncertainty and variability?

It seems that this is not so, at any rate in the case of a painting seen by the artist's contemporaries at a time in history when there is an accepted style of painting, that is, a general mode of depiction everyone is used to. First, it is clear that the external world is continually changing, as is only too obvious to those who try to paint, say, a landscape on

[1] An outline of the ideas developed here was published by the present writer in 1944. Similar views, with a wealth of detailed illustrations, will be found in Professor Gombrich's book (1960).

location, whereas the painting does not change in this way. A portrait, for instance, does fix a certain aspect of the sitter. Furthermore, reality is often confusing—and so in fact are many photographs. But the artist, even if he does not actually rearrange his subject, may at leisure choose his standpoint, his lighting and create a clear and coherent picture.[1]

The main difference between perception of reality and perception of a representational painting, however, is caused by the very limitations of the artist's perception of reality. These limitations must result in a reduction of the play of perception in the spectator who views the artist's work. For even the most realistic paintings can only contain a restricted number of visual elements taken from reality. This is an essential property of all representational art.

Note on the historical evolution of the theory and use of perspective

The method of pictorial representation practised for thousands of years by the Egyptians, for instance, never made use of linear perspective in the full modern acceptation of the term (Fig. 12.5). Before the middle of the sixth century B.C., there are hardly any instances even of the use of foreshortening in the art of any nation. The ancient mode of depiction is, however, based implicitly on precise optical laws, but these laws consist of little more than one single theorem of perspective.

The central projection of a plane figure upon a plane parallel to that of the figure, is a figure which is geometrically similar to the original one (Fig. 12.6). The Egyptians drew separately in this way the main features of the objects, animals and men they wished to represent. These features, each of which can roughly be regarded as flat, were drawn one by one in the plane of the picture, independently of their relative orientation in space— hence the well known fact, for instance that the picture of a human head combines the profile of the head with a frontal view of the eye. This mode of depiction bears some resemblance to the folding of the leaves of a plant specimen when it is pressed to be dried flat before being mounted in a herbarium. The organization of these component parts into a single whole, such as a human body, was to a great extent conventional. There were definite rules to be obeyed in Egyptian paintings and bas-reliefs. These

---

[1] While the interpretation of the picture of a single object separated from its context often is wildly mistaken when it is presented to a subject under difficult conditions of observation, the interconnections between the various components of a complicated picture by a good artist seem much less liable to misinterpretation under such conditions. Experiments have been made on vision at low luminance levels, in which the observer was shown an engraving by Hogarth ('Hudibras beats Sidrophel and his man Whacum', 1726) in such a dim light that many of the details were impossible to see (Pirenne, Marriott and O'Doherty, 1957). Under those conditions, a number of different observers who were merely informed of the general contents of the picture (a magician's cave) all gave of it rather similar descriptions with relatively few mistakes.

12.5 Egyptian limestone bas-reliefs of the XIth Dynasty, *c.* 2100 B.C.

From the tomb of Tjetji, in Thebes, showing a man and a woman carrying food for the dead man. (British Museum, London.)

Note the life-like realism of the representation of the ducks; and the fact that the woman is depicted as having a right hand on her arm.

rules were applied more strictly in the case of important personages than in that of servants, captives and unimportant objects and animals. Again the Egyptian style became freer for a while, during the Amarna period (1375–1355 B.C.), but the ancient Egyptians, and their contemporaries, never used linear perspective to produce a unified picture of a whole scene giving a representation in depth of the component parts with their apparent

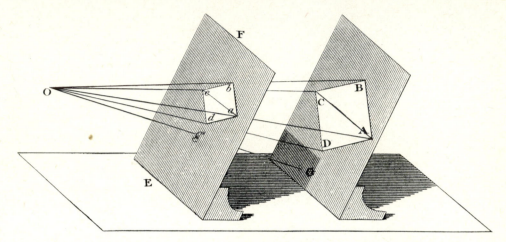

12.6   Central projection of a plane figure on another plane parallel to the plane of the figure
The figure *abcd*, which is the projection of *ABCD* on the plane *EF* parallel to that of *ABCD*, is geometrically similar to the figure *ABCD*. (From Brook Taylor (1811), *New Principles of Linear Perspective.*)

size and position (Schäfer, 1963; Harris, 1966). Yet it has been seen in Chapter 5 that the main fact of *natural* perspective, namely the apparent diminution in size of distant objects, was known in the seventh century B.C. and it may be surmised that it was known from prehistoric times.

The Egyptian mode of depiction led to results which may appear very odd to the modern eye, as in the drawing of a woman looking at her reflection in a mirror to paint her lips, reproduced in Fig. 12.7a and b. This method, however, presents the advantage that it gives unambiguous information about the main shape of the constituent parts of the scene or objects represented, rather like certain engineering drawings. Foreshortening, on the other hand, may lead to ambiguities. Thus the paintings on Greek vases of the classical period contain foreshortened, elliptical, representations of warrior's shields, which might lead to the view that the actual outline of the shields were elliptical, whereas in fact these were circular in shape.

The ancient mode of depiction does not by any means preclude realism; in certain respects many Egyptian and Assyrian paintings and reliefs are most realistic. This is not surprising since the drawing of *individual* pictorial elements, corresponding to the method

12.7a

12.7b

12.7a, b   Egyptian drawing of a woman painting her lips

From the erotico-satirical papyrus, Turin (Cat. No. 2031). XXth Dynasty, *c.* 1190–1075 B.C.
(12.7a: Museo Egizio di Torino. 12.7b: line drawing made from the original, published by Dr
J. R. Harris in his book *Egyptian Art*.)

of projection of Fig. 12.6, is no in way conventional. It is interesting to note that, as this method belongs to central perspective, a whole façade may be drawn in exactly the same manner in Renaissance paintings as the individual elements made use of in Egyptian art. This is so for example in many paintings by Piero della Francesca which contain buildings the façade of which is parallel to the picture plane; circles belonging to the façade are then represented as circles, squares as squares.

The profile of the heads appearing on coins is drawn according to the same principle. Held in the right position, the small profile on the coin could be made to coincide visually with the actual profile of the person represented.

This should not be dismissed as an obvious fact, by saying that such circles, squares, human profiles, are simply drawn 'as they are'. For usually they are much larger in the original than in the representation, which merely is *geometrically* similar to the original. As Mach (1911) pointed out it is not obvious why two figures which are geometrically similar can *look* similar to the eye. The empirical reason for this seems to be that they can be superimposed visually on one another; and this ultimately is due to the fact that light travels in straight lines.

To this it might be objected that the same superposition could be achieved for *any* central projection of the flat object on a surface. But projecting a flat object on a plane parallel to its own plane presents the advantage that when the projection, or the object itself, is placed in front of the eye perpendicularly to the normal direction of sight, its appearance undergoes less alteration when the head moves to a certain extent, than when it is placed in any other position. Thus the outline of a coin held in this way in the frontal plane subtends at the eye a right circular cone which suffers relatively small changes when the position of the eye is slightly changed, whereas the flattened cone which is subtended at the eye by the outline of a coin held inclined to the frontal plane becomes more markedly altered when the position of the centre of rotation of the eye is altered.

The Greeks were the first to introduce perspective into pictorial representation, at any rate in a fragmentary, and possibly purely empirical way. From the end of the sixth century B.C., Greek painted vases show in the drawing of the human body foreshortening and perspective effects of a kind quite unknown in earlier times. Most unfortunately, none of the large-scale works of Greek painters has come down to us. Reflections of these works occur in Greek painted vases of the classical period (Richter, 1966, 1970). But the curved surface of these vases would not lend itself to elaborate perspective effects. On the other hand certain architectural views unearthed at Pompei (destroyed A.D. 79), are probably based on earlier Greek original paintings, and contain the representation of parallel lines perpendicular to the picture plane, of which many (but not all) converge towards a single point. In two paintings from the Augustan period recently discovered in Rome, such lines converge almost (but not quite) without exception onto one point (Gioseffi, 1966a). The Naples Museum contains an amazing collection of paintings and mosaics of all kinds, from Pompei and Herculaneum, which strangely foreshadow many of the paintings of the Italian Renaissance. There is no doubt that the main features of modern perspective were fully used, at any rate empirically, in Greco-Roman times.[1]

There are no texts, however, to prove definitely, to everyone's satisfaction, that the basic principle of perspective, namely the section of the visual pyramid, was fully understood by the artists of the classical Greek, Hellenistic and Roman periods. Euclid's *Optics* and his *Elements* potentially contain all the principles of linear perspective[2] but the *Optics* is essentially a treatise on natural perspective, not on linear perspective, and the section of the visual pyramid (see Lejeune, 1948). On the basis of the whole evidence (texts and paintings still extant) Gioseffi (1966a) concludes that the optical basis of perspective was clearly understood already by the classical Greek painters, and therefore was merely *re*-discovered at the Renaissance—but this is not universally accepted.

Many of the paintings from Pompei and Herculaneum contain perspective depictions of round objects such as circular tables, dishes and goblets. Their circular outlines are drawn as more or less regular ellipses. Now there is no indication that the great axes of such ellipses deviate systematically from the horizontal for objects near the edges of the picture, as they should be expected to do according to the strict rules of geometrical perspective (Figs. 9.15 and 16). Since as a rule Renaissance artists also fail to observe the rules in such cases, however, this does not provide any clear evidence as to whether perspective was used purely empirically (as it seems to have been used by Giotto and the brothers Van Eyck, for instance) or whether the exact optical theory was known but left unheeded for artistic or other reasons.

The loss of the great works of Greek artists is particularly regrettable, for they would have given most important information on the passage from the pure Egyptian mode of depiction to the elaborate perspective representation which have survived from Greco-Roman times. As has been pointed out, the use of perspective may have tended to come into conflict with the realism already present in the old mode of depiction. Central perspective introduced new elements of realism, of a new, different, kind. It would have been most interesting to know how this change of style, the most momentous change

[1] Dr G. M. A. Richter's (1970) book discusses the development of perspective from about 800 B.C. to A.D. 400 on the basis of the paintings still extant. See also Beazley and Ashmole (1966.)

[2] It is none the less strange to consider that the first work giving the solution of the general problem of the vanishing point of a set of parallel straight lines (not parallel to the projection plane) was only published 1900 years after Euclid (Ubaldi, 1600, Prop. XXXII and Corr. 1). Ubaldi gives a long geometrical demonstration. A simpler demonstration may be obtained on the basis of the theorem of Euclid's *Optics* which prove that the angle under which one sees the separation between two parallel lines decreases as the distance from the eye increases.

which ever occurred in the history of painting, exactly took place. It is hardly conceivable that it was quite a sudden one, so that works of the transitional period might have appeared to some as giving the worst of both worlds. It is possible that some of Plato's strictures against the art of his time were connected with this problem (see Schuhl, 1963).

Once perspective had been widely used and accepted, there was no return to the pure pre-Greek mode of representation. Elements of foreshortening remain present in Byzantine and in Western medieval art, even though the paintings as a whole are no longer constructed on the basis of a central projection from one single point (Bunim, 1940; Gioseffi, 1966a).

Perspective in the full meaning of the term was discovered (or possibly only rediscovered) in the Renaissance. The Italian architect Brunelleschi (1377–1446) constructed the picture of an architectural view on the principle of the section of the visual pyramid, and arranged it to be viewed in a peep-show so that the spectator's eye was being kept in a fixed position. According to Gioseffi (1966a), Brunelleschi's first experiment was probably made between 1401 and 1409. Here again, unfortunately, our information is secondhand and incomplete: but many other Renaissance texts show that the main optical principle, the section of the visual pyramid, was definitely understood. It appears likely that in Brunelleschi's experiment the picture in perspective, since it was viewed with one eye kept fixed at the centre of projection, was seen in a truly three-dimensional manner, whereas, as has been argued in the present book, the perception or ordinary paintings viewed binocularly in the usual manner is much more complex on account of the spectator's awareness of the painted surface. As shown in previous chapters, this considerable complication was in effect taken into account by Renaissance artists in the depiction of objects having curved surfaces. And it seems clear that it lay at the root, for instance, of Leonardo's strugglings with the problem of linear perspective.

In the present century, photography and methods of mechanical pictorial reproduction are playing an immense role in everyone's life. The photographer has to a large extent replaced the artist in the production of pictures serving as records, illustrations, portraits. Again reproductions of an immense variety of works of art of all origins have become readily available in illustrated books. As photography automatically gives pictures in central perspective, there seems to be little doubt that many artists in fact have reacted to this 'unfair competition', preferring to use modes of depiction as different as possible from photographic perspective, and often inspired by works from distant times and places. Yet, perforce, all men continue to see in 'natural perspective'.[1]

---

[1] For further information on the history of perspective, see Carter (1970), Gioseffi (1957, 1957–8, 1966a), Ivins (1938, 1964) and ten Doesschate (1964). The book by Brücke (1878) also contains valuable remarks on perspective, its history, and practical problems such as the hanging and lighting of paintings.

Conclusion

The considerations developed in this book show that there is no reason to think that the main essential characteristics of human vision have changed in the course of history, or even prehistory. What has changed in the course of time are the methods of depiction used by artists—and also, naturally, what they depicted. All methods of representational painting rest on empirical optical facts.

The alleged possibility of producing a complete, perfect, imitation of visible reality is a myth. The opposite belief, namely that there are no permanent optical laws relating to human vision, and that the evolution of art must be explained entirely on subjective grounds, for instance, on the basis of varying concepts or intuitions of space, is another myth.

The main conclusion of the present study, however, is that under usual conditions ordinary representational paintings do not give us a simple kind of illusion. Their perception is a complex process because it invokes in the spectator a special kind of awareness of the characteristics of the painted surface itself. This complicated state of affairs, which is also discussed in Michael Polanyi's Foreword,[1] has important implications, for instance, with regard to the practical usefulness of pictures as representations. From the standpoint of aesthetics, it increases the range of possibilities open to the artist in the way he can use linear perspective to compose his painting, and it entails that a representational painting can contain the same kind of aesthetic elements as a purely non-representational, 'abstract', painting.

[1] See also Polanyi (1970).

Bibliography

Abbot, W. (1950). *The theory and practice of perspective*. London and Glasgow: Blackie.

Alhazen (Ibn Al-Haitham). *See* Winter (1954); Schramm (1963); Lindberg (1967).

Allport, G. W. and Pettigrew, T. F. (1957). 'Cultural influence on the perception of movement: the trapezoidal illusion among Zulus.' *J. abnorm. soc. Psychol.* **55**, 104–13.

Asher, H. (1961). *The seeing eye*. London: Gerald Duckworth.

Barlow, H. B. (1963). 'Slippage of contact lenses and other artefacts in relation to fading and regeneration of supposedly stable retinal images.' *Q. Jl exp. Psychol.* **15**, 36–51.

Barre, A., and Flocon, A. (1968). *La perspective curviligne: De l'espace visuel à l'image construite*. Paris: Flammarion. With Bouligand, G., Flocon, A. and Barre, A. 'Etude comparée des différentes méthodes de perspective: une perspective curviligne.' From *Bull. Ac. R. Belgique*, Séance du 7 mars 1964.

Beazley, T. D. and Ashmole, B. (1966). *Greek sculpture and painting to the end of the Hellenistic period*. Cambridge: University Press.

Blank, A. A. (1962). 'The Luneburg theory of binocular vision.' In S. Koch (ed.), *Psychology: a study of science*, Vol. 1, *Sensory, perceptual, and physiological formulations*, 395–426. New York, Toronto, London: McGraw-Hill.

Blavier, A. *See* Pirenne, M. (1954).

Blumenfeld, W. (1913). 'Untersuchungen über die scheinbare Grösse in Sehraume.' *Z. Psychol. Physiol. Sinnesorg.*, Abt. 1, **65**. 241–404.

Bouligand, G., Flocon, A. and Barre, A. (1964). *See* Barre and Flocon (1968).

Brook Taylor. *See* Taylor, B.

Brücke, E. (1877). *Bruchstücke aus der Theorie der bildenden Künste*. Leipzig: Brockhaus. French translation: *see* Brücke (1878).

Brücke, E. (1878). *Principes scientifiques des beaux-arts: essais et fragments de théorie*. Paris: Bibliothèque Scientifique Internationale, Librairie Germer Baillière. (Trans. of Brücke, 1877.) Published with H. Helmholtz, *L'Optique et la Peinture* (trans. of Helmholtz, 1871–3). A fourth edition was published in 1891 by Alcan.

Bunim, M. S. (1940). *Space in medieval painting and the forerunners of perspective*. New York: Columbia University Press.

Burke, J. (1955). *See* Hogarth (1753).

Burton, H. E. (1945). 'The optics of Euclid.' *J. opt. Soc. Am.* **35**, 357–72.

Bury, R. G. ed., and trans. *See* Sextus Empiricus (1961).

Carter, B. A. R. (1953). 'The perspective of Piero della Francesca's "Flagellation".' This is Pt II of the paper by Wittkower and Carter (1953), *J. Warburg and Courtauld Inst.* **16**, 292–302.

Carter, B. A. R. (1967). 'The use of perspective in Saenredam.' *The Burlington Magazine* **109**, 594–5.

Carter, B. A. R. (1970). 'Perspective.' In H. Osborne (ed.), *Oxford companion to art*. Oxford: Clarendon Press.

Choisy, A. (1904). *Histoire de l'architecture*. 2 vols. Paris: Rouveyre.

Clerc, L. P. (1946). *Photography: theory and practice*, 2nd edn. London: Sir Isaac Pitman and Sons.

Cox, A. (1956). *Optics: the technique of definition*, 11th edn. London and New York: The Focal Press.

Descartes, R. (1637). *Discours de la méthode pour bien conduire sa raison, et chercher la vérité dans les sciences, plus la dioptrique, les météores et la géométrie, qui sont des essais de cette méthode.* Leyden.

Dinsmoor, W. B. (1950). *The architecture of ancient Greece: an account of its historic development*, 3rd edn. London, New York: Batsford.

Dirac, P. A. M. (1958). *The principles of quantum mechanics*, 4th edn. Oxford: Clarendon Press.

Euclid (*c.* 300 B.C.). *Optics. See* Burton (1945); Ver Eecke (1938).

Ferree, C. E., Rand, G. and Hardy, C. (1931). 'Refraction for the peripheral field of vision.' *Archs Ophthal. N.Y.* **5**, 717–31. (Publishers: American Medical Association, Chicago. Ill.)

Fick, A. (1879). 'Dioptrik: Nebenapparate des Auges: Lehre von der Lichtempfindung.' In L. Hermann (ed.), *Handbuch der Physiologie*, Vol. III, Pt 1, *Gesichtssinn*. Leipzig: Vogel.

Fielding, H. (1932). *The history of Tom Jones, a foundling*. London: Dent; New York: Dutton. (Everyman's Library.)

Gibson, J. J. (1950). *The perception of the visual world*. Boston: Houghton Mifflin Co.

Gioseffi, D. (1957). *Perspectiva artificialis; la storia della prospettiva; spigolature e appunti*. Istituto di Storia dell'Arte Antica e Moderna, No. 7, University of Trieste.

Gioseffi, D. (1957–8). 'Complementi di prospettiva', 1 and 2. *Critica d'Arte*, 1957, 468–88 and 1958, 102–49.

Gioseffi, D. (1959). *Canaletto; il quaderno della Gallerie Veneziane e l'impiego della camera ottica*. Istituto di Storia dell'Arte Antica e Moderna, No. 91, University of Trieste.

Gioseffi, D. (1963). 'Prospettiva.' In *Enciclopedia universale dell'arte*, Vol. XI, 115–59. Venice and Rome: Istituto per la Collaborazione Culturale.

Gioseffi, D. (1966*a*). 'Perspective.' In *Encyclopedia of world art*, Vol. XI, 183–221. New York, Toronto, London: McGraw-Hill. (English language edition of *Enciclopedia universale dell'arte*. Venice and Rome: Istituto per la Collaborazione Culturale.)

Gioseffi, D. (1966*b*). 'Optical concepts.' In *Encyclopedia of world art*, Vol. X, 758–70. New York, Toronto, London: McGraw-Hill. (English language edition of *Enciclopedia universale dell'arte*. Venice and Rome: Istituto per la Collaborazione Culturale.)

Gombrich, E. H. (1960). *Art and illusion. A study of the psychology of pictorial representation*. London: Phaidon Press; New York: Pantheon Books.

Graham, C. H. (1951). 'Visual perception.' In Stevens (ed.), *Handbook of experimental psychology*, 868–920. New York: John Wiley.

Grimaldi, F. M. (1665). *Physico-mathesis de lumine, coloribus, et iride, aliisque adnexis libri duo*. Bononiae.

Guillot, M. (1967). 'Vision des couleurs et peinture.' *J. Psychol. norm. path.*, **64**, 385–402.

Hardy, A. C. and Perrin, F. H. (1932). *The principles of optics*. New York and London: McGraw-Hill.

Harris, J. R. (1966). *Egyptian art*. London: Spring Books.

Hartridge, H. (1919). 'The limit to peripheral vision.' *J. Physiol., Lond.* **53** (*Proc. Physiol. Soc.*), xvii–xviii.

Hauck, G. (1875). *Die subjektive Perspektive und die horizontalen Curvaturen des Dorischen Styls*. Stuttgart.

Hazlitt, W. (1936). 'On genius and common sense: the same subject continued.' In *Table Talk*. London: Dent; New York: Dutton. (Everyman's Library.)

Helmholtz, H. von (1866). *Handbuch der Physiologischen Optik*. 1st edn. Hamburg and Leipzig: Leopold Voss. 2nd German edn, see Helmholtz (1896). 3rd German edn, see Helmholtz (1909–11).

Helmholtz, H. von (1867). *Optique physiologique*. Trans. by E. Javal and N. T. Klein. Paris: Masson.

Helmholtz, H. (1871–3). *Optisches über Malerei*. Republished in Helmholtz (1884). For French translation *see* Brücke (1878).

Helmholtz, H. von (1884). *Vorträge and Reden*. 2 vols. Brunswick: Fr. Vieweg und Sohn.

Helmholtz, H. von. (1896). *Handbuch der Physiologischen Optik*. 2nd edn. Hamburg and Leipzig: Leopold Voss. This edition, revised by Helmholtz, contains new material based mostly on the work of his collaborator A. König. It also contains a bibliography, complete to the year 1894, prepared by König.

Helmholtz, H. von (1903). 'On the origin and significance of geometrical axioms.' In *Popular lectures on scientific subjects*, Second series, 27–71. London: Longmans, Green. (Translation of Helmholtz (1884).)

Helmholtz, H. von. (1904). 'The recent progress in the theory of vision.' In *Popular Lectures on scientific subjects*, First Series, 175–267. London: Longmans, Green. (Translation of Helmholtz (1884).)

Helmholtz, H. von (1909–11). *Handbuch der Physiologischen Optik*. 3rd, posthumous, edn, 3 vols. This consists of the text of the first edition (1866) with supplements by A. Gullstrand, T. von Kries and W. Nagel. Hamburg and Leipzig: Leopold Voss.

Helmholtz, H. von (1962). *Treatise on physiological optics*. Trans. and ed. by J. P. C. Southall, 3 vols. bound as 2. New York: Dover; London: Constable. This edition, first published by the Optical Society of America in 1924–5, is a translation of Helmholtz (1909–11).

Hirschberg, J. (1899–1908). 'Geschichte der Augenheilkunde.' In *Graefe-Saemisch Handbuch der gesamten Augenheilkunde...*, 2nd edn, Vols XII and XIII. Leipzig: Engelmann.

Hogarth, W. (1753). *The analysis of beauty, written with a view of fixing the fluctuating ideas of taste*. Edited with an introduction by J. Burke (1955). Oxford: Clarendon Press.

Hultsch, F. (1899). 'Winkel-messungen durch die Hipparchische Dioptra.' *Abh. gesch. Math.* **9**, 208.

Huygens, C. (1888–1950). *Oeuvres complètes, publiées par la Société Hollandaise des Sciences*. Vol. XV: *Observations astronomiques. Travaux astronomiques 1658–66*. La Haye.

Ibn Al-Haitham. *See* Alhazen.

Ittelson, W. H. (1952). *The Ames demonstrations in perception*. Princeton, N. J.: Princeton University Press.

Ivins, W. M. Jun. (1938). *On the rationalization of sight*. New York.

Ivins, W. M. Jun. (1964). *Art and geometry: a study in space intuitions*. New York: Dover. (Reprint of the work first published by Harvard University Press in 1946.)

Jammer, M. (1954). *Concepts of space: the history of theories of space in physics*. Cambridge, Mass.: Harvard University Press.

Javal, E. *See* Helmholtz (1867).

Johnson Abercrombie, M. L. (1960). *The anatomy of judgment: an investigation into the processes of perception and reasoning*. London: Hutchinson. Reprinted 1969, Harmondsworth, Middlesex: Penguin Books.

Jopling, J. (1835). *See* Taylor (1811).

Jurin, J. (1738). *Essay upon distinct and indistinct vision*. Published as an appendix in R. Smith's (1738) *Opticks*.

Kepler, J. (1604). *Ad Vitellionem paralipomena, quibus astronomiae pars optica traditur*. Francofurti.

La Gournerie, J. de (1859). *Traité de perspective linéaire contenant les tracés pour les tableaux plans et courbes, les bas-reliefs et les décorations théatrales, avec une théorie des effets de perspective*. 1 vol. and 1 atlas of plates. Paris: Dalmont et Dunod; Mallet-Bachelier.

Latham, R. E., trans. (1958). *Lucretius: the nature of the universe*. Harmondsworth, Middlesex: Penguin Books.

Le Grand, Y. (1948). *Optique physiologique.* Vol. II, *Lumière et couleurs.* Paris: Ed. de la 'Revue d'Optique'.

Le Grand, Y. (1952). *Optique physiologique.* Vol. I, *La dioptrique de l'oeil et sa correction,* 2nd edn. Paris: Ed. de la 'Revue d'Optique'.

Le Grand, Y. (1956). *Optique physiologique.* Vol. III, *L'espace visuel.* Paris: Ed. de la 'Revue d'Optique'.

Le Grand, Y. (1957). *Light, colour and vision.* Trans. of Le Grand (1948) by R. W. G. Hunt, J. W. T. Walsh and F. R. W. Hunt. London: Chapman and Hall.

Lejeune, A. (1947). 'La dioptre d'Archimède.' *Annls Soc. scient. Brux.* **61**, 27–47.

Lejeune, A. (1948). *Euclide et Ptolémée: deux stades de l'optique géométrique grecque.* Louvain: Université; Recueil de travaux d'histoire et de philologie.

Leonardo da Vinci. *See* McMahon (1956), Pedretti (1964), and Richter and Richter (1939).

Letarouilly, P. (1840–57). *Edifices de Rome moderne.* 2 vols. and 3 vols. of plates. Paris.

Lewes, G. H. (1879). *Problems of life and mind.* London: Trübner.

Lindberg, D. C. (1967). 'Alhazen's theory of vision and its reception in the West.' *Isis,* **58**, 321–41.

Lucretius. *See* Latham (1958).

Luneburg, R. K. (1947). *Mathematical analysis of binocular vision.* Hanover: Dartmouth Eye Institute.

Mach, E. (1911). *Die Analyse der Empfindungen und das Verhältnis des Physichen zum Psychischen.* 6th edn. Iena: Gustar Fischer.

McMahon, A. P. (1956). *Treatise on painting (Codex Urbinas Latinus 1270) by Leonardo da Vinci.* Vol. I, translation; Vol. II, facsimile. Princeton, N. J.: Princeton University Press.

Maffei, F. de' (1966a). 'Perspectivists.' In *Encyclopedia of world art,* **11**, 221–43. New York, Toronto, London: McGraw-Hill. (English language edition of *Enciclopedia universale dell'arte.* Venice and Rome: Istituto per la Collaborazione Culturale.)

Maffei, F. de' (1966b). 'Pozzo, Fra Andrea.' In *Encyclopedia of world art,* **11**, 560–2. New York, Toronto, London: McGraw-Hill. (English language edition of *Enciclopedia universale dell'arte.* Venice and Rome: Istituto per la Collaborazione Culturale.)

Magendie, F. (1833). *Précis élémentaire de physiologie.* 2 vols. Paris.

Marini, R. (1959). *Andrea Pozzo, Pittore.* Trent: Arti Grafiche 'Saturnia'.

Ministry of Education (1960). *First report of the National Advisory Council on Art Education.* London: Her Majesty's Stationery Office.

Müller, J. (1826). *Zur vergleichenden Physiologie des Gesichtssinnes des Menschen und der Thiere, nebst einen Versuch über die Bewegungen der Augen und über den menschlichen Blick.* Leipzig.

Newton, Sir Isaac (1730). *Opticks, or a treatise of the reflections, refractions, inflections and colours of light.* 1st edn, 1704; 4th edn, 1730. London. The fourth edition, the last corrected by Newton, is available in a modern reprint, 1952, New York: Dover.

Ogle, K. N. (1962). 'The Optical space sense.' In H. Davson (ed.), *The eye*, Vol. IV, 211–417. New York and London: Academic Press.

Panofsky, E. (1927). 'Die Perspektive als symbolische Form.' *Vorträge der Bibliothek Warburg* 1924–5, 258–330. Leipzig–Berlin.

Panofsky, E. (1940). *The Codex Huygens and Leonardo da Vinci's art theory*. London: The Warburg Institute.

Pascal, B. (1939). *Pensées*. In J. Chevalier (ed.), *Oeuvres*. Paris: Bibl. de le Pléiade.

Pedretti, C. (1964). *Leonardo da Vinci on painting: a lost book (Libro A)*. Berkeley and Los Angeles: University of California Press. British edition (1965) London: Peter Owen.

Piéron, H. (1952). *The sensations: their functions, processes and mechanisms*. Trans. by M. H. Pirenne and B. C. Abbott. London: Frederick Muller.

Pirenne, M. (1954). 99 *Reproductions d'oeuvres de Peintre*. Texte d'André Blavier. Verviers: Ed. 'Temps Mêlés'.

Pirenne, M. (1958). *Dessins*. Verviers: Ed. 'Temps Mêlés'.

Pirenne, M. *See* Vandeloise (1970).

Pirenne, M. H. (1944). 'Peinture, photographie et réalité.' *Bulletin de l'Association des Etudiants Belges en Grande-Bretagne*, No. 8, Été 1944, 30–3.

Pirenne, M. H. (1948). 'Independent light-detectors in the peripheral retina.' *J. Physiol., Lond.* **107**, 47 P.

Pirenne, M. H. (1950). 'Descartes and the body-mind problem in physiology.' *Brit. J. Phil. Science*, **1**, 43–59.

Pirenne, M. H. (1952). 'The scientific basis of Leonardo da Vinci's theory of perspective.' *Br. J. Phil. Sci.* **3**, 169–85. (This paper has been partly superseded by Pirenne (1963). See above, Chapter 8, pp. 99–100, footnote.)

Pirenne, M. H. (1963). 'Les lois de l'optique et la liberté de l'artiste.' *J. Psychol. norm. path.* **60**, 151–66.

Pirenne, M. H. (1967a). *Vision and the eye*. 2nd edn. London: Chapman and Hall Ltd and Science Paperbacks.

Pirenne, M. H. (1967b). 'On perspective and the perception of pictures.' *J. Physiol., Lond.*, **192**, 7–9 P.

Pirenne, M. H. and Marriott, F. H. C. (1962). 'Visual functions in man.' In H. Davson (ed.), *The eye*, Vol. II, *The visual process*, 3–320. New York and London: Academic Press.

Pirenne, M. H., Marriott, F. H. C. and O'Doherty, E. F. (1957). 'Individual differences in night-vision efficiency.' *Spec. Rep. Ser. med. Res. Coun.*, **294**.

Polanyi, M. (1958). *Personal knowledge: towards a post-critical philosophy*. London: Routledge and Kegan Paul.

Polanyi, M. (1962). 'Tacit knowing: its bearing on some problems of philosophy.' *Rev. mod. Phys* **34**, 601–16.

Polanyi, M. (1970). 'What is a painting.' *British Journal for Aesthetics*. In the press. Also in *The American Scholar*. In the press.

Polyak, S. L. (1941). *The retina*. Chicago: University of Chicago Press.

Pozzo, A. (A. Putei) (1707). *Rules and examples of perspective proper for painters and architects. In English and Latin. Done into English by Mr John James.* London. (English edition of Putei, 1693.)

Putei, A. (A. Pozzo) (1693–1700). *Perspectiva Pictorum et Architectorum Pars Prima— Secunda.* (Latin and Italian.) Rome. (For the English edition see Pozzo, 1707.)

Raeder, H., Strömgren, E. and Strömgren, B., trans. and (eds.) (1946). *Tycho Brahe's description of his instruments and scientific works as given in Astronomiae Instauratae Mechanica.* Copenhagen: Det Kongelige Danske Videnskabernes Selskab.

Rayleigh, 3rd Baron (1910). 'Diffraction of light.' In *Encyclopaedia Britannica*, 11th edn, Vol. VIII, 238–55.

Richter, G. M. A. (1966). 'Linear perspective in representations of Greek and Roman furniture.' Appendix in *The furniture of the Greeks, Etruscans and Romans.* London: Phaidon.

Richter, G. M. A. (1970). *Perspective in Greek and Roman art. A study of its development from about 800 B.C. to A.D. 400.* London: Phaidon.

Richter, J. P. and Richter, I. A. (eds.) (1939). *The literary works of Leonardo da Vinci compiled and edited from the original MSS. by J. P. Richter, 2nd edn enlarged and revised by J. P. and I. A. Richter.* 2 vols. (Italian and English). London: Oxford University Press. Reprinted 1970, London: Phaidon.

Robertson, D. S. (1964). *A handbook of Greek and Roman architecture*, 2nd edn., reprinted with corrections. Cambridge: University Press.

Roger Marx, C. (1963). 'Centenaire de Delacroix. Le plus grand des critiques d'art.' *Revue de Paris*, April 1963, 101–11.

Ronchi, V. (1956). *Histoire de la lumière.* Paris: Armand Colin.

Rosenfeld, L. (1936). 'La première phase de l'évolution de la théorie des Quanta.' *Osiris* **2**, 149–96.

Rosser, W. G. V. (1964). *An introduction to the theory of relativity.* London: Butterworths.

Rudaux, L. and Vaucouleurs, G. de (1959). *Larousse encyclopedia of astronomy.* London: Hamlyn.

Saenredam, P. J. *Catalogue raisonné of the works by Pieter Jansz. Saenredam published on the occasion of the exhibition Pieter Jansz. Saenredam, 15 September–3 December 1961.* Utrecht: Centraal Museum.

Schäfer, E. A. (1894). 'Organs of the senses.' In *Quain's Elements of anatomy*, (eds.) Schäfer, E. A. and Thane, G. D., Vol. III, Pt III, 10th edn. London: Longmans, Green.

Schäfer, H. (1963). *Von Ägyptischer Kunst*, 4th edn prepared by E. Brunner-Traut. Wiesbaden: Otto Harrassowitz.

Scheiner, C. (1619). *Oculus; hoc est fundamentum opticum...* Oeniponti.

Schlosberg, H. (1941). 'Stereoscopic depth from single pictures.' *Am. J. Psychol.* **54**, 601–5.

Schramm, M. (1963). *Ibn Al-Haythams Weg zur Physik.* Wiesbaden: Franz Steiner.

Schuhl, P. M. (1963). *Platon et l'art de son temps (arts plastiques)*. Paris: Alcan.

Schwarz, H. (1959). 'The mirror of the artist and the mirror of the devout: observations on some paintings, drawings and prints of the fifteenth century.' In *Studies in the history of art, dedicated to William E. Suida on his eightieth birthday*. London: published by the Phaidon Press for the Samuel H. Kress Foundation, New York.

Segall, M. H., Campbell, D. T., and Herskovits, M. J. (1966). *The influence of culture on visual perception*. Indianapolis, New York, Kansas City: The Bobbs-Merrill Co., Inc.

Sextus Empiricus (1961). *Outlines of Pyrrhonism*. Edited and trans. by R. G. Bury. London: Heinemann; Loeb Classical Library. Cambridge, Mass: Harvard University Press.

Signac, P. (1899). *D'Eugène Delacroix au néo-impressionisme*, 4th edn, 1939. Paris: Floury.

Smith, R. (1738). *A compleat system of opticks* with J. Jurin's *Essay upon distinct and indistinct vision*. Cambridge.

Taylor, B. (1811). *New principles of linear perspective: or, the art of designing on a plane, the representation of all sorts of objects in a more general and simple method than has been hitherto done*, 4th edn (reprint of the 1719 edn). London: J. Taylor. The first edition was published in 1715, the second in 1719. Another edition with additions by J. Jopling was published in 1835.

Ten Doesschate, G. (1962). 'Oxford and the revival of optics in the thirteenth century.' *Vision Research*, **1**, 313–42.

Ten Doesschate, G. (1964). *Perspective: fundamentals, controversials, history*. Nieuwkoop: B. de Graaf.

Ten Doesschate, G. and Kylstra, J. (1956). 'The perception of parallels.' *Ophthalmologica*, **131**, 61–5.

Töpffer, R. (1865). *Réflexions et menus propos d'un peintre genevois sur le beau dans les arts*. New edn. Paris: Hachette. Töpffer died in 1846; apparently, the first edition of this work was published posthumously in 1848.

Trevor-Roper, P. D. (1959). 'The influence of eye disease on pictorial art.' *Proc. Roy. Soc. Med.* **52**, 721–44.

Tycho Brahe. *See* Raeder, Strömgren and Strömgren (1946).

Ubaldi, G. (1600). *Perspectivae libri sex*. Pisauri.

Valéry, P. (1939). 'De la ressemblance et de l'art.' *Prométhée*, June 1939, 159–65.

Vandeloise, G. (1970). *Maurice Pirenne*. Verviers: Ed. 'Temps Mêlés'.

Ver Eecke, P. (1938). *Euclide: l'optique et la catoptrique*. Paris, Bruges: Desclée de Brouwer.

Vinci, Leonardo da. *See* Leonardo da Vinci.

White, J. (1949). 'Developments in Renaissance perspective—I.' *J. Warburg and Courtauld Inst.* **12**, 58–79.

White, J. (1951). 'Developments in Renaissance perspective—II.' *J. Warburg and Courtauld Inst.* **14**, 42–69.

White, J. (1956). *Perspective in ancient drawing and painting*. London: Society for the Promotion of Hellenic Studies.

White, J. (1957). *The birth and rebirth of pictorial space*. London: Faber.

Winter, H. J. J. (1954). 'The optical researches of Ibn Al-Haitham.' *Centaurus*, **3**, 190–210.

Wirth, A. (1968). 'Patologia oculare e arti figurativi.' *Atti della Fondazione Giorgio Ronchi*, **23**, 445–66.

Wittkower, R. and Carter, B. A. R. (1953). 'The perspective of Piero della Francesca's "Flagellation", I and II.' *J. Warburg and Courtauld Inst.* **16**, 292–302.

Wood, R. W. (1934). *Physical optics*. 3rd edn. New York: MacMillan.

Young, T. (1807). *A course of lectures on natural philosophy and the mechanical arts*. 2 vols. London.

Zanetti, M. (1951). 'Una proposta di reforma della prospettiva lineare.' *L'Ingegnere*, **25**, 945–51.

Zanetti, M. (1959). 'Architectura e prospettiva.' (Note sul 'Brunelleschi' di G. C. Argan.) *L'Architetto*, September 1959, No. 9, 33–8.

Zanetti, M. (1960). 'Prospettiva, pittura et architettura.' *L'Architetto*. September 1960, No. 9, 28–34.

Zanetti, M. (1968). 'La géométrie du champ de regard et le postulat des parallèles.' *Revue d'Optique théorique et expérimentale*, **47**, 15–18.

Index

Abbot, W., 76 n
abstract painting, 114, 183
accommodation of eye, 29; and perspective, 78–9
achromatic optical systems, 46 n
albino animals, eyes of, 29, 31; retinal images in, 63–71
Alhazen (Ibn Al-Haitham), 7–8, 15
alley experiments, 147
Allport, G. W., and T. F. Pettigrew, 162 n
Ames, A., Jun., 151, 152, 162 n
anaglyphs, xvii, 99, 160, 163–4
ancillary parallel through eye, 59, 67, 70, 139, 140, 141
aperture of pinhole camera, effects of: position of, 14; size of, 16–20, 34 n; size of, in relation to aperture/screen distance, 23
apertures, vision through, 5–7, 35 n, 45, 56, 110–11
aqueous humour of eye, 30, 31
Arch of Janus, Rome: photographs of, with different planes of projection, 103–6, 110, 139–41
Archimedes, 56
Arnheim, R., xvi
artists: avoid exact perspective, 122, 123, 125–6, 132, 135; personal psychology of, 11 n; psychological problems of, 168–74; reactions of, to photography, 182; representational paintings not the percepts of, 10
Asher, H., 96 n
Assurbanipal of Assyria, 59
Assyrians, art of, 178
astigmatism: effects of, 43–4; irregular, 42 n; peripheral, 38–40; regular, 40–2
astrolabes, 52
astronomy: perspective in, 58; refraction in, 52–4
Austin, A., 64
awareness: focal, xvi, 114; subsidiary, of

surfaces of pictures, xvi, 12, 114, 161, 166; see also surfaces

balusters, perspectives of, 130–2, 143–5
Barlow, H. B., 8 n
Baroque artists, 91, 110
Barre, A., and A. Flocon, 149 n
bas-reliefs: Egyptian, 176, 177; painted, as trompe-l'oeil, 93 n
Beazley, T. D., and B. Ashmole, 181 n
'Big Brother', photograph of photograph, 96, 97, 99
Biot, J. B., 173
black objects, scattering of light by, 14
blackness of pupil of eye, 30–1
Blank, A. A., 147
blood supply of retina, 25
Blumenfeld, W., 147
Borromini, F., 152, 154, 162
Bouligand, 6, 149 n
Brahe, Tycho, 52
brain: retina as expansion of, 25; visual cortex of, 9, 10
Brücke, E., 166 n, 167, 182 n
Brunelleschi, F., 182
Bunim, M. S., 182
Burton, H. E., 60 n

Calza-Bini, S., 86, 87, 89, 90
camera obscura: eye as, 1, 8, 31, 50; with lens and plane mirror, used by artists, 123 n
camera, photographic, with lens, 46–9; fish-eye, 149; purposes of, 49–50
camera, pinhole, 14, 15–19, 49; diffraction of light in, 18–20, 49 n; luminance of image in, 23–4
Canaletto, A., 102, 103, 123 n
cardinal points of eye, in Gaussian theory, 32, 34

Carter, B. A. R., 59, 75, 135, 149 n, 182 n
cat, pupil of eye of, 7, 31
cataract, 30 n
central projection, 72–6; in eye, 38, 50; of lens and pinhole cameras, 49–50, of linear perspective, 78–9; in Pozzo's painted ceiling, 79, 84, 85, 88–91; of spheres, 116, 121; of straight lines, 136–45
Cézanne, P., 161 n
Charterhouse, Rome: cloister at, 125
checkerboard, subjective curvatures, 145–6
Choisy, A., 150
choroid of eye, 25, 27
chromatic aberration, 46 n, 48
ciliary processes of eye, 28, 29
Clerc, L. P., 20, 48
colour vision, 27, 44 n, 167
columns, perspectives of rows of, 124–32
cone cells of retina: cease to function at low intensities of light, 45; colour vision mediated by, 167; in fovea, 27, 29, 44; numbers of, 29; see also rods and cones
contact lenses, 42 n
cornea of eye, 1, 25, 28; astigmatism caused by, 40–1; reflection of light by, 30–1; refraction of light by, 31–2, 37–40
corneal reflex, 30
correspondence, point to point, between object and image on retina, 3–5, 8
Cox, A., 48
cubes, perspectives of, 126, 127
curvatures, subjective, 57, 138, 145–50
cylinders, perspectives of, 124–32

daguerreotypes, 168
dark adaptation of eye, 45
deformations: in anaglyphs, xvii, 163–4; in perspectives (of cubes), 126, 127, (of cylinders), 124, 125, 144–5, (of spheres), 118–32; in photographs of photographs, 96–8; in pictures, viewed from wrong position, 12, 79, 136, 154–60, 162; in Pozzo's ceiling, viewed from wrong position, xv, xvii, xviii, 85, 87, 96, 137, 151
Delacroix, E., 114
Democritus, 14
depth of field: of cameras, 48, 49, 50; of eyes, 111
Descartes, R., 1, 2, 9 n, 37 n, 63
diffraction of light, 5; in lens camera, 49; limits accuracy of image, 44, 52; not explained by corpuscular theory, 13; in pinhole camera, 18–20, 49 n
diffraction fringes, 20, 21

Dinsmore, W. B., 149
dioptric apparatus of eye, 30, 31, 32–3
Dirac, P. A. M., 22 n
distance: apparent diminution of objects with increase of, 59–60; limit of, for seeing an object, 61; subjective estimation of, 78, 147
distance points, 142–3, 144
distortion in pictures, see deformations
Divini, E., 170
divisionisme, 166 n
Doric temples, curvatures in, 149–50
Douglas, C. G., 30 n

Egyptians: bas-reliefs by, 176, 177; pictures by, xxi, 175, 178–9
Einstein, A., 99–100
El Greco, fallacy concerning, 43, 44, 145
ellipse, projection of sphere as, 116–23
emmetropia, 35 n
energy of a quantum, 24 n
entrance pupil, of eye and camera, 55
Epicurus, 14
Etana, legend of, 59
Euclid, xxi, 171 n; *Elements* by, 51, 61, 62, 181; experiments illustrating theorems of, 66, 67; *Optics* by, 7, 56, 60–2, 148, 181; 'visual rays' of, 7, 34
Euclidean space, 51
Evett, A. S., 18, 91, 150 n
Exell, A. W., 162 n
eye, 1–7; acuity of, 44–5, 61; astigmatism of, 38–44; centre of rotation of, 55, 62, 72; compound, of insects, 4, 8, 50; efficiency of, as detector of light, 24, 45; experiments on, 63–71, 136; fixation reflex of, 27, 35; floating spots appearing before, 10; focus of, 30, 32, 35, 40, 50; movements of, 8, 9 n, 34, 50, 55, 61, 139; oldest diagram of, 37 n; optical system of, 25–35; peripheral vision by, *see under* vision; reflection of light from, 30–1; refraction of light in, 31–2, 35 n, 37–40; visual field of, 35–7, 62, 87 n
eyeball, 25, 26

Ferree, C. E., G. Rand, and C. Hardy, 40
Fick, A., 38, 39, 41, 42
field of view, 35, 37
Fielding, H., 165
focus: of eye, 30, 32, 35, 40, 50; images in and out of, 5–7, 47–8
Folkes, Martin, 147
Fontana, F., 170
foreshortening, 180, 182

fovea of eye, 26–7, 29; image on, 32, 33, 50

frame of picture, 77, 114

Galen, 7
Galileo, 170
Garrick, David, 165
Gassendi, P., 170
Gauss, C. F.: on image formation, 32–5, 37; triangulation measurements by, 51
gestalt psychology, xvi, xvii
Gibson, J. J., 43, 61
Gioseffi, D., 93 n, 123 n, 149 n, 181, 182
Giotto, 174, 181
Gombrich, E. H., xxi, 174 n
Graham, C. H., 148
Grassi, O., 80
great circles, 136–7
Greeks: theories of vision of, 7; use of perspective by, 180–2
Grimaldi, F. M., 19–20
Guillot, M., 44 n

Hardy, A. C., and F. H. Perrin, 20, 48
Harris, J. R., 178, 179
Hartridge, H., 36
Hauck, G., 148
Hazlitt, W., 173
Helmholtz, H. von, 1; on achromatic optical systems, 46 n; diagrams from 3, 27, 28, 29, 33, 37, 146; invents ophthalmoscope, 31 n; on optics and painting, 167; *Physiological Optics* by, 8 n, 31 n, 32, 77, 78
Hermann, L., 38, 39, 41, 42
Hevelius, J., 170
Higgins, R. A., 101
Hipparchus, 52 n
Hirschberg, J., 8 n
Hogarth, W., 169, 175 n
Hoogstraaten, S. van, 85 n
horizon, in linear perspective, 141, 142, 143, 144
Hultsch, F., 52 n
human figures, perspectives of, 123, 180
Humphrey, G., 9 n
Huygens, C., 99, 170, 171, 172
hypermetropia, 35 n

iconoscope, 96 n
'illusionistic' painting, 85
illusions: of perspective in architecture, 152–4, of reality in pictures, awareness of surface and, 12

image, retinal: 1, 2, 3; of ancillary parallel line, 70; experiments on geometrical properties of, 63–71, 136; Gaussian theory of, 32–5; inversion of, 3, 5, 8–9, 66; as link in process of seeing, 9, 50; not itself seen, 8–10, 44, 148; not what artists paint, 9 n; in perspective, 76; point to point correspondence of object and, 3–5, 8; as a whole, 35–7
images: conveyed by light, 14; formed by biconvex lenses, 46–8; in pinhole camera, 16, 23; wave theory of formation of, 22–4
imagination, xviii, xix
imitation in painting, 165–83
impressionist painters, 9 n
insects, compound eyes of: 4, 8, 50; erect images in, 5, 9
integration, of distorted aspects of a picture, xvii, xviii
interference phenomena, 21, 22
inversion, of image on retina, 3, 5, 8–9, 66
inverting spectacles, learning to use, xviii
iris of eye, 25, 28
Ittelson, W. H., 151
Ivins, W. M., Jun., 182 n

Jammer, M., 51
Javal, E., 96 n
Johnson Abercrombie, Mrs, 168, 170
Jopling, J., 138
Jurin, J., 18

Kepler, J., 1, 13, 31 n, 36
knowledge, is personal, 11 n
Kottenhoff, H., xviii

La Gournerie, J. de, xxi, 76 n, 121, 122, 135, 159, 161
Larkin, F. M., 127
Latham, R. E., 14 n
Le Grand, Y., 9, 32, 33, 40, 43
Lejeune, A., 56, 181
lens of eye, 1, 7, 26, 28, 29–30; astigmatism caused by, 42; reflection of light by, 30; refraction of light by, 31–2, 37, 40; yellow colour of, 30, 30 n
lenses: of cameras, 23, 46–8, 50; convex, formation of images by, 46–8; of spectacles, 35 n, 42
Leonardo da Vinci, xxi, 8; on evolution of painting, 174; and perspective, 33–4, 56, 182; on pinhole camera, 14, 15–19, 24; and

Leonardo da Vinci, (*cont.*)
projection of sphere, 121; representational painter, 165; on vision, 96 n
'Leonardo window', 73, 74, 77, 104, 116, 138
Letarouilly, P., 125, 154
Lewes, G. H., 172–3
light: concept of rays of, 13–15, 17, 20, 34 n; corpuscular theory of, 13, 21; diffraction of, 5, 13, 18–20, 44, 52; efficiency of eye as detector of, 24, 45; main rays of, 3, 17, 33, 34, 47; propagated in straight lines, 11, 52, 61, 71; quantum properties of, 21–2, 24, 45, 61; reflection of, by cornea and lens of eye, 30, 31; refraction of, 1, 47, 52–4, (in eye), 31–2, 35 n, 37–40; vision at low intensities of, 24, 45, 167, 175 n; wave length of, 44; wave properties of, 19, 21–2, 45, 52
Lindberg, D. C., 14
Lucretius, 14
luminance: of pinhole camera image, 23; range and level of, in photographs, paintings, and nature, 166
Luneburg, R. K., theory of binocular vision of, 147–8

Mach, E., 180
McIlroy, M. D., 127
McMahon, A. P., 15 n, 96 n, 121
Maffei, F. W., 79 n, 85 n
Magendie, F., 63
magnitudes, objective and visual, 60
Mantegna, A., 123 n
Marini, R., 79 n
Masaccio, 174
Medd, S. A., 150 n
Mesopotamia, cosmology of, 60
Michelangelo, 152
migraine, 10
mirror: ancillary parallel in, 59; convex, 149; presents reality, 11 n, 163
moon: angle subtended at eye by diameter of, 53; eclipses of, 54; refraction of light of, 54
moonlight, 23, 45; paintings of scenes in, 166, 167, 168
motion parallax, 61, 78 n
Müller, J., 4
Murillo, 167 n
myopia, 7, 35 n

neo-impressionism, 166 n
nerves, *see* optic nerves
Nevile's Court, Cambridge, 152

Newton, Isaac, 13, 46 n, 48; corpuscular theory of light of, 21–2
Nixon, President, photograph of photograph of, 98, 99
nodal points in eye, 32, 33, 37, 38, 55

Ogle, K. N., 147, 148
ommatidia, of insect eye, 4
ophthalmoscope, 31
optic disc of eye, 25, 26, 27
optic nerves, 1, 4, 9, 27; number of fibres in, 29; retina as expansion of, 25
optical centre: of eye, 32, 38; of lens, 47
optical media of eye, 30
orthogonal projection, 102
orthogonals to plane of projection, 141–2, 143, 144

Paestum: Basilica at, 124, 125; curvatures in temple at, 149; photographs of temple at, with different planes of projection, 107–9, 110; steps of temple at, 150 n
painting: abstract, 114, 183; 'illusionistic', 85; imitation in, 165–83; representational, 10, 11, 12, 114, 165, 183
Palazzo Barberini, Rome, 94
Palazzo Spada, Rome: perspective arcade in, 152, 153, 154
Panofsky, E., 93 n, 148
parallel lines, 57–8; ancillary, passing through eye, 59, 67, 70, 139, 140, 141; images of, on retina, 64–71; projection of, on planes at different angles, 137–43; vanishing point of, 139, 140, 141, 142, 143, 181 n
parallels, postulate of, 62
Parthenon, Athens, curvatures in, 149
Pascal, B., 173
Pedretti, C., 93 n
peep-shows, 85, 95 n
penumbra, 20
perception: of pictures, 95–115; psychology of, xxi; of reality and of representational pictures, 175; visual, 10
perspective: binocular vision and, 77–8; 'curvilinear' systems of, 149 n; exact, avoided by artists, 122, 123, 125–6, 132, 135; Greek use of, 180–2; historical evolution of theory and use of, 93 n, 175–82; Leonardo da Vinci and, 33–4, 56, 182; linear, xxi, xxii, 11–12, 56–7, 71, 72–94; marginal distortions of, 12; natural, xxi, 34, 56–62, 74, 182 n; in photographs, 50; teaching of, xxi; theoretical ambiguity of, 151

perspective illusions in architecture, 152–4

perspective projection, 57, 74, 163 n

perspectivic pictures, seen as such only from centre of projection, xv

perspectivists, 85 n

photographs: not perfectly representational, 166, 168; of photographs, 96–8; of pictures, taken at an angle, xvii; primitive people and, 162; wide-angle, 123

photography: lens and pinhole cameras for, 49; 'unfair competition' of, with painting, 182

photons, 21, 24

Piazza of the Capitol, Rome, 152, 155, 156, 157

pictures: awareness of surfaces of, see surfaces; integration of distorted aspects of, xvii, xviii; imitation in, 165–83; limitations of representation in, 166–8; perception of, 95–115; preconceived ideas in looking at, 151–4; and reality, xviii, 10, 174–5; stable elements in, 160–1; trompe-l'oeil, see trompe-l'oeil pictures; viewed with one eye, 78, 95–6, 182; viewed from wrong position, 12, 79, 136, 154–60, 162

Piero della Francesca, 74, 75, 142

Piéron, H., 95 n

pigment, lining iris and choroid of eye, 25, 28, 29

pinhole camera, see camera, pinhole

Pirenne, Mrs K. A. M., 150 n

Pirenne, M., xxii

Pirenne, M. H., 3, 5 n, 9 n, 24 n, 31 n, 45 n, 100 n, 113, 119, 120, 171 n, 174

Pirenne, M. H., and F. H. C. Marriott, 24 n, 45 n, 168

Pirenne, M. H., F. H. C. Marriott, and E. F. O'Doherty, 175 n

ploughed field, parallel furrows of, 59

point image: of ancillary parallel line, 70, 71; not formed in astigmatism, 41, 42

'point in the eye', 33, 34 n, 54–5; Euclid and, 56, 57, 61, 62

point of sight (centre of projection; point of view), 57, 76, 88

pointillisme, 166 n

Polanyi, M., 11 n, 114, 183

Polyak, S. L., 37 n

Pompei and Herculaneum, paintings from, 133, 180, 181, 182

portrait, apparent direction of eyes of, 160

Pozzo, Andrea (A. Putei), picture by, on ceiling of Church of St Ignatius, Rome, xv, 10, 79–94, 132, 167; deformations in, when viewed from wrong position, xv, xvii, xviii, 85, 87, 96, 137, 151

preconceived ideas, in looking at pictures, 151–5

presbyopia, 29, 35 n

primitive people, and photographs, 162

principal point 139 n, 141, 143, 144

projection: advantage of plane surface of, 136–7; central, see central projection; centre of (point of sight, point of view), xv, 57, 76, 88; distance of centre of, in photographs, 101–3; frontal, 141–2; orientation of plane of, 103–10, 140–1; orthogonal, 102; several centres of, in one picture, 121, 122, 123

psychological compensation, 99, 162

psychological constancy, 59, 60

psychological problems of artists, 114–15 n, 168–74

psychology: gestalt, xvi, xvii; of perception, xxi; personal, of the artist, 11 n

Punch (1849), 168

pupil of eye, 1, 25, 28, 29, 55; blackness of, 30–1; glow of, 31 n; size of, 23

Putei, A. (A. Pozzo), 79

pyramid of sight, see visual pyramid

quantum properties of light, 21–2, 24, 45, 61

Raeder, H., E. Strømgren, and B. Strømgren, 52

railway lines, perspective of, 57, 66

Raphael, 121–3

Rayleigh, Lord, 23

realism, in pre-Greek art, 178, 180, 181

reality: pictures and, xviii, xix, 10, 174–5; presented by mirror, 11 n, 163

reflection of light: by cornea and lens of eye, 30, 31; by mirror, 11 n, 59, 163

refraction of light, 1; astronomical, 52–4; in eye, 31–2, 37–40, (errors of), 35 n; by glass lenses, 47

relativity, theory of, 51–2, 148

Rembrandt, 173

representational painting, 10, 11, 12, 114, 165, 183

resolving power of optical instruments, 22

retina, 1, 9, 24 n, 25, 26, 27, 29; curvature of, 38, 39–40, 50; image on, see image, retinal; mosaic of receptors on, 44, 45, 61, 167

Riccioli, G. B., 170

Richter, G. M. A., 180, 181 n

Richter, J. P., and I. A. Richter, 14 n, 15 n, 16, 33 n, 34 n, 96 n, 174, 180
rifle: in picture, 160; sighting with, 52
Robertson, D. S., 149
Rock, I., and C. S. Harris, xviii n
rod cells of retina: at low intensities of light, 24, 45, 167; numbers of, 29
rods and cones of retina, 9, 25, 26, 27
Roger Marx, C., 114
Ronchi, V., 8 n
Rosenfeld, L., 21
Rosser, W. G. V., 52
Rubens, P. P., 167 n
Rudaux, L., and G. de Vaucouleurs, 54 n, 58

Saenredam, P. J., 134, 135
St Bavo Church, Haarlem, 134, 135
St Ignazio Church, Rome: balustrade on roof of, 132, 143–5; painted ceiling and cupola of, see Pozzo; spheres on roof of, 118
St Maria Maggiore Church, Rome, 150 n
St Maria del Popolo Church, Rome, 94
Saturn, planet, 170, 171, 172
Schäfer, E. A., 26
Schäfer, H., 59, 178
Scheiner, C.: drawings by, 37 n, 170; optical experiments by, 2, 5–7, 45, 63, 111 n
Schlosberg, H., 95
Schramm, M., 14
Schuhl, P. M., 182
Schwarz, H., 149
sclera of eye, 25, 27, 63
Segall, M. H., D. T. Campbell, and M. J. Herskovits, 162 n
Seurat, G., 165, 166
Sextus Empiricus, 7 n, 171 n
shooting stars, 58, 145–7
Signac, P., 167 n
Smith, R., 6, 47, 53, 54, 58, 123 n, 147
space: curvature of, 51; Euclidean, 51; representation of, xxii, 11; 'visual', of Luneburg, 147
spectacles, design of, 35, 40, 42
spheres: perspectives of, 116–23; projection onto surface of, 136–7, 141 n; as surface of projection, 120
stereoscopic devices, xvii, 77, 96 n, 163, 167; see also anaglyphs, three-dimensional effects
Stoy, J. E., 127
straight lines: central projection of, 136–45; light propagated in, 11, 52, 61, 71; in pictures 160
subjective curvatures, 57, 138, 145–50

sun: angle subtended at eye by diameter of, 53; eclipses of, 52, 54 n; light of, compared with moonlight, 23; refraction of light of, 53–4
sunbeams, 57–8
surfaces: curved, perspectives of, 116–35, 136–7; of pictures, awareness of, xvi, xxii, 12, 93, 95, 99, 113–14, 132, 161, 166, 182, 183; of pictures, three-dimensional effect in absence of awareness of, 111–13, 115, 116–17; plane, advantages of, for pictures, 49–50, 136; of Pozzo's ceiling, 'invisible', 84, 85, 92–3
suspensory ligaments, of lens of eye, 28, 29

tapetum of cat's eye, 31 n
Taylor, Brook, 72, 73, 78, 79, 167, 178
telescopes, 22, 23, 48, 52
ten Doesschate, G., 8 n, 93 n, 148, 182 n
Thebes, Egypt, bas reliefs from tomb at, 176, 177
theodolite, 52
three-dimensional effect: of pictures seen with one eye, 78, 95–6, 182; of pictures seen without awareness of surface, 111–13, 115, 116–17; of Pozzo's painted ceiling, xv, xvii, 84, 85, 86, 87, 92–3; of trompe-l'oeil pictures, xxii, 93–4; see also anaglyphs, stereoscopic effects
Töppfer, R., 168, 174
trapezoidal window illusion, 162 n, 163 n
Trevor-Roper, P. D., 44 n
Trinity College, Cambridge, Nevile's Court in, 152
trompe-l'oeil pictures, xviii, xix, xxii, 95, 163; Pozzo's ceiling as, 10, 93–4, 132

Ubaldi, G., 181 n

Valéry, P., 168 n
Van Eyck brothers, 165, 181
Vandeloise, G., 191
vanishing points, 139, 140, 141, 142, 181 n
Vatican, trompe-l'oeil in, 94
Ver Eecke, P., 60 n
Vermeer, Jan, 165
Vesalius, 37 n
vision: an active process, 8; binocular, 77–8, 96 n, 147–8; centrifugal and centripetal theories of, 7–8, 14 (see also visual rays); of colour, 27, 44 n, 167; Kepler's theory of, 1; at low intensities of light, 24, 45, 167, 175 n; Luneburg's theory of binocular, 147–8; peripheral, 36, 37–40, 61, 145–6, (in rabbit), 68, 70, 76 n; retinal image as link in process

vision, (cont.)
    of, 9, 50; through apertures, 5–7, 35 n,
    45, 56, 110–11; uniocular, 62 n, 72, 78,
    95–6, 146, 182
visual acuity, 24, 44–5, 61
visual angles, 34, 54, 56, 60; and perspective,
    57, 137, 139, 140; for two eyes, 77
visual field, 35–7, 62, 87 n
visual pyramid (pyramid of sight), 17, 33–4,
    56, 62, 181, 182; perspective projection as
    section of, by a surface, 74
visual rays, theory of, 7, 8, 14 n, 17, 34, 61
Vitellio, 7
vitreous humour of eye, 30, 31

wall opposite observer, perspective of, 57, 68,
    137, 138

Walters, H. B., 101
wave properties of light, 19, 21–2, 45,
    52
Wheatstone, C., 96 n
White, J., 93 n., 149
Wiertz, A., 95 n
Winter, H. J. J., 14
Wirth, A., 44n
Wittkower, R., and B. A. R. Carter, 75
Wood, R. W., 20, 23
Wren, Sir Christopher, 152
Wundt, W., 78

Young, Thomas, 20–1

Zanetti, M., 62 n, 93 n, 149
Zulus, and perspective illusions, 162 n–163 n